D0924858

WHEN ORACLES SPEAK

WHEN ORACLES SPEAK

Understanding the
Signs & Symbols All Around Us

Dianne Skafte, Ph.D.

A publication supported by
THE KERN FOUNDATION

Theosophical Publishing House

Wheaton, Illinois ♦ Chennai (Madras), India

Copyright © 1997, 2000 by Dianne Skafte

First Quest Edition 2000

All rights reserved. No part of this book may be
reproduced in any manner without written permission
except for quotations embodied in critical articles
or reviews. For additional information write to

The Theosophical Publishing House
P. O. Box 270
Wheaton, IL 60189–0270

A publication of the Theosophical Publishing House,
a department of the Theosophical Society in America

Library of Congress Cataloging-in-Publication Data

Skafte, Dianne.
[Listening to the oracle]
When oracles speak: understanding the signs & symbols all
around us / Dianne Skafte. — 1st Quest Books ed.
    p.   cm.
"A publication supported by the Kern Foundation."
"Quest Books."
Originally published: Listening to the oracle. San Francisco,
Calif.: HarperSanFrancisco, c 1997.
Includes bibliographical references and index.
ISBN 0–8356–0791–7
1. Divination.   2. Oracles.   I. Kern Foundation.   II. Title.

BF1751.S54 2000
133.3—dc21   00–041756

6   5   4   3   2   1   *   00   01   02   03   04   05

Printed in the United States of America

Contents

To my parents,
Lucille C. Lane and Samuel R. Lane

Acknowledgments

The voices of many others have mingled with my own to create this book. I thank Candice Fuhrman for her guidance through every stage of the process. My friends, Dana Cavallero, Barbara Walker, and Tom Davis have contributed wonderful material to the narratives. I am grateful to colleagues and students at Pacifica Graduate Institute for their encouragement all along the way. Special thanks are due to Stephen Aizenstat, Charles Asher, Lionel Corbett, Ginette Paris, and Mary Watkins. Lee Ann Morgan located many fine treasures in our research together. Peter Skafte's work with Nepalese shamans has expanded my vistas greatly. I also wish to express my gratitude to Malvina McNeill for her steadfast warmth and insight.

Chapter 1

Receiving an Oracle

Preparations and Expectations

"**O**racles are coming back into the world." These words rang clearly in my awareness, though I heard no actual sound. What did they mean? I recalled the oracle of Delphi, silent for fifteen hundred years now, its altar stones scattered on the hillside. Surely that temple would not rise again. But the message repeated itself distinctly. I knew then that I was being addressed by a mysterious source beyond myself. "Well, I answered silently, "if oracles are coming back into the world, tell me what I can do to welcome them."

Several years have passed since I was touched by the quiet voice that turned the course of my work. This book is a response to that voice, a way of welcoming it into daily life. I understand now that oracles never really left the world. They went on speaking through the cries of birds, the patterns of light upon a wall, and the thousand little signs showing us the way. They continued to live with native peoples who kept ancient folkways alive. Even while suffering ridicule by the culture at large, oracles stayed faithful to practitioners of divination, trance, mediumship, and other "sacred arts."

It is we, carriers of modern culture, who have turned away from oracles. Bird calls mingle with the airplane roar overhead, but we pay no attention. Strange coincidences urge us forward or caution us back, but we see no meaning in them. Our society harbors a great fear of anything that ushers the mind into dark, unknown regions of psychic life. In an atmosphere of such profound distrust, the art of communicating with oracles has fallen, unsurprisingly, on hard times.

But a homecoming is at hand. Signs of spiritual renaissance are everywhere, as evidenced by our interest in angels, miracles, apparitions, magical animal encounters, and extraterrestrial contacts. In quieter ways, people are discovering the beauty of simple ritual and devotional practices. We are also finding a new, revitalized connection with religions of our ancestors. Judaism, Christianity, and Islam, as well as traditions from Asia, Africa, Native America, and old Europe, speak to the heart with fresh meaning. Expanding knowledge of early goddess worship has brought the Divine Feminine back into our experience.

Oracles fulfill a profound need in spiritual life. We long to be addressed in an intimate, helpful way by something wiser than ourselves. We yearn to feel our connection with the larger matrix of existence. The soul feels at home in realms beyond time and space, as Thomas Moore said, and it yearns to feel the brush of "otherness."[1] We grow weary depending solely on personal resources day after day. The old heroic "I can do it alone" attitude often leads to despair, especially when social and ecological crises are spinning out of control. When an oracle appears from nowhere (or so it seems) and offers its perfect, elegant guidance, we know that something sublime has happened. A stranger's voice speaks from the crowd at just the right moment, providing an answer to our question. The *I Ching* illuminates a relationship problem as lucidly as a good counselor. In our dream, we see a vision of the place where we will someday work. Oracles like these not only guide and inform us; they demonstrate that we are not alone in the universe.

Before exploring these thoughts further, I want to clarify how I will be using the word "oracle." A term loses power if it tries to encompass too many meanings. For example, if receiving an oracle is identical with mysticism, occultism, prophecy, synchronicity, divination, psi phenomena, and confrontations with the unconscious, then there is no point in using the word at all. Placing a few markers around our subject will orient us to the work ahead.

According to the *Oxford English Dictionary*, an oracle is the instrumentality or medium by which a deity makes known its will. Often a priest or priestess serves as the mouthpiece for supernal intention. Communications inspired by divine inspiration are also known as oracles. To avoid confusion between the message and the messenger, I will use the term "oracle-speaker" when referring to a human agency and reserve the word "oracle" for all other purposes.

Dictionary descriptions provide a starting point for identifying our subject, but they leave out the most important element from a psychological viewpoint—the experience of receiving an oracle. Since we can only begin to know oracles through our contact with them, let us frame a definition that speaks to this relationship.

To receive an oracle is to receive guidance, knowledge, or illumination from a mysterious source beyond the personal self.

Each element of this definition is important. Notice that it begins with the words "to receive". Oracles always provide us with something we can carry home, so to speak. They may provide information we need, warn of danger, open a new perspective, or nudge us in a different direction. Glimpses of the future are sometimes given in oracles, but just as often they illuminate past or present concerns. Some oracular visions terrify us with specters of a reality we hate to see. King Saul found this out when he sought revelation from the wise-woman of Endor (see chapter 2).

Our English word "oracle" derives from the Latin *orare*, meaning "to speak." When something speaks, it does not merely make sounds or flash signs at random. It communicates with purposeful intention. Of all the qualities we associate with oracles, this one is the most important. The significance of an oracular message penetrates our entire being. Sometimes we are unable to understand all dimensions of its meaning in precise terms, for oracles love to speak in metaphors and images. But the message is so perfectly configured that it passes unhindered through many gates of the unconscious. This is why we often feel a soft underground "boom" when an oracle hits its mark. In classical times, the shock was imagined as the touch of a deity. Or sometimes the statue of a god or goddess could be seen to nod (*nuere* in Latin) its head in answer to a question. In Roman religion, *numen* was a word for divine power or intention. The term gave rise to our English word "numinous," signifying a powerful experience of the holy.[2]

Oracles speak "from a mysterious source beyond the personal self." We always experience these communications as coming in from elsewhere. One may imagine that oracles issue from a domain of the human psyche or from a realm existing independently from us. But their nature will always remain a mystery. Socrates, whom the oracle of Delphi called the wisest of humans, relied on oracular communications to guide him in daily life. He practiced divination, communicated with birds, and took direction from a voice he called his "daimon." But when asked to explain what oracles were and where they came from, the philosopher declined. He would only call them "Divine Somethings."

Nearly anything may serve as a channel for oracles. Dreams, inspired trance states, spontaneous encounters with the natural world, inquiry through divination, and revelation through music and art are some of the means through which messages of guidance come. Oracles may address consciousness through any of the senses or through imaginal productions of the psyche. A dog's howling at dusk or the memory of a face from elementary school can deliver powerful communications when conditions are right.

However, not every psychic or spiritual encounter should be considered an oracle, and our guidelines can help us differentiate these experiences. For instance, research on telepathy suggests that people can receive thoughts, images, or impressions from others in their dreams and waking life. But unless this material contains a meaningful message for the recipient, I would not classify it as an oracle. Also, in certain mystical experiences, a person may feel he or she dissolves into a universal presence so sublime and encompassing that it is "ineffable"—incapable of being described in words. But oracular encounters rarely dissolve personal identity. We *can* talk about the encounter because the conscious self remains an active participant. Oracles are more awesome than everyday events but far less awesome that mystical raptures. Perhaps they form a contact point between heaven an earth.

Receiving an oracular communication is nearly always a positive experience, and people cherish the guidance they gain from it. Yet all practices have a shadow side. People run into trouble if they abandon common sense and allow themselves to be swept away by oracular encounters. They may begin seeing signs everywhere and blindly follow their lead, eventually losing all sense of orientation. Individuals with fragile or immature self-structures may not be able to handle oracular experiences well. They are also vulnerable to manipulation by egoistic leaders who use spiritual ideas to attract followers. The rational self must always be a full and equal participant in any venture into otherworld realities.

Other shadows abound in the realm of oracles. Con artists posing as spiritual guides take advantage of our desire for numinous encounters. I remember my own feelings of shock and betrayal when I invested trust in such a charlatan. This experience is related in chapter 5, which deals with the dark side of oracles. We must remain aware of the hidden, unsavory, or dangerous aspects of this domain, for unless we are willing to peer into the darkness, our work will always remain at half strength.

A Camellia, An Oracle, An Initiation

If someone had told me that a life-changing event would unfold on a sleepy afternoon in my office, involving nothing other than a camellia flower, I would have laughed. But oracles are strange stage masters. I was reading student term papers, and I had paused to gaze out the windows, unfocusing my eyes. For several minutes I drifted along in a no-thought sort of place, waiting until I felt ready to enter the material again. Suddenly a loud hollow "pop" went off close to my head. The noise startled me an inch out of my chair, reverberating in some strange way against my insides. I whirled around to see what had happened. Nothing was there. Then I realized that a heavy blossom from my vase of camellias had dropped from its stem and thudded onto the wooden file cabinet below. I stared in disbelief at the soft agent of such a hard sound. "How could a small flower possibly make a noise like that?" I wondered. My thoughts were scrambled and my heart was beating too fast. In an effort to compose myself, I picked up one of my term papers and tried to read the title.

But now my attention was pulled back to the file cabinet. I distinctly felt a strong presence in that corner of the room. I rose from my chair as though to greet a visitor, knowing full well that no one was there. Then I saw it. The camellias was looking at me. A radiant intent was pouring from its layered petals, and this intent was focused on me. Never before had I seen a flower look like that. The being seemed so alive and conscious that I almost expected it to begin speaking in a human voice. I heard nothing. But I felt a warm pulselike sensation against my chest that seemed to address me in an intimate, reassuring way. I knew that the flower was communicating with me in a language of its own.

The word "oracle" flashed into my mind. "So this is an oracle!" I thought breathlessly. I was familiar with the word, of course, but until that moment I had never comprehended its meaning *from the inside*. I suddenly understood what ancient writers meant when they said that crows had told them the way home, that oak trees had whispered the answer, that surging springs had healed their sorrow. They, too, had felt the presence of a mysterious "other" that seemed to transfer parts of its own consciousness into them. It seemed clear that the camellia was rapping on my personal door to tell me something. Then I heard a sentence speak distinctly in my mind. "Oracles are coming back into the world," it said. I wasn't entirely sure what it meant, but a joyful feeling swept through me. I sensed that I and many others were part of an important event that I could not grasp. We were being given a job assignment of sorts. And without realizing it, I had longed for this assignment all my life.

I looked again at the flower resting on my cabinet and saw that its intensity had dimmed. The numinous opening had closed. The communication was over. Feeling that the camellia would want to spend its last hours in nature's arms, I cradled it outside to a little bed of leaves in the shade. I then thanked it for the cherished gift I had received that afternoon.

In the months that followed, I walked around in a happy haze. Acquaintances told me how healthy I looked, or they commented that I seemed happier than usual. When people would ask, "So what's been happening?" I had to quell a desire to blurt out the whole story of my flower oracle. I intuitively knew that the encounters of this nature need time to incubate in silence before they hatch into narrative. Perhaps this is why participants in the Eleusinian mysteries and other ancient rites pledged themselves to secrecy about their experiences. The purpose was not to "hide" important spiritual information from the world but to shelter the gift their soul had received.

My oracular experience had unexpected effects on my patterns of work. I lost all interest in my formerly intriguing research projects. Stacks of books on now-abandoned academic subjects collected dust in my library. I remember delivering a lecture during this period on "women and medicine in the nineteenth century" (a research specialty of mine) before an out-of-town group. I discovered with alarm that my interior connection to this material had dissolved. I still remembered certain facts and ideas, but they drifted like disabled satellites outside the orbit of my concern. The only way I could cope with delivering my speech was to pretend I was an actress playing the role of a psychology professor who was very interested in women and medicine during the nineteenth century. Even then, the words felt dry in my throat. My soul now belonged to another mystery, and everything else paled in its light.

I began sneaking away to the library at odd times, as though to meet a clandestine lover. I haunted the bookshelves and pestered reference librarians to find everything related to oracles in ancient and modern life. My long hours in the company of Herodotus, Plutarch, Iamblichus, and others were among the happiest in memory. I felt very much at home exploring oracular practices in indigenous and folk cultures around the world.

By what means did ancient peoples find guidance and illumination from dreams, divination, the voices of nature, and inspired oracle-speakers? What can we learn from their example? How can we open our own line of communication with oracles? What dangers might await us there? Questions such as these never left my side as I explored the far reaches of psychic life. By the end of a year, many realities had shifted for me. A gateway to my future work had opened wide. In fact, my studies seemed to generate energy for their own accomplishment. Even after working long hours in the day and attending to family matters in the evening, I eagerly turned to my arcane texts in the last hour before bedtime. Most importantly, I no longer felt marooned in a barren world from which signs and wonders had fled. I knew now that the oracular "others" were with us and had never departed. The task ahead, I realized, was to start *remembering.*

As a way of remembering, let us look at several examples of oracular encounters from ancient and modern life. Just as a glowing wick bursts into flame when a lighted candle is brought near, our own oracular consciousness may be kindled by drawing close to those who have communed with oracles. Sharing in their experiences will also provide clues on how we can invite messages of guidance into our own lives.

When Crows Point the Way Home

Many ancient accounts describe how birds may guide, warn, and assist human beings. (See chapter 2 for a Native American account.) One of the most inspiring stories I have found from classical times was related by Appian of Alexandria, a Roman author who lived in the second century of the common era.[3] His experience reminds us that oracles may come from overhead just when we need them most.

It was a time of war, and Appian was stranded alone in enemy territory. His only chance for survival was to reach the river several miles away. A Roman trireme waited there, and it was due to sail for Pelusium, an allied territory. Unsure that he could locate the river and avoid hostile troops on his own,

Appian implored an Arab traveler he had met to serve as his guide. The old Arab agreed, but for a price.

As the two men snaked their way through trees and thickets, they heard the insistent cawing of a crow overhead. The guide's face darkened in concern. "Bird-Speaker warns us that we have lost our way," he whispered. Abruptly he made a sharp turn and began walking toward the east. Appian had no choice but to follow blindly. Soon, more calls rang out. "We are hopelessly lost," he moaned. "The oracle tells us we have strayed very far from our course." Both men huddled in the bushes, not knowing what to do next. Appian bitterly regretted having employed the so-called guide. He felt his chances would have been better searching for the river himself. Time was flying, and the boat was scheduled to leave at sundown.

Suddenly, a clear, sharp call penetrated Appian's ears, then another and another. The guide leaped up as though stung by a wasp. "This is wonderful news!" he exclaimed. "The Bird tells us that we will live to bless this day!" With a confident step the guide turned to the right and marched unafraid into a grove of trees. Then both men saw it: a beautiful river shimmered just beyond the clearing.

Appian started running, heedless of enemies. But when he reached the water's edge, he went numb. This was the wrong river. None of its features matched the description he had been given, and he saw no Roman galley. Little daylight remained. His cause was lost.

"One river is like another river," the guide shrugged. "Fear not. Everything will be blessings, everything will be blessings." Appian stared ahead darkly and said nothing. A group of strangers approached the Arab and began jabbering in a foreign tongue. After a few moments, they all tugged Appian by the arm and pushed him into a dilapidated boat. "Take a guess where they are heading now," the guide grinned. "Pelusium!"

Appian waved back to his Arab friend as they pushed from

the shore. As the gentle waters carried him to safety, he thought for a long time about the strange crow and the remarkable old man. The oracles had surely saved his life that day. But one more astonishment awaited Appian when he reached Pelusium. Upon landing at the harbor, he heard a group of people talking in sad tones about a Roman trireme that was scheduled to arrive that night. It had been captured by enemy forces shortly after departing the bank, and all aboard were killed. If Appian had succeeded in reaching his original destination at the river, he would have been among the casualties.

The augury witnessed by Appian is one of the oldest known forms of divination. To receive an augury was to receive a "bird telling" according to Latin etymology. Something became "auspicious" when it was blessed by a favorable *av-is spex*, a "bird-beholding." From archaic times, birds have been associated with oracular states of consciousness. Shamanic practitioners in cultures around the world have utilized bird images and power objects (especially feathers and claws) to carry them on flights into other dimensions of reality. Myths and stories abound that express our reverential feeling for birds. Although these stories originated long ago, they speak to a place of timeless knowing. Thus, the art of augury might still provide a framework of meaning through which the divine can tell, show, and bless. More than that, it celebrates the sweet and exhilarating discourse between the race of humans and the race of birds.

Divine Messages from Voices in a Crowd

One of the most welcomed forms of oracular messages one could receive in the classical world was a *cledon*, words heard at random or out of context that had precise meaning for the recipient at a given moment. These messages usually were uttered unknowingly by strangers, children, or passersby. Sometimes whole sentences would loom out from voices in a

An ancient Etruscan augur receives oracular communication from birds as he whirls, probably in a trance state. (Wall painting from the Tomb of the Augurs, Tarquinia, Italy, 550 B.C.E.)

crowd, offering directions or advice. A person was considered fortunate when Divine Intention chose to express itself spontaneously through the lips of another.

Herodotus, a Greek historian in the fifth century B.C.E., related an interesting example of how a cledon affected the king of Sparta.[4] The king was deliberating on whether or not to launch a particular military campaign. He was troubled by the questions because certain factions were putting pressure on him to go ahead with the campaign yet wondered whether his plan accorded with the will of Destiny. One question kept drumming in his mind: Would the deities guide his army? One evening, while the king was preoccupied with this problem, his attention suddenly fixed upon one particular man standing nearby. On impulse, he said, "Tell me, oh guest from Samos, what is your name?" "Hegistratus," the guest answered. This name meant "army guide." The king laughed out loud and shouted, "I accept the oracle!" He felt that the deities were giving him a sign that they would lead his troops to victory just as a good guide leads the army safely to its destination.

With confidence and zeal, the ruler mobilized his forces and made ready for the march. The guest from Samos was invited to accompany them as a kind of good luck charm, since the deities had spoken through his mouth. He readily accepted. From the campaign's beginning to its successful end, everything went uncannily well, and the king offered thanks for the inspired oracle he had received.

Cledons provide a good example of how oracles depend upon recipients as much as recipients depend upon oracles. The Spartan king yearned for a sign of reassurance from the deities. His desire sensitized him to any response that might be offered. But the likelihood of being spoken to by a god at a dinner party surely seemed remote. Without realizing why, the king's intuition honed in on a particular stranger in a roomful of guests, and he asked the one question that would prove important.

Furthermore, the king allowed his oracular consciousness to work for him after the stranger's name was spoken. It forged the necessary link between the meaning of "Hegistratus" and the king's own burning issue.

Many of us have received messages from the chance hearing of words without knowing about the tradition of cledons. I remember an incident from my own experience; though it lacked the drama of a war campaign, it certainly meant a lot to me at the time. I was scheduled to give a two-hour guest presentation one evening on the subject of folk medicine and shamanic healing. I knew a great deal about the subject, but I felt terribly unsettled about what I would say. My audience would include people who had studied shamanic traditions extensively, as well as those who knew nothing about the subject. I kept changing my mind about what material I should present. What would the audience really want to hear, I wondered? Everything I thought of saying seemed too general or too specific, too well known or too esoteric. Meanwhile, I stopped at the grocery store that afternoon to pick up something light for dinner. Shuffling behind the other customers at the deli counter, still worrying over my speech, I paid little attention to my surroundings. I was dimly aware that an endlessly long conversation was going on between the woman behind the counter and a man in front who was praising her elegant salads in the display case. From the drone passing between them, once sentence emerged very clearly. "It doesn't matter what you put there," the woman said. "It's all in the presentation." Then, unexplainably, the volume of her voice increased three times. To this day I feel certain that she shouted, not spoke, the sentence again. "Y'know what I mean?" she blared out. "It's all in the presentation.

Suddenly, I had the solution to my quandary. It didn't matter what material I chose to present that evening. The key was to present it in a lively, personal manner, staying close to my own experiences. Immediately, several interesting topics suggested themselves. My revelation put me in a soaringly happy mood. I knew with certainty that the speech would go well that night. By the time my turn came at the deli counter, I could hardly contain my gratitude. Leaning forward to receive my bundle of Jarlsberg cheese, I blurted out, "Thank you. Thank you very, very much!" The woman drew back and peered at me warily. I could not blame her for failing to understand. After all, her job description said nothing about speaking oracles to customers in need.

When Leaves Whisper and Gnarly Oaks Scowl

Citizens of the premodern world expected to receive oracles from every possible source imaginable. But they looked most often to the realm of nature for unfailing guidance. Plants and animals, stars and heavenly bodies, faces of the great weather, and even the earth underfoot poured out their splendid thoughts. It made sense to our ancestors that the teeming life-matrix should desire to stay in communication with parts of its own body.

Two examples of nature oracles, one ancient and the other modern, give us a flavor of these communications. The accounts are separated by twenty-five hundred years and half the globe, but they both demonstrate how human beings have always taken wise direction from the ground of being on which they stand.

One of the most revered oracles of antiquity was a great oak tree growing at Dodona in northwestern Greece. For countless centuries, supplicants traveled to this site seeking oracular guidance from its whispering voice. We do not know exactly how petitioners made inquiries to the great tree, but judging from the practices at other oracle sites, it is likely that they would pray, purify themselves, and make an offering to the tree itself. We can imagine them climbing up into the oak's sturdy branches or

How Oracles Atrophy into Superstitions[5]

IMAGINE THAT A YOUNG MAN LIVING IN OLD EUROPE decides to buy a horse. One day he comes across a mare with one white foot. The horse pleases him immensely, for her foot looks like a bright torch that she carries with her always. The man suddenly knows that he must have this animal, and so he buys her. Sure enough, she proves to be the best steed he has ever known.

As time passes, the owner keeps thinking about that one white foot and how it led to such a good purchase. He decides that a principle is at work here. Horses with a single white foot must be superior animals.

Someone from the past must have had an experience like this, because a superstition has persisted that "if a horse has one white foot, buy it." From the 1400s onward, we find this piece of advice being recorded in almanacs and collections of folk sayings all over Europe.

Most superstitions had their beginning in the oracular experience of an individual or group. Then the experience became codified into a rule of action. If the young man had focused on his own intuitive abilities, he would have received continual guidance in all areas of life. Such a gift is infinitely more valuable than learning to count white feet!

lying on the ground beneath its foliage and speaking the concerns weighing on their hearts. From the silence would emerge a stirring, brushing-together, a breathing like that of great creatures, until distinct words formed within the rich, complex sounds. The answer would fall into place, and yes, they would know intuitively that it was right. After giving a thank-offering to the oak tree for its beneficent help, the pilgrims would start for home with a new sense of peace and resolution. They had heard the words of divine presence that day, and those messages were fashioned for their ears alone.

In the earliest legends about Dodona, oracles were delivered by the oak itself, without the assistance of human channels or interpreters. It was also said that birds who happened to alight on the tree would suddenly begin speaking in human voices. The Dodonan oak was such a mighty presence that even planks of wood fashioned from its limbs had the power to utter oracles. One myth recounts how Greek argonauts fitted a piece of the sacred tree into the keel of their ship. When danger was near it called out a warning, and on several occasions the wood advised them to change their course. By the time of the Homeric writings (around 800 B.C.E.), a group of oracle-interpreters called the *selloi* had established themselves at Dodona. A passage in the *Illiad* tells us that the selloi "were of unwashed feet and slept on the ground." No one today understands the story behind this description, but it is possible that these religious officials were barefoot and left dust on their feet as an expression of reverence for the earth. Sleeping on the ground was often practiced as a way of receiving oracular dreams wafting up from the underworld.

Dodona's great oak seems to have stopped speaking altogether by the year 500 B.C.E. Classicist H. W. Parke has suggested that the tree might have died around this time. He has based his calculations on the fact the Odysseus was said to have consulted the oak sometime during the Trojan War period—around

1200 B.C.E. Since the life span of this species is eight hundred years at the most, the tree could not have survived long past the beginning of the sixth century. No account can be found of anyone receiving an oracle directly from the oak after this time. The site became an oracle of Zeus, and priestesses channeled the god's messages. But the legendary tree's magical leaves and branches were never forgotten, for the oracle-speakers called themselves "Doves."[6]

Like the oracles of Dodona, most numinous messages offer encouragement or guidance. But they also issue stern warnings when we violate sacred principles. The earth itself may lash back in no uncertain terms when humankind refuses to respect its boundaries. Communications of the *genius loci*, the daimon or spirit of a place, should always be honored.

A builder in northern California learned this lesson too late. In the early 1990s, architectural consultant Rosmarie Bogner was asked by a client to help design a state-of-the-art home in a beautiful rural area called Story Hill.[7] Before agreeing to any job, Bogner always made it her practice to visit the intended site and stay there until she knew what relationship she should have to the project. If the *genius loci* of the region registered consent, she proceeded with confidence. But if negative messages came in, Bogner knew that the plans should be modified or abandoned. She trusted the dreams, images, physical sensations, and direct intuitive feelings that came to her while communing with the land.

Bogner drove to Story Hill and set up a little tarp for the night. Almost immediately her attention was drawn to a gnarled dwarf oak hunkered down into the earth. Dry, twisted, and windblown, it seemed centuries old. The area's *genius loci* embodied itself in this strange being, she knew. "I'll call you 'Gnarly'," Bogner said, walking toward the tree. But she felt a surge of annoyance shoot back at her. Gnarly hated being disturbed. Human beings were intruders into its ancient domain, and they had no place here, now or ever. She could almost hear a croaking grunt, warning her to stay back.

"Have I offended you?" Bogner asked timidly. As though answering, a rag of fog tore loose from a large cloud bank overhead and raced toward her. At the same time, she noticed that round insects were crawling all over her tarp—Rocky Mountain ticks, potential carriers of deadly tick fever! Alarmed, she leaped backward right into a thicket of poison ivy. The land's displeasure seemed to be assaulting her from all sides. It did not want her there! Quickly she packed up and left the place.

Bogner knew that she had received an oracle telling her that Gnarly would not bless the house they had envisioned. Returning home, she advised her client either to select a different building site or to reorient the building's position to work more harmoniously with the environment. But since she could not support her opinion with convincing practical reasons, the client proceeded with his plans. Before long, bulldozers were rolling across Story Hill. Here is Bogner's account of the events that followed:

> A year later, the house was featured in *Architectural Digest*. That same month, the outside stairway separated from the building and its front door decided to move into the driveway. Two years later, the house was written up in Italy's *Arbitare*. By then, all the French doors facing west had warped from the assault of battering winds. Rivulets of water and mud were seeping into oak floors and kilims. In the third year, a critical volume of water accumulated in the subfloors of the deck above the bedroom. The occupants were out to dinner when the bedroom ceiling collapsed onto their bed. They arrived home to find the canopy holding a grotesque mud sculpture; the figure was curled into a sleeping mound, resembling a homunculus, its mouth wide open. Gnarly was yawning.[8]

Bogner, like an increasing number of architectural professionals today, is dedicated to the idea that we must invite psyche into the process of building and dwelling. The *genius loci* of
each place wishes to be heard, recognized, and taken as a partner in our work. Then it may support what we build and infuse
our creations with its own spirit. Inspiration for further developing this relationship may be found in the rich legacies of geomancy, the art of divining sacred intention within the signs and
features of the landscape. *Feng shui,* the ancient Chinese art of
positioning structures, buildings, and interior in accordance
with the spiritual presence of a place, is capturing the interest of
many Westerners. Realization is dawning that we cannot bull-
doze our way into a relationship with nature. Perhaps, as
philosopher Richard Tarnas has suggested, the passion of the
Western mind is now to reunite with the ground of its own
being.[9] As we follow this passion, oracles of the earth can help
show us the way

Opening Expectation

Looking at oracles in different periods of history helps us
cultivate our own ability to receive oracular guidance. We can
foster this work by adopting an attitude of "warm expectation."
I use the word "adopt" because it suggests a deliberate, conscious
taking on of something. We test an attitude to see where it will
carry us. Carl Jung made this psychological move when he
decided to *assume* that dreams were meaningful. "I cannot prove
that dreams have meaning," he said, "but I must regard them as
hypothetically meaningful to find the courage to deal with them
at all."[10] Nurtured by this assumption, Jung's work flourished.

Trying on an attitude is easier than struggling to believe
something. We can enter into oracular consciousness without
believing that disincarnate spirits send messages or that the gods
and goddesses make known their wills. Oracles may speak to us

even though we have no inkling of their source. The true origins of deep experiences will always remain veiled, for the human psyche cannot step outside of its own process to observe itself from a totally separate vantage point. The best one can hope for is to embrace good working theories that make sense of things and open new possibilities.

What does it mean to hold an attitude of warm expectation? Personally, I enter the experience by recalling times in my life when I quietly and pleasantly expected something to happen. Friday afternoons in school were sweet because I knew the long, leisurely weekend stretched ahead. I kept an ear attuned to the telephone because I expected my best friend to call. No designated hour had been set, but I looked forward to the inevitable ring. I knowingly waited for the moon to rise, the puddles to freeze, the squirrels to snatch peanuts from a plate In recalling these kinds of experiences, I am trying to evoke a sense of expectation that is grounded in repose. Tension, anxiety, and overexcitement tend to shut down oracular messages. (Exceptions are found during intense emergencies when oracles may rush in to lend assistance. But our aim is to cultivate oracular knowing in daily life.) One thing I learned during my camellia experience was that oracles like to reach us through a place of inner quietude. If we prepare a hushed, inviting chamber within, the guests will be drawn to our door.

Daring to Trust

To anticipate something pleasantly is difficult when the soul feels jeopardized. Our greatest fear about courting oracular guests is that we will end up in the arms of something evil. What if we invite the light but darkness rushes in?

These fears must not be shut off or glossed over, for they point to genuine psychic realities. There are realms of experience that are too terrible to hold. Forces from within or without may invade the personal self and shatter it like a vase. From the earliest times, shamans and folk healers knew that the dark, terrifying, dismembering forces of life existed side by side with the radiant, restoring forces. In modern practice, psychotherapists are keenly aware that the fragile and beautiful mind-body-spirit unit can fall apart at any time. Our fear of the unknown is sometimes justified. Getting in touch with our worst imaginings about oracles will strengthen our practice. I frequently review my own cautions, fears, and alarming images. For example, a voice in me sometimes says, "Maybe you're fooling yourself about this whole thing. Perhaps these so-called oracular experiences are nothing more than fantasy creations, concocted to wrest meaning from a boring existence. You love the idea of voices, messages, and portents filling the air. But maybe the ethers are as empty and silent as your own soul." When I hear this voice, I reach out to it as a sad and frightened figure within me. I carry on a dialogue with her and ask questions, trying to probe the roots of her/my feelings. In this way, I become more deeply acquainted with these anxieties and with my own psychological process.

Losing contact with the outside world is another fear I encounter in oracular work. It is easy for me to slide into a dreamy, receptive, slightly entranced state of awareness. A cherished feeling of "coming home" always greets me when I enter that place of experiences. But my joy is disturbed by a sense of unease. Unless I remain partly vigilant and aware, a voice warns, something terrible will happen—not to my soul, but to my body. Harm may befall loved ones as well. Images such as these arise: *I am suspended deep in an alternate reality; strangers break into the sanctuary with shouts and crashing; I am ripped away from my communion; my body is battered, violated. Others, others are screaming also. We should have been watching, we should have been watching!* Is this a memory from another existence or from the collective memory pool of humankind? Is it a glimpse of things to come? I only know that vague dread has always kept me from surrendering to totally dissociated states of consciousness. For this reason, I have never mastered channeling or mediumistic trance.

Certain fears have little power to claim me. The likelihood of becoming engulfed or possessed by alien psychic forces seems remote. I am not afraid of losing my mind, losing touch with "reality" or losing my way in oracular space. A deep trust abides in my heart concerning the unseen worlds. Intuitions like these can only be reported, not explained.

I encourage you to explore you own fears around oracular engagement. Your purpose is not to dispel anxieties but to understand them more intimately. You may decide (perhaps with the assistance of a therapist or mentor) that opening yourself to oracles and other psychic communications is not wise. Jung thought that some people should not attempt to probe the unconscious (and the psychic realm) because of the severe disruption it could cause in their lives. Jung even refused to hear the dreams of some patients.

After we have identified, dialogued with, and evaluated our apprehensions about oracles, we must take a stand. Either we will proceed onward or we will bless the subject and walk away from it. To proceed means to adopt an attitude of trust toward the process. It might be helpful to imagine that oracular forces bear a kinship to us, even though we cannot comprehend their identity. We willingly invite kinfolk into our homes. But if it seems that they may hurt or threaten us, we withdraw our trust and protect ourselves fully. By honoring both caution and desire in oracular work, we can position ourselves at the perfect point between safety and daring.

Speaking with Oracular Guests

Having adopted an open attitude and worked with our fears, conditions are right for receiving oracles. They appear through a variety of channels. Dreams, signs from nature, voices in a crowd, and spontaneous happenings in daily life all may carry personal messages for us. For example, a graduate student, whom I will call Alice, was trying to decide whether to continue in school during the next term or to take a leave of absence. The months ahead would be busy ones, for she planned to get married, go on a honeymoon, and change her residence. Alice felt exhausted and longed to take time off, but she hesitated to interrupt her education. Persuaded at last by her sense of duty, Alice bought a large stack of textbooks and trudged to the registrar's office to enroll for the term. As she set her heavy load on a small end table, she heard a loud cracking sound. The table actually broke in pieces, spilling everything on the floor.

Alice instantly knew that she had received an oracle. "Don't carry to heavy a load," it seemed to say, "or you might crack." But she decided to override its warning. Something in her character simply could not stop pushing forward. The next months turned out to be among the worst of her life. Everything went wrong on her honeymoon trip abroad. She and her new husband met with one difficulty after another in their move, and Alice became seriously ill for a long period of time. Unable to complete all of her coursework that term, she received the lowest grades of her academic career. Later, Alice told me, "I wish I had listened to the oracle!"

An oracle's meaning sometimes leaps out with dramatic clarity. Then we must consult our intuitive knowing and common sense to see whether its directive should be followed. Deep down, Alice felt that she should relax and leave school for a while. But her ingrained patterns of behavior won the day. Oracles never force us to do anything. They suggest, advise,

warn, or point the way. But our free will ultimately has authority to make the final decision.

What if an oracle does not speak clearly? Sometimes you
feel that a dream or a sign is important, but you cannot fathom
its message. When this happens, you might hold the communication gently in your mind without trying to wring meaning
from it. Relax into an attitude of "tell me more" while turning
the sound or images of the oracle over and over in your awareness. Then allow your mind to drift away from the communication into a place of stillness. The act of de-centering opens a
space in which the psyche's meaning-making function may
roam free. Allow all thoughts, feelings, and images to arise
without judging them or selecting among them. Within
moments, a gentle knowing may begin to emerge. But if nothing happens, you may store the experience away for a while. Its
meaning may become perfectly clear later.

As a way of paying honor to the oracles who drop into your
life, you might write about them, inscribe their images in art,
include their words in songs and poetry, or fashion them into
ritual objects. Not only will you remember the communication
by recording them in this way, but your relationship with them
will continue to evolve long past the moment of original transmission. Enacting or inscribing oracular experiences enjoys a
long historical tradition. Most of the world's tribal art was
inspired by divinatory in-breathings. We all have encountered
masks, statues, or images that still emanate a certain psychic
presence after many centuries. Shamans and folk-healers on all
continents utilize mantras (chains of words that are believed to
carry power) in their spiritual work. Each mantra was originally
received through a dream or empowered state of consciousness;
later it was passed on from teacher to student for many generations in the conviction that it would continue to activate
patterns of divine force. We may follow the ancient example
and create short chants or songs based on oracular experiences.

Each time they are sung, an echo of their first bright sounding will be heard.

I always feel moved when I think about how intimately connected to the matrix of life ancient peoples felt, how reverently they attended to its movements and sounds, how grateful they were to be addressed by its communications. Those of us who catch our breath in pleasure when a gray sparrow hops on our doorstep can fully appreciate what the word "auspicious" means. As we begin the new millennium with a commitment to global consciousness, we may find special value in learning about traditions that take *anima mundi*—an ensouled world—as their starting point. We shall then discover that the voices of Earth speak to us today with as much beauty and meaning as they did in ages past.

Chapter 2

Listening to the Oracles of Earth

"**L**ong ago, when plants and animals talked freely with human beings..."

Many folk tales begin with these words. A haunting memory stirs when we imagine how it would be if oak trees whispered words of counsel or we understood the language of wolves. Biblical accounts assure us that donkeys sometimes carried on conversations with their human companions. An Ojibwa Indian legend says that butterflies taught the first babies to walk by enticing them to their feet. African Americans in the Old South listened to owls and learned when the fish would bite. Ravens and moles, thunder above and lava below—they all have something important to tell if we have ears to hear.

Ancient peoples saw and heard oracles everywhere because they lived in an ensouled world. The phrase "ensouled world" may inspire us today, but perceiving everything around us as truly alive, brimming with consciousness, intently present, and gazing back at us is an experience of a different order. Few adults living in modern cultures are able to sustain an ensouled relationship with creation for more than a few moments at a time. Then we lapse back into a way of experiencing that the philosopher Martin Buber has called "I-it."[1] In this mode, my personal subjectivity (which feels alive) stands separate from the rest of the world (which feels like a collection of objects). Even animals and people can seem like "its" when I fail to remember that they, too, are looking out on reality from their own vantage points.

Like most people, I sometimes feel exquisitely open to the aliveness of things. I step outside my door and am snagged by a shrub. Tiny purple flowers spread themselves across my arm like stars. Suddenly, I wake up and see that the plant is not a stage prop. It breathes and moves and watches from its quiet station. My entire day changes when I can momentarily enter into a relationship like this. Then I wonder why I had never really noticed "who" the bush was before.

Material objects may also carry a psychic presence. Sometimes we glance at an ordinary fork or chair and are struck by its perfection. The photographer Jerry Uelsmann is famous for creating lyrical, otherworldly images out of everyday scenes. When students enroll in his photography class, he sends them straight to the garbage dump for their first photo session. Many express shock at receiving such an assignment. "We want to photograph beautiful things, not revolting garbage!" they protest. But Uelsmann is trying to teach them that everything exudes its own special beauty. So his students trudge down to the dump and snap pictures for a whole smelly afternoon. When they later develop their photos, they murmur in surprise. Even the grossest material has complex dimensions of form and shadow that make it look like a work of art. "I never realized the garbage had so much soul!" they say.

Was there a time when humanity lived in such close alliance with all creation that everything sparked with life? Might the voices of earth speak freely with us again? To answer these questions we must explore nature oracles and learn about their special ways of communicating. We will review accounts of people who have received important messages from insects, animals, plants, weather, and landscapes, studying their experiences for how we might open our own earth senses further. Though it's not immediately appealing, the practice of necromancy, receiving communications from the buried dead, deserves mention here. This art belongs to the earliest layers of earth worship and offers many revelations about our connections with life.

Deep in Conversation with the Bees

We have all heard the soft zithering sound of bees, but how many of us have actually *listened* to it? More is to be found in their voices than mere humming. An Englishwoman told me that her mother, Annie Burt, kept bees all of her life at their country farm in Upton. Annie was often seen sitting alone on a milking stool near the hives, talking to her special friends. She told them all the news of the family, being especially careful to mention any recent illnesses or deaths. It was important to her that the bees knew what was happening in their shared community.

Annie also brought her personal problems to the bees. She could be seen talking to them a long time, explaining a troublesome situation in detail. Then she would incline her ear toward the hive and listen carefully. The family noticed that she always returned from these sessions with a different air about her, like one who had found relief and peace. When Annie's children came to her with a heartfelt concern, she would hear them out and offer what motherly advice she could. But when the problem was especially difficult, she would put her arm around their shoulders and say softly, "We'll take it to the bees, darling. We'll take it to the bees."[2]

Tears came to my eyes when I first heard this account. I felt moved to learn that an oracular tradition thousands of years old had survived well into the twentieth century. At one time, peoples of early Europe paid homage to many bee deities. The German-Roman bee-goddess, Nantosvelta, was portrayed as carrying a staff crowned with a beehive. Early Poles and Silesians worshipped Babios and Austeia, male and female bee deities. And the Russians celebrated their bee-god, Zosim, who brought agriculture to humanity.

When Christianity came to Europe, the honeybee made its way into the lives of many saints and church histories. It is said that thieves who stole the honey hives of St. Medard, an early French monk, were pursued around the whole countryside by angry bees until they fell at the saint's feet and begged for forgiveness. An Irish abbess from the sixth century, St. Gobnat of

In cultures around the world, bees were worshiped as divine forces who assisted human beings and carried messages to heaven. These Minoan bee goddesses dance in celebration of life. (Crete, circa 1800. B.C.E.)

Ballyvourney, was known as the patroness of bees. With the help of her small friends, she performed many miracles for people in need.

Because bees are closely associated with souls of the dead, they deliver news of death and other events to the deities. People all over Europe believed it was important to tell the bees what was happening so that they could come into better alignment with the Otherworlds. In England and Ireland, families often draped black crepe over their beehives when someone died. French citizens celebrating a wedding could be seen placing threads from the bride's dress on honey hives so that bees could share their happy day.

Traditions such as these formed the background for Annie's daily communion with the bees. How did she actually receive messages from her guides? She did not describe this experience to anyone, but we can draw upon our knowledge of oracular practices to make an educated guess about her methods. First, she must have seen the creatures as holy beings. Approaching their hives, she'd perhaps feel a little tingle down her spine as she came into the presence of a hallowed Intelligence who could not only hear her words but answer back. The attitude of anticipation always opens up oracular receptivity. Speaking one's concerns out loud is a very powerful act, for it mobilizes psychic energy around the issue at hand and invites mysterious Others to participate in the cosmic moment. Expectation is warm, the heart is open, needs and concerns are laid before the altar. Conditions are perfect to receive an oracle.

Annie inclined her head and listened to the bees. To appreciate this experience, we must place our ear near a beehive. Thrums and murmurs a hundred layers deep carry the soul into a thick, teeming, centerless place. The sounds drone past our ears and permeate every cell of the body. We feel like an instrument being tuned to a new frequency. Then the humming begins to gather into something that resembles words. Yes, a

The Bee Was Sacred to Gods and Mortals

DEITIES HAVE ALWAYS LOVED HONEYBEES.[3] The Egyptian god Ra wept tears that turned into bees when they reached the ground. Honey was placed on the mouths of sacred statues in Sumeria, Babylonia, and other parts of the ancient Near East to bring life into their forms. In Hindu mythology, Indra, Vishnu, and Shiva were called the "nectar born" ones.

Priestesses of Rhea (ancient Greek mother of the gods) and Demeter (goddess of the fruitful earth) were addressed as "Melissa," the word for bee. Hesiod and Sophocles were said to gain divine literary gifts after bees pressed honey into their mouths. The Koran records Muhammad as saying that God speaks directly to only one animal on earth—the bee. In ancient Mayan texts, deities and heroes appear in the form of bees. Pre-Christian Europeans in Poland, Germany, Russia, and elsewhere worshiped their own bee-god and bee-goddess.

Bees were revered as powerful oracle-bringers. In African American folklore, to dream of bees swarming portended death; to dream of bees making honey was a sign of future prosperity. With legends such as these shining in our collective experience, it is not surprising that we feel something special has happened when a honeybee meanders across our path.

gentle whirring voice is speaking from the din. "Beee comforted. Beee comforted, " it intones. "All will beee well."

Whether Annie heard actual words during her sessions with the bees is unknown. Like many of us, she might have felt messages register in her body or watched them take form in visual images. Once a person slips into oracular space, oracles may come in through a variety of sensory channels. We can be sure that the beehive's humming sounds carried Annie's consciousness into a receptive state. Perhaps its unique harmonics stimulated brain-wave frequencies associated with active imagination and dreaming. Or from a psychoanalytic perspective, the hive's pervasive droning may have created a "white sound" screen upon which unconscious contents would be projected. In any case, these communications gave Annie beneficial assistance and comfort all of her life. Her experience reminds us why humankind has long treasured its friendship with the royal house of bees.

Mysteries of Augury:
How Birds Show Us the Way

Augury, the art of receiving oracular messages from birds, is one of the oldest forms of divination known to us. A cave painting from southern France dating some thirty thousand years ago shows a figure believed to be a shaman lying down next to a bird poised on top of a staff. Some anthropologists have suggested that the shaman may be in an empowered state of consciousness while he or she journeys on a soul-flight into other worlds. The bird lends its flight-power to make the journey possible. In native cultures today, birds still perform this function in shamanic undertaking. The creature's feathers, talons, and bones are regarded as spiritual allies that assist the work.

Accounts from China, India, Persia, and many other regions of the world demonstrate how carefully people attended to the

voices and movement of birds in order to understand Divine
Intention. But practically no information survives about the
methods used by augurs. All we know is that they observed
birds in painstaking detail and then used complicated codes
to interpret their findings. For example, a Tibetan text from
the ninth century (derived originally from Sanskrit) is entitled
"Kakajarita." The document gives instructions for divining the
meaning of crow cries. When you hear a crow call out, it advises, first determine from which direction the sound came. Now
note the time of day, for communications mean different things
at different periods of the morning, midday, afternoon, and
night. If possible, try to see where the bird is and what it is doing
while calling. Turning to the Kakajarita, you can now derive
oracular meaning from the cry. For example, if a crow calls at
1 P. M. from the north, it portends the arrival of a good friend.
But if the cry comes from the southeast, watch out, for an enemy
is on the way.[4]

Portions of augury codes may be found scattered in other
ancient writings. But I, for one, gain no inspiration from
reading them. I cannot believe that augury (receiving "bird-
tellings") gains its magic from a set of codes and signals. The art
must originally have been founded on an intimate rapport
between birds and humans. Myths and legends from around the
globe speak of a time when we received messages from birds
directly, without the need for interpretation manuals. One
account, found in the tribal records of the Coeur d'Alene
Indians, demonstrates this art with power and simplicity.

The Coeur d'Alenes, who called themselves the Skistwish
before Europeans came to America, lived in the territories
around northern Idaho.[5] In 1740, one of their chiefs acquired
the name Circling Ravens after the life of his band was saved by
a raven oracle. A group of about a hundred people had ventured
into enemy territory in order to hunt buffalo, for food was
scarce. As they camped, the chief suddenly fell into an empow-

ered state of mind and began singing a prophecy song. He sang that three ravens would soon fly overhead to give them news. Everyone should listen carefully to what the Bird People told them, he said, for their voice is wisdom.

A few moments later, three great ravens appeared from nowhere and encircled the camp. Three sharp caws rang out, and then the birds disappeared. The chief asked his companions if they had understood what the ravens had said. "No," they answered, "we don't know their language." But the chief comprehended it all perfectly. He told them that enemy tribes already knew where they were camped and would attack very soon. "We should fight valiantly," he instructed, "but after enemy blood has been spilled seven times, we should all make a swift retreat. If we try to press our advantage, some of us will die this day. The ravens told us to beware and follow their counsel."

Almost immediately a great commotion broke out as the band was attacked by a group of Absorka Indians and their allies. But the Absorka soon discovered what fierce fighters they had taken on, and several of their warriors received wounds. The chief kept count of enemy injuries, and when the number reached seven, he signaled a retreat. Everyone followed his lead, though some of the young men mumbled that the fighting was just beginning to get good. Arriving at their new camping place, the Skitswish found that no member of their band had received so much as a scratch. From that day onward, the chief was called Circling Ravens, and many stories are told about his remarkable talks with the Bird People.

Accounts such as this suggest that augury does not need to depend upon an organized system of signs. People may enter into a mystical participation with bird-consciousness and receive oracles through this channel. But when oracular consciousness is distrusted, the psychic field uniting animals and humans begins to perforate. Direct rapport is replaced by more analytical methods of interpretation. Printed augury texts are passed around as a replacement for the forgotten skill. With time, augury is discounted as a useless form of superstition.

Yet we never entirely forget our bond with the race of birds. When we hear the bright trilling of a wren overhead, we come close to recalling something important. "If only a small gear would click into place," we think, "this language would become transparent to me."

If our collective psyche retains knowledge of how to commune with animals, then surely the art can be revitalized. The best place to begin is at our own doorstep. Many people have spontaneous experiences of rapport with birds, and birds themselves seem to have uncanny ability to pick up our thoughts and feelings. A parrot of mine, who slept in my bedroom, always knew the instant I awoke in the morning. I would lie in bed without moving a muscle or opening my eyes. I even controlled my breathing to keep it as slow and steady as possible, trying to prevent the bird from screeching in happiness. But I never fooled him, not once. The instant my consciousness dawned, he welcomed me back into the world with ear-splitting shrieks.

In the spirit of sharing bird augury accounts, a friend of mine named Anthony told me about direct assistance he once received from a blue jay. His account provides important hints about how ancient peoples might have been guided by animals. This description tells the story from Anthony's perspective, and it reflects the events as he related them to me.

Late afternoon at home. Should finish the graphics piece for my boss, but feel tense and brooding. Can't work. This dialogue in my head won't stop. In my mind I'm telling my friend Kristin about the nature of sexual love and how it is similar to religious passion. I'm sharing many details from my own experiences with both kinds of love. In my fantasy she listens with rapt attention and offers beautiful reflections of her own. We finish talking, and the whole thing starts over again. I hate being possessed by this damned dialogue. It really has a hold on me. I feel a mad desire to phone Kristin and talk to her in person, just to get it out of my system.

But of course I won't do that. She's only been at the company a few weeks, and it would be very uncool of me to bring up a steamy topic like that so soon. What if Kristin thinks I'm putting a sexual harassment number on her? Or if she did decide to warm up to me, what then? We're both married to other people, both have kids. Fan a spark at the wrong moment and the whole barn goes up in flames. Two families burnt, two jobs lost, two lovers blackened with guilt and blaming each other. I've been there before. Unfortunately. That settles it! I'll stay away from her. Keep my distance in word and deed. Damn, I want to call her. Maybe I'll just dial her up to see if she's home or not.

Suddenly a blue jay pops out of nowhere and lights on the fence a few feet away outside my window. I don't know why, but it gives me a start. Last thing I expected to see. It's a big California jay, very dark blue color. A strong, beautiful bird. She (it seems female, somehow) stands there peering right into my eyes. You know, when you really look deep into a bird's eyes, a creepy feeling comes over you. It's like looking into something alien. Then you remember that they walked around with the dinosaurs. In fact, some biologists say they are actually dinosaurs with feathers. That really makes you feel weird.

I expect the jay to fly away any second, but she locks her eyes on mine for a long time. I stare at her like someone under a spell. Suddenly she looks very old to me. I get the distinct feeling that I am looking into the eyes of an old woman, an ancient woman. And, this is strange, but I feel she has wisdom, knows a lot about life. She almost seems to care about me at the moment. So I beam a thought at her and say, "Tell me what to do about Kristin. To call or not to call?" Ordinarily I'd feel idiotic asking advice from a bird, but something different is happening now, and it seems like the right thing to do.

No sooner do these words leave my mind than the jay gives a little shudder. She fluffs out all her feathers and seems to sink into her own feet. Her whole body turns into a fluffy ball. Even her neck disappears into a bed of down. But those eyes never leave mine.

My body relaxes with hers. I can't help it. My shoulders sink. I let out a long breath. I realize now how knotted up I've been over this Kristin thing. I've been obsessing about all these different scenarios, trying to calculate all the outcomes ahead of time. Suddenly, I know that it doesn't matter whether I call Kristin or not. Things have their own way of working. Who knows whether she will want a friendship with me? Who knows whether I will want a friendship once I get to know her? Right now I'm driving myself crazy on fantasy material. Just relax. Let it all go for now. That's what the bird is showing me.

The blue jay springs to attention, like she heard my thoughts. She hop-turns to the right and to the left, then resumes a forward position. I swear it looked like a salute. "Congratulations!" she seems to say. "You got it, Bub!" I laugh out loud. Then she does something more amazing. She bobs her head and chest up and down three times very distinctly, very vigorously. It looks like she's saying, "Yes, yes, yes!" I'm flabbergasted. Now I'm sure that this creature is communicating with me. I raise my hand to my forehead in a salute and silently say, "Thanks." A flash of blue, and she's gone.

The effect of all this stays with me for many days. There's a happy feeling in my heart. That's the best way I can describe it. My life seems like a good thing to me. I get in touch with how much I love my wife and my little girl and my work. My churning thoughts about Kristin have calmed way down. Yet when I talk to her I know something special is there between us. I decide just to let it be and not look far ahead. If I feel any tension creeping up on me, I remember the jay settling down in a fluff ball, and I can relax.

About a week later, Kristin comes up to me and suggests we have lunch together. I accept the invitation with a calm "let's see what happens" attitude. We talk about this and that at lunch. I can definitely

feel erotic sparks between us. But they become part of the back-
ground. Something other than romance is happening between us, and
we both sense it. Then as the waiter is pouring coffee, an impossible
thing happens. Kristin says, "Have you ever thought about the fact
that romantic love and the love for God have a lot in common?" It's
fortunate that I'm in such a mellow state of mind, or I'd drop my
cup. We now get into an incredible conversation. Kristin is making
statements that are lifted word for word out of the dialogues I had in
my mind. We get so absorbed that we're both late getting back to
work. I'll never forget that afternoon.

Anthony told me about these events two years after they
had happened, but he recalled them as though they had taken
place yesterday. I asked him what direction his relationship with
Kristin had taken. He said that they have formed a deep friendship with each other that continues to grow all the time. More
than that, they have the strange feeling they are doing important "work" together even though they only talk. They wonder
whether someday they might not team up in a more formal way
with a joint project.

As for the romantic potential, it still hovers there but never
presses very hard on them. Kristin and Anthony came across an
idea in the *Celestine Prophecy* (a novel based around spiritual
themes) that helped them put things in perspective.[6] The idea
is that spiritual forces sometimes draw two people together, but
it is important not to let the attraction automatically turn into
romantic love. Romance funnels psychic energies into a narrow,
obsessive channel. The partners attach all of their hopes and
dreams to each other instead of staying in relationship with the
"third," the greater force moving between them. Later they may
feel bitterly disappointed when the love affair fails to bring them
what they longed for. But if they both focus on the "something
greater" that drew them together in the first place, they will stay
on course with their own souls and with their love.

With this notion to guide him, Anthony feels he is on solid ground. He knows for certain that the destiny of his unusual relationship with Kristin is good, if he follows its spiritual lead. And he can almost see the jay bobbing up and down with a wholehearted "Yes, yes, yes!"

Let us review Anthony's bird communication from a more analytical perspective, trying to identify patterns common to all nature oracles. Looking at this experience may also give us clues on how communication with birds took place long ago.

First, Anthony's state of mind before the oracle appeared was agitated; he felt confused and "not himself." A force more powerful than his personal will seemed to be stirring up unwelcome thoughts and emotions. One could say that he was in a mild state of dissociation or trance. Just as figures in a dream generate speeches all on their own, the dreaming-while-awake part of Anthony's psyche was busy creating dialogues without asking his permission. He hated this experience at the time. But it fostered ideal conditions for receiving an oracle.

While Anthony was in his preoccupied, almost entranced state of mind, the blue jay appeared. Its sudden arrival shocked his system. Naturally, he had seen hundreds of birds in his life, and there was nothing unusual about this one. But recipients of oracles often describe a similar kind of psychic jolt. I believe this shock of contact occurs when something "other" makes an appearance to the personal self. What the "other" really is can never be known. But a feeling of awe passes through us when we register its presence. Many people report that their emotions and thoughts take unusual turns during oracular encounters. Even life-long patterns may change in a twinkling. Perhaps the shock effect of oracles dislodges certain psychic structures so that something new can enter.

Anthony felt intensely absorbed in the jay's every motion. The rest of the world faded away. Oracles entrain our awareness, pulling us like a tractor beam into another consciousness. Then the smallest detail shines with special meaning, and each sound, movement, or touch is experienced as an intentional act. Oracles gain power to speak by drawing us into a relationship of rapt rapport. How did Anthony receive messages from the bird's movements? The sight of a blue jay cannot, in itself, provide guidance about a complex relationship issue. A mediating force must enter the process, breathing life and significance into mere form. We can give names to this mediating force (such as the transcendent function, mythopoetic imagination, or Divine Inspiration), but we can never comprehend its identity. The best we can say is that Anthony entered into partnership with something that helped him have an oracular experience.

The oracle continued to unfold long after its messenger saluted and flew away. When Kristin called Anthony on the phone, he responded to her with tranquility rather that agitation. Later, the attracting force between them flowed into its rightful channel and served their mutual benefit. Clearly, oracular communications offer more than glimpses of the future. They provide a new dynamic principle for organizing present experience. Before long, not only feelings but external events begin to shift into alignment with the principle.

In summary, we might say that the Bird People are most likely to contact us when we are somewhat entranced or dissociated. Using the universal power possessed by all living creatures, they exert a kind of magnetic pull on our awareness. Information or guidance is transmitted in whole units and is often channeled directly through the body. But our own oracular knowing must be willing, ready, and able to receive these messages, or they will fly right by us. The entire process can be described but never really explained. If someone asks us how we can be so sure of our oracular knowledge, we can only answer that "a little bird told us."

Orpheus, a healer, musician, and oracle speaker, played the lyre so sweetly that birds floated down from the trees to gather near him. (Etruscan tomb painting, Tarquinia, 470 B.C.E.)

Building a Soul-Bridge to Animals

One of the most lucid descriptions of communicating with animals is offered by J. Allen Boone in his classic work *Kinship with all Life*.[7] Originally released in 1954, the slender volume still inspires thousands today. No one who reads the author's experiences can ever look at animals or insects as "lower forms of life" again. Boone's interactions with Strongheart, a dog of movie fame, can help us piece together how ancient peoples were able to talk with animals, and they offer us useful suggestions for how to build a bridge of rapport with our nonhuman peers.

Boone was surprised when a movie studio manager asked him to become the companion and caretaker of their most valuable film dog, Strongheart. As an author of screenplays, he possessed no special expertise in canine care. But he did have plenty of time and a comfortable home in the hills of Hollywood. Boone shrugged and accepted the job, not realizing how his entire relationship with life would change as a result of this simple decision.

Strongheart was a large, beautiful German shepherd who had been trained as a war dog in Germany before being shipped to the United States. Due to his remarkable intelligence and ability to understand the intentions of people around him, he had no trouble adjusting to the peaceful work of film acting. Nor did the shepherd register surprise when Boone picked him up and led him on a leash to the front door of his bungalow. Strongheart opened the doorknob with his teeth, trotted in, and explored every corner of the place.

The first few nights required adjustments from both dog and man. It was agreed that they would share the large bed, but the relative positions of their bodies became an issue of dispute. Strongheart insisted on lying with his hindquarters brushing up against Boone's face. After several nights of fitful tossing and turning, Boone crossly told the dog that he must angle himself in another direction or sleep on the floor. As soon as the words were spoken, Strongheart tugged at his master's sleeve and pulled him to the French windows nearby. Using his teeth, the shepherd repeatedly opened and shut the windows, demonstrating that they did not stay closed. Then Boone understood. Strongheart wanted to keep his snout pointed toward the most vulnerable entrance in the room. He was only trying to protect the household from a potential break-in. The problem was solved by reversing the bed so that both dog and man faced the windows.

After a few weeks, the companions fell into a pleasant rhythm with each other. They ate, slept, went on walks, and sometimes just sat outside beneath the evening sky. But Boone began to sense that he only understood the exterior part of Strongheart. His invisible, interior part remained a mystery. How was he able to react with such intelligence to situations, Boone wondered? How could he carry out complicated feats on movie sets after being instructed only once? Was it possible that a dog could really understand human speech and read people's intentions even before words were spoken? Boone's respect for Strongheart was growing by the hour. No longer could he think of this individual as "only an animal."

Then one day something happened that turned everything in a whole new direction. Boone was sitting at his typewriter pounding out prose in fits and starts. Staring at the page and hitting a few more keys, he suddenly decided that the day was too beautiful for staying inside. Yes, in a few minutes he would stop writing and go for a drive with the dog. At that instant, Strongheart raced into the room from nowhere and licked Boone's hand. Then he dashed into the closet and brought Boone the old sweater he always wore on outings. Another scamper to the bedroom and Strongheart dragged out a pair of blue jeans; then came Boone's boots, one after the other.

Springing happily into the air and barking, the dog made it clear that they should leave immediately.

Boone gasped in amazement. He was sure that Strongheart had been nowhere around when he'd made the decision. And he thought that his body had betrayed no outward sign. But the shepherd had picked up his thoughts clearly. Now things began to fall into place. Strongheart could give remarkable performances on the screen because he knew what people expected of him. He could live harmoniously with his human companion because he attuned himself to that companion's thoughts and feelings. The dog was a telepath!

But the telepathic messages only traveled one way. Boone felt humbled by the realization that he did not possess an ability that came so naturally to his canine friend. He decided to become Strongheart's pupil rather than his master. Each day he watched his teacher attentively, appreciating the animal's sense of wonder, love of life, and complete absorption in whatever he was doing in the moment. Boone talked to his friend often and then listened for any answers that might be given. Nothing came through, but Boone found the whole experiment was educational.

One afternoon, Strongheart and Boone went on an outing to one of their favorite spots in the hills overlooking a beautiful wilderness area. The dog loved to sit there for long periods and gaze at the horizon as though deep in meditation. Boone sat a short way behind, staring at the back of his companion's head. Mentally, he began asking the dog all kinds of intimate questions about himself, such as what his life had been like in Germany, whether he had sired puppies, how he felt about human beings, and what forces beyond himself operated through him. Boone really didn't expect any answers, and when the questioning was over, he just relaxed into a pleasant feeing of drifting. His mind was fuzzy and blank.

Suddenly, Boone saw the dog turn its head around and stare

straight at him. The eyes were like X rays, seeming to penetrate his bones. How long the two comrades stayed locked in that gaze was difficult to say. But after a time, Strongheart turned away and looked out into space again. And then, easily, without effort, Boone knew the answers to every one of his questions. He was able to verify many of them later by checking into Strongheart's history. The dog had responded to him in a direct transmission, using that ancient wordless language in which all life speaks whenever hearts and minds are attuned.

Now that Boone and Strongheart were synchronized, their lives became almost as one, and their intimate conversations took on universal dimension. The author's own description of one of these sessions expressed what they shared.

> The most memorable of our silent talks took place out under the stars where he and I would sit shoulder to shoulder in shared contemplation like a couple of cogitating philosophers. We would first saturate ourselves with distance. We would watch the lovely designs and purpose operating in all things, and we would wonder, and marvel, and ponder. . . . At intervals Strongheart and I would pull in our thinking from distant spiraling and silently talk with each other on matters of mutual interest. I would ask him a specific question. When the answer came, it arrived with the gentlest kind of impact. It came as a "still small voice" whispering the needed information within.[8]

Boone said that when the answers came, he never had to make any conscious transition between knowing and not knowing. The experience was like remembering something he had always known. His own consciousness expanded greatly as a result of communicating with Strongheart. He began noticing the presence of an illimitable, eternal mind that continually moved through everything everywhere. His rapport with Strongheart remained as a spiritual force in his life even after the dog passed away a few years later.

The author had many other telepathic encounters with animals and insects of all descriptions, and he learned that the Voice of Existence knows no barriers of time, space, or species. Those of us who have enjoyed a close relationship with animals can relate to many of Boone's experiences. One does not have to find a gifted animal like Strongheart in order to exchange telepathic communications with nonhuman beings. But one must put side certain prejudices and misconceptions for the bridge to be built. We cannot view the other creature as inferior because its abilities are different from ours. Boone offered a useful image to express this principle. He said that a mental bridge had to be extended to Strongheart before communications were freely exchanged. If Boone forgot their basic kinship and mentally elevated himself over the dog, then his end of the bridge was held too high and he could not receive anything. But once the structure was level, communications could flow across easily.

How can we build bridges of rapport with creatures who have so much to offer? First, we reeducate our vision to see them as equal partners with us on earth. It is one thing to say "this animal is equal to me" and another to really experience it. Boone worked hard to change his old limited ideas about dogs. He did everything he could to imagine Strongheart as an equal in every way. At night he read poetry and favorite passages of philosophy to his friend. He discussed events of the day with him (as one would "tell the bees") and mentally stayed open to any response he might receive. Rather than take charge of all their activities, Boone allowed the shepherd to take the lead every other day and choose sites he might want to visit. These methods slowly worked their magic. The bridge between man and dog leveled out and created a wonderful passageway.

Boone's experiences remind us that a part of our psyche is always ready to commune with animals, even if the encounter frightens us a bit. One night I got up to check whether a front door was locked. In the dim light I saw my cat sitting on the couch. She was not stretched out on the seat or curled up in customary feline fashion. No, she was poised upright on her haunches, leaning against the back cushion while her two front arms dangled alongside her body—exactly as a person would sit! I froze with a chilling feeling that this was not my cat at all, but an entity unknown to me. She did not move a muscle but continued to gaze at me with such awareness and deliberate intent that my heart began thundering. I wish now that I could have kept my composure and opened my mind to her transmission. But I had not yet studied these matters and was caught unprepared in the middle of the night. So I raced for the bed and shut my door.

Experiences like these are important, alarming as they may be. My conception of "cat" cracked open at the moment and allowed something new to enter. To say, "This is not an animal but an entity unknown to me" is the first step to experiencing the animal's "otherness." We can enter into true dialogue with an intelligent other, but not with a cardboard mock-up that we call "my pet." Communication failed during my own late-night encounter because I dropped my end of the bridge too low, out of fear! But from that moment onward I became more attuned to the mystery and power of all cat-beings.

Another way of building a bridge to animals is to notice their fine qualities. Boone spent a lot of time just admiring Strongheart's beauty and watching the way he loved life. Aesthetic pleasure is a powerful oracular tool. It primes the soul for many extraordinary experiences. Naming the specific points of magnificence you admire in a creature will help create a bond between you both. A specific exercise to strengthen rapport with animals is described in chapter 8.

We must talk about our animal encounters so that we can learn from one another. We need to identify the shades and variations of our experiences in order to build more descriptive vocabulary. In a typical thesaurus, one may find twenty-five words for feeling "angry." But how many terms are listed for receiving a mental transmission from an animal? Indigenous peoples who have stayed in touch with ancient folkways may offer clues about communicating with the non-human world. Once we remember that it *can* be done, the actual doing will come more easily. Then perhaps we will piece together what was scattered across the centuries.

Oracles of Earth — The Deep Below

All that lives rises from the body of Earth, and to that body all shall return. Our ancestors never lost sight of this truth. They constantly paid honor to the Fruitful Provider, often imagined as a Great Mother. Grain from the first harvest of every season was offered back to her, and nourishing gifts of milk, wine, or blood were poured directly into the ground as an expression of gratitude. Remnants of these traditions still survive, even in modernized countries. Lithuanian scholar Marija Gimbutas noted that her father arose each morning and poured a libation of wine into the soil as a thank-offering to the earth.[9]

Earth is also home to the dead. Agricultural peoples all over the world planted their dead into the ground like seeds, expecting them to be born again from another woman's womb, to spring up new in the body of a plant or animal, or to linger in the underworld. Spirits who joined with all-knowing Earth became wise. They acquired power to see the future, reveal secrets, and provide beneficial guidance. If a living person contacted them, he or she could gain knowledge of many hidden things. This is why the biblical King Saul violated his own law and sought out a wise-woman in the town of Endor, who knew the art of necromancy—receiving oracles from the dead (see sidebar, p. 54).

The word "necromancy" (with its somber root in *necro*, dead body) evokes so many unpleasant associations that few people wish to dwell on the subject for long. But we should remember that traditional peoples did not share our modern horror of death. Their daily experience was interlaced with images of being pulled from the womb and being laid in the grave, of growing strong and decaying away, of eating feasts and being eaten by worms. Nor were corpses to be shunned. In fact, many ethnic groups considered it cozy to bury the dead right under the living room floor so that they could remain close to the family. The Estonians of eastern Europe liked to throw banquets in the graveyards and eat with the departed. They put a few delicacies on each tombstone in a spirit of friendly sharing. On certain days when the dead returned home for a visit, bathrooms were kept heated and food was laid out in festive array. Necromancy holds a place of honor among ancient oracular arts. Shamanic practitioners have always received training in the art of summoning departed spirits. The dead were thought to be skillful at diagnosing illness and prescribing cures.[10]

I was fortunate to witness a Nepalese shaman named Jebi make contact with a spirit and channel its communications during a healing ritual. The patient, a Westerner named Jeanine, had experienced a stabbing sensation in her chest area from early childhood, but doctors could find no physical reason for it. So she decided to take her problem to the native healer. Though Jeanine kept an open mind, her faith in being healed was not particularly strong.

After Jebi entered an empowered state of consciousness through drumming, dancing, and chanting, he became possessed by a spirit who identified itself as a female ancestor of Jeanine. It was eerie to watch the shaman speak in a strange rasping monotone while his face and body jerked with rhythmi-

John Dee (1527–1608), famous mathematician, philosopher, and astrologer for Queen Elizabeth, holds a torch while an adept necromancer consults with a spirit. (19th-century engraving)

cal spasms. His eyes stared dully ahead with a glassy, unseeing expression, looking very much like the image of death. Through his halting words, we learned that the pain was an ancestral wound. A woman relative (now a spirit) had been stabbed to death and no one knew about it. The crime was recorded on Jeanine's body. After Jebi came out of the trance, he performed rituals to help the spirit let go of her trauma. He also performed rituals for the patient and told her certain procedures she must perform each day for three weeks. Jeanine told me that her pain was gone when she awoke the next morning. She was so astonished that words could not describe her feelings. When I checked with her a year later, the pain still had not returned. Those of us who saw the event never forgot it. We could not fathom who or what really spoke through the shaman, but no one could deny that a healing miracle had taken place that day in the name of necromancy. And we witnessed a living demonstration of practices as old as humankind.

Necromancy was well developed among the Egyptians, Assyro-Babylonians, and Etruscans of the ancient world. Citizens in classical times revered their *necromaneia*—oracles of the dead—and often made pilgrimages to them. A famous oracle of this type was located at Epiris in a hillside cave directly above the point where two rivers (the Cocytos and Acheron) met. The legendary hero Odysseus summoned the dead at Epiris and obtained valuable guidance for his journey home. This site was associated with the worship of Persephone, goddess of the underworld, and later with Hades, god of the dead.

During the medieval and Renaissance periods of European history, summoning the dead was practiced as a normal part of life. Wise-women and wise-men in the countryside conjured up departed spirits to help diagnose illnesses and prescribe cures. Families prayed to dead relatives for guidance, asking them to appear in dreams or otherwise make their presence known. Departed spirits were especially skilled at helping to find missing persons or lost treasures. They also felt impelled, like the ghost of Hamlet's father, to expose secret crimes that had been committed. Catholic priests practiced their share of necromancy in centuries past, a matter rarely discussed in church histories!

Scholars and professors sought knowledge of hidden things by communing with spirits of the dead, even though such activities were often punishable by death. A nineteenth-century engraving shows the scholar John Dee and his colleague standing in a graveyard late at night. A magic circle etched with signs of the zodiac and other arcane symbols encompasses their feet. Rising from a moonlight-shocked tomb is a frightful looking corpse, ready to impart its unthinkable secrets. Necromancy played a central role in the Faust legend, and communications from the dead even found their way into Charles Dickens's tale of Scrooge. Images such as these hint at the exceedingly old practice of communicating with the dead.

Few of us will ever practice necromancy. But we may expand our personal range of experience by giving more thought to the dead and their role in our lives. A Brazilian friend told me that on a recent visit home she and her cousin spent a heartwarming day at the cemetery renewing their friendship with those who had died. Since graves in Brazil often display the picture as well as the name of the deceased, it was easy to make a connection with relatives and friends who had passed away. The two women talked at length to many deceased people, asking them questions, telling them recent news, and wishing them well. Passersby smiled understandingly as the two friends joked and laughed with the dead. At the day's end, their hearts felt rich and full. They had extended a bridge between this world and the next, and both sides undoubtedly profited by it. I regret that many modernized countries no longer celebrate a "day of the dead." The deceased seem to have no place, no usefulness, in a culture devoted to industrial production. Individual friends and

King Saul Talks to the Dead
(I Samuel, chapters 28 and 31)

KING SAUL WAS DESPERATE. THE PHILISTINES WERE
planning to attack the city, and his own people were
turning against him. Day after day, Saul prayed to God
for a sign of reassurance. But he received no answer. In
desperation, the king disguised himself and traveled to
see a wise-woman who lived in Endor. "I pray thee,"
he said, "consult with your familiar spirit and bring up
a certain soul of the dead."

"Do you want me killed?" the woman cried. But
Saul assured her she would not be punished for calling
up spirits. "I see gods ascending out of the earth," the
seeress cried while in trance. "And they gather in the
form of a man covered with a long mantle." Then
Saul bowed low, for he recognized the spirit of his wise
counselor, Samuel.

But harsh words rushed from the spirit's mouth.
Saul was condemned for breaking his agreement with
the Lord and told that tomorrow he would die. Upon
hearing this prophecy, the king collapsed into a heap.

The next day, Saul's troops were decimated, and
he was mortally wounded. As for the wise-woman, she
must have thought it sad and ironic that the man who
persecuted the ancient arts so viciously should ultimately turn to them in his hour of need. In the mean-
time, she would continue her work in secret.

relatives are remembered, but we extend no hand of greeting to the multitudes of dead as a community. Our lack of hospitality in this respect separates us from an important human tradition. Perhaps we are missing many opportunities to receive direct assistance from the "friendly dead" who still take interest in our lives.

I believe that we can strengthen our connection to oracles by devoting mindful thought to images of bodily decay. I realize how strange this statement may sound. Only after studying ancient practices for a long time did I finally recognize the intimate connection between oracles and the buried dead. I began to understand that in the earliest times people looked downward into the earthy dark for guidance and comfort. The caves, the snug womb-like shelters, the moist hollows in rocks and trees—these were our first temples. The earth pressed oracles upon us, body to body. And where the body is, death will naturally follow.

Learning about ancient folkways also made me aware of how shielded most of us are from the physical realities of death. We see images of violent murder on nearly every media broadcast, but dead bodies are immediately whisked out of sight. I wonder what would happen if a newspaper or television station presented close-up pictures of corpses in various stages of decay? Horrified viewers would be outraged. They might demand that new censorship laws be enacted to prevent exposure of such material. Killing is acceptable, but the dead are off-limits. Our deepest terrors are revealed by peering into our taboos.

When consciousness of death is blocked, awareness of oracles will also be blocked. To say that people fear an encounter with the unknown misses the bigger point. What they really fear is an encounter with the dissolver, the undoer, the decayer. The spacious dark of oracular presence bears an ominous likeness to the darkness of the crypt.

In some traditional cultures today there survives an awful and awe-filled practice: disinterment of corpses and the reading of human bones. For example, anthropologist C. Nadia Seremetakis has published a detailed account of such practices in Inner Mani, a province in Greece.[11] Of Greek descent herself, Seremetakis lived with old women in a particular village, sharing their housework and conversing with them in their native language. After several years of friendship, she gained admittance to the inner sanctum of pre-Christian spiritual traditions. These traditions included reading dreams, speaking prophecies, and exhuming the dead.

Seremetakis noted that exhuming the dead is an activity that belongs exclusively to women in Greece, and older women gain spiritual weightiness from knowing secrets of the grave. Even the most respected community members cannot belong to the inner circle of those who "have seen." In fact, the researcher commented that no matter how close she got to the old women, there was always something missing in the relationship. They treated her with an attitude of "You're still young," not because of her age, but because she was ignorant of certain mysteries. But after Seremetakis expressed her desire to witness an exhumation, their attitude changed. Now she could begin to fathom their most important truths.

Drawing upon Seremetakis's extensive interviews, I have reconstructed the following account of an exhumation. It condenses a large amount of information while remaining as close as possible to the thoughts and experiences of the Greek women as they were recorded in the researcher's interviews.

A corpse is exhumed three years after the burial. If the crypt can't be opened at that time, you must wait until the fifth year. Even-numbered years are dangerous, for the dead could drag you along with them into the grave. In the old days, members of the village used to stream in from all over the countryside and witness the "opening." They would wail loudly in memory of their great loss. The dead felt comforted to be mourned by the people who loved them. Nowadays, few people have exhumations, and the old folks think it's a shame. To open your first grave is called "the first facing." A woman must call upon great inner strength within herself or she will not be able to do it. You can barely sleep or eat for a whole week beforehand, fearing what you will see and feel. On the appointed day, you set out early with a bucket of water, sponges, and vinegar. You also bring a cask along for holding the bones. Arriving at the crypt, you start to chisel away plaster from around the door until it gets loose enough to move. Then you slowly push open the heavy slab. That's a strange moment. You may see something like a little shadow escape through the door and vanish from sight. You squeeze your eyes shut in fear. You don't want to look at it, the body, the corpse. But you must face it, you must look.

The coffin has disintegrated into soft brown splinters that lie in little heaps everywhere. Nothing is left of the person you loved. Two teeth and a shrunken eyeball—that is all you can see of her face. Bits of clothing cling to the body in shreds. Strangely, one foot still wears a stocking, but it crumbles when you put your hand on it, and you see the little toenails plop into the dust. The only thing in the whole coffin that has not dissolved is a polyester handkerchief. The body looks charred, like it's been torched. A sick feeling goes through you to see how time burns everything away.

But you recover your heart and begin the work. First you brush away all the splinters, straw, and clothing. The stench is not that of the new-dead, but heavier and darker. It gets into your lungs and will never really leave as long as you live. But the work must go on. First you remove the head and place it in the bucket. Then the large arm and leg bones; shoulders, ribs, hips, spine, everything. You can't leave a single bone. It's very bad for you and family if anything is left behind. We have hundreds of bones, especially in the hands and feet. In the little toe alone there are many little pieces.

Now you wash the bones thoroughly with vinegar and water. You must scrub hard sometimes to get the old flesh off. All of the brain must be dug out. Wash and rinse, wash and rinse. It takes a long time to clean a skeleton. So many thoughts go through your mind while washing the corpse. You remember how this person used to cook food at the stove and hand each kid a warm piece of bread. The way she laughed when her little puppy skidded into a mud puddle— you think about these things.

The bones shine white in the sun after you lay them out to dry. This tells you that all is well with her in the afterlife and that she has come to peace with her former life. Bones that turn black, that is bad, very bad. Then you know that something isn't right with the person. Maybe there's a dark secret in the family that wants to be revealed. One time a man was disinterred and his muddy-looking bones revealed that things were not at rest in his soul. It turned out that he had molested his daughter many times, and no one knew. You have to pray for the soul of a man like that, and for his daughter, too. Sometimes the corpse writes letters on its skull or breast bones to communicate with the living. Then the old women get together and interpret their meaning, for the dead go to a lot of trouble to speak that way.

Finally, the bones are dry. You wash them all again and dry them again. It takes a long time. Then you put them into the cask. The skull must always be on top. You take the cask to the priest for a blessing, and he pours oil into it and says a few words over the bones. The poor bones, they look a mess swimming in oil, but you dry them out again in the sun. Now you take the loved one's remains to the family crypt and lay them down beside other relatives. You can feel good then because you know you've done the right thing for your loved one. This is how people should treat one another.

After the first facing, you are never the same. It hurts because you see that in the end we become a handful of bones, just like a dog, just like a goat. We all look the same in the grave. It makes no difference who you are, for you'll soon melt into the earth like everything else. Once you face the dead with open eyes, you never can be blind again.

Reading about the women of Inner Mani and how they encounter the dead fills me with wonder and respect. How many of us could dig our fingers into the rotted cavity of a corpse? How would we feel afterward? Like the old women of Mani, we would never be the same.

Each encounter with death scrapes away a layer of defense from our psychic structure. Terror follows, but if the experience is contained in a ritual framework, new vitality surges through the self. From a psychoanalytic perspective, we might say that the energy we had used to repress our fear of death is now liberated and can be used for living life. Freud pointed out long ago that people who repress large amounts of unconscious material seem pinched and drained. They have little zest for life, and even small tasks deplete their spirits. But as soon as repression lifts, liberated energy flows freely. Sorrow, rage, and fear are keenly felt. But the soul is alive.

In Freud's time, people commonly repressed knowledge of their sexual fantasies and desires. Today, we repress knowledge of our own approaching death. Sogyal Rinpoche, a Buddhist lama raised in Tibet, said that he was shocked to see how Westernized countries shield their citizens from the images, sounds and sensations of dying.[12] He expressed concern over this attitude of denial, for death is the teacher who shows us how to live. We should take time to contemplate the last hours of our earthly existence, Rinpoche says. We should meditate often on our death, not in a morbid way, but with mindful thought about the impermanence of all things. Then we should ask, "How can I conduct my life today in such a manner that I will have no regrets in those final hours?"

Oracular receptivity opens wide when awareness of death is no longer blocked. This is why people caught in life-threatening emergencies are often flooded with messages of guidance from a transcendent source. Similarly, those who have accepted the fact they are dying from cancer, the AIDS virus, or other illnesses may be visited by remarkable oracles on a daily basis. Numinous voices and caresses are ever near for those who reach out to them. The realms of Deep Earth bear special love for those who will soon return to its embrace. And that includes all of us.

Eco-theologian Thomas Berry has suggested that in this confused and desperate era, our cultural institutions may not be able to help us.[13] He says that we need to go to the earth and ask for its guidance. Earth holds within itself the psychic and physical form of every being who now lives or has ever lived. Somewhere in the expanse of its wise intelligence, we may be able to find ourselves.

Earth's guidance is readily available to us. We make connection with it by following our hunches and feeling free to experiment. I believe that nature oracles want us to enjoy them, to play with them, to exchange love talk. Once a heart is open to the kinship of all life, loneliness cannot last very long or run very deep, even in the face of death.

The world's oracular traditions drew their original inspiration from the Earth. No one knew this reality better than the priestesses of an oracle site whose very name sets the imagination turning. To learn more about their way of working we next journey to Delphi.

Chapter 3

Delphi's Enduring Message

Delphi. The name is like no other. From classical times to the present, people have revered Delphi as the paragon of all oracle sites. Every broken stone and worn inscription from the temple grounds has been palmed over a thousand times in hopes of discovering new clues to the ancient wonder. The priestess herself, enthroned upon a three-legged platform, eyes closed in trance, has inspired the imagination of writers and poets for thousands of years. Even though she uttered her last words over fifteen hundred years ago, we have never let her voice fade from memory.

What is the basis of our enduring fascination with Delphi? I believe the answer runs deeper than we suspect. Thinking about the oracle of long ago stirs our own archetypal ability to commune with numinous forces. Delphi reminds us that oracular ways of knowing used to have a place in everyday life. We revere the shrine not for its historical importance but for its spiritual power. This chapter explores the mystery of Delphi, asks what meaning it holds for us today, and examines modern descendants of ancient oracle-speakers.

Let us begin with an old legend of how the oracle at Delphi was founded. The story comes to us from Roman historians writing in the first century B.C.E., more than five hundred years after the shrine first gained fame in the Greek world.[1] I find this particular legend to be very instructive, for it seems to carry an underlying message about the nature of our own oracular abilities.

Long before Delphi's great marble temple was built, the area was a track of wilderness. One day, a goat herder wandered into the area, lazily nudging his animals forward with a long staff. Suddenly, he noticed something strange up ahead. A few of the goats were leaping around in a most peculiar way, throwing their heads back and emitting hoarse, urgent cries. They trembled all over as though chilled to the bone. Drawing closer, the herder saw that some of his goats had clustered around a fissure in the earth from which vapors were rising. They were staring into the crack with intent interest.

"What's down there?" the herder wondered. He craned his neck over the fissure and peered into the swirling mist. Within moments an exalted feeling of inspiration swept through his body. Leaping back from the chasm, the herder danced and whirled among his goats, singing joyful songs of praise for all creation. So much knowledge poured through his mind that he could not possibly tell it all in a hundred years. Scenes from past history played before his eyes, and he saw events from the future unfold with bright clarity. The herder lost all track of time and wanted to stay in that place forever and ever.

Relatives became concerned when the herder did not arrive at his destination as expected. They sent out a search party to comb the area, and it was not long before they found him sitting in the grass among his goats, chanting to himself. He was brought to a nearby settlement and put to bed. No one could figure out what was wrong with the man. Had he eaten the poison honey that was known to cause madness?

The herder awoke a day later and seemed calmer. When a young woman brought him a bowl of goat's milk, he smiled and said, "Thank you maiden. I know that the man you wish to marry carries a spear-point in his leg, but don't worry, the point will work its way out before tomorrow has passed. He'll be quite fit for the wedding." Everyone gasped. How could this stranger know such a thing? Only yesterday the girl's parents had expressed doubts about the warrior's health, for he was feverish from a wound in his thigh. The herder went on talking to no one in particular. "Don't send your prayers to distant corners of the sky," he said in a dreamy voice. "The deities are nearer than your breath. It is love that binds them to us." Now everyone took a step backward. An ignorant shepherd with greasy hair speaking for the gods? This was impious, impertinent, outrageous. But rather wonderful.

People from all around began streaming into the village for a look at the stranger. Sometimes he told them what their problem was before they even spoke; at other times he listened patiently while they asked his advice. His words always hit the mark, and he seemed to possess knowledge of both worldly and otherworldly matters. Soon the herder was revered as an oracle-speaker.

News of the amazing chasm spread far and wide. Its vapors came from the divine realm of Earth, people said, and those who inhaled them mingled with the breath of Earth and gained sublime knowledge. And it seemed to be true. Pilgrims to the site were filled instantly with divine inspiration. Everyone was speaking oracles, seeing into mysteries, and dancing in joy beneath the cliffs of Mount Parnassus. In their rapture some individuals threw themselves into the crevasse and were never seen again.

Village leaders soon became alarmed. "This strange trance poses a danger to the community," they said. "It is our duty to protect citizens from destroying themselves." So they roped off the chasm and posted guards around the area. This measure proved to be very unpopular, however, and people began clamoring for access to the wonderful oracular portal. Finally, it was decided that access to the fissure would not be denied completely. One person alone would be appointed to inhale the vapors and serve as the community's official oracle.

The people reluctantly agreed to this plan. A woman was selected who possessed a fine character and was practiced in many mysteries. Once a year, the priestess was escorted to a three-legged stool positioned over the abyss. As the vapors enclosed her body like a divine cloak, she entered into an inspired trance and gave counsel to those who asked. As years passed and with increasing frequency, elaborate structures were built over the site. Soon the great institution of Delphi became renowned throughout the land.

Many elements of this legend invite reflection. I am struck by the idea that oracular consciousness is a natural gift emanating from the earth itself. As we know, Ge (also called Ga, Gaea, Gaia, and Ma) was worshiped from very early times as the living Earth Matrix whose boundless generative power creates and sustains all things. When its vapors (an image of soul) mingle with our breath, we partake in the vast consciousness of Gaea and become oracle-speakers.

The Delphic legend implies that divinely inspired vision is available to any human being. Oracular abilities are not the exclusive property of a few gifted individuals, nor do they belong to the priestly classes alone. A personal connection with divine presence is available to all who draw near the source. Perhaps there was a time in history when human beings enjoyed free access to inspired intuition. Or perhaps the phrase "long ago" is a metaphor for a place in the psyche where oracular knowing always flow freely.

What happens next in the story is astonishing, for it seems to forecast two thousand years of Western history in one swoop.

Expanded states of consciousness were condemned as dangerous because they operated outside of the rules of rational thought. Any threat to rationality was deemed a peril to society itself. So oracular knowing was placed off-limits. If people wanted to receive information from transrational sources, they now had to journey long distances and petition a selected individual who was kept under close observation. It is true that the oracle-speaker was highly celebrated and revered. But her richness only underscored the poverty of others, for people eventually forgot their own oracular birthright.

Delphi stirs our wonder because it preserves the memory of a consciousness almost lost. Having been banished from the place where Deep Earth breathes up to us, we long to find one last sanctuary where oracles still might live. We would gladly journey miles over rough terrain (like pilgrims of old) to witness divine counsel pouring through human lips.

The Pythoness Delivers Oracles

The priestess at Delphi felt deeply honored to be addressed as the "pythoness" (also called the "pythia"). Her name recalled the ancient she-serpent of Ge, whose shrine consecrated the site long before the temple of Apollo was built. Serpents were revered as manifestations of divine Earth power and presence. A pythoness was one who drew upon vast resources from realms below the surface world. From the earliest times, these realms were associated with dreams, healing, communication with the dead, artistic inspiration, prophecy, and second sight.

Before entering the temple, the pythoness acknowledged deities who inhabited the sacred site. We have a glimpse of what this invocation may have been like from the opening scene of a Greek play, The *Eumenides* by Aeschylus.[2] First, homage was paid to Themis and Phoebe (daughters of Ge), who were the first oracle-speakers at the shrine. The priestess then saluted

Apollo, Dionysus, Poseidon, Zeus, and the nymphs of the Corycian cave. Finally, she closed with a prayer that Apollo would guide her lips and enable her to speak the truth. It was important that the priestess address by name every deity who empowered Delphi.[3] Because the gods and goddesses were experienced as living entities, as real and vital as any person, she needed to affirm her bond with them and ask for their blessing. Only they could make the magic happen.

The priestess made a burnt offering of laurel leaves and barley meal on a temple altar. Because laurel was the heraldic emblem of Apollo, she possibly placed a few leaves of the plant in her mouth as well. Some modern writers have speculated that the pythia chewed quantities of laurel in order to enter a trance state by biochemical means. But most authorities doubt this claim. Spiritual practitioners in antiquity were quite capable of entering altered states of consciousness without chemical assistance. Furthermore, chewing a quantity of laurel leaves would probably have brought on severe headaches and nausea in the poor priestess—a condition not very conducive to inspiration.

Entering the *adyton* (holy chamber) beneath the nave of the temple, the priestess mounted a tall chair that resembled a covered bowl with three legs. In one hand she held a branch of laurel. For some time she sat quietly upon her throne, recessed in meditation. Then suddenly the laurel branch in her hand began to move. First it twitched almost imperceptibly; then the motions intensified until each separate leaf trembled violently. The movements spread up the pytheoness's arm to her shoulder and chest until her whole body vibrated as though shaken by an invisible hand. By this sign, priests knew that she had surrendered to the state of *enthousiasmos*—divine ecstasy. Trembling was regarded as a sacred phenomenon signaling that the deity's presence had come into her body.

"I greet thee," a voice said. It was the priestess's voice, but her tone was deep and round, like someone speaking from a

Who Was the Pythoness of Delphi?

How old was she? The priestess was required to
be at least forty-five or fifty years of age. In the very
early years of Delphi's operation, she might have been
selected from among younger women.

How was she chosen? We do not know. But she had
to possess a fine character and spiritual mindedness.

What was she like? In classical times, she appeared
to be a cultivated woman who could utter oracles in
refined verse. By the first century of the common era,
it was preferred that the priestess have no education or
worldly experience.

What was her life like at Delphi? She lived a devotional existence in a community of priests and temple
attendants. Her practice probably included
fasting, prayer, and the performance of many rituals.
The pythoness was required to live a life of "purity,"
but it is unknown whether she was expected to be
celibate. Standards for sexual conduct probably
varied over the centuries.

How often did she deliver oracles? In early
centuries, oracles were delivered once a year. Sessions
increased to once a month as the temple gained in
fame. At times, three priestesses lived at the shrine
to serve the many pilgrims seeking audience.

*In this early Greek image of the Delphic oracle, the pythoness
sits serenely on her sacred tripod with a laurel branch in
one hand and a shallow bowl in the other, preparing
to address a petitioner. (5th century* B.C.E.)

well. Each word seemed to fill the entire room with its uncanny
fullness. Sometimes a fragrance of unusual beauty drifted
through the room where the pythoness sat entranced. Yet no
one could identify its source.

Questions were now read to the pythoness. She listened to
each one, was silent for a moment, then responded with a
haunting chant or song. Sometimes the message was simple and

direct. But often the words were arranged into elegant hexameter verses, a style of poetry used for religious discourse. Considerable talent was required to fashion answers spontaneously into this complex form of verse. It has been claimed that the phythia's actual words were barely understandable and that priests translated them into poetry. But there is no evidence to support this prejudice, and early Greek writers expressed no doubt that the oracle-speaker's verses came from her own mouth. In later centuries, however, the literary quality of oracles declined sharply, and they were no longer given in verse.

What did the priestess herself feel during entranced sessions? Since oracular practice in Greece was built upon the earlier shamanic traditions, we can gain insight from looking at the work of shamans today. All over the world, trembling is recognized as a signal that the practitioner is entering an empowered state of consciousness. Many shamans plunge so deeply into trance that they experience themselves being possessed by a deity, spirit, or otherworldly entity. Sometimes they remember nothing of the episode later. Yet they continue to drum and dance while in a profoundly dissociated state of mind. Moments later, some of their self-awareness returns, and they carry out complex ritual procedures on behalf of their patient. Shamans are able to accomplish such feats because they are very skilled at moving between different levels of consciousness.

It is likely that the pythoness of Delphi exercised a similar ability. There were times when she allowed the supernal Other (who was identified as Apollo) to take over her identity completely. She may have remembered nothing of these sessions when they were over. On other occasions the oracle-speaker might have chosen to remain in a light trance, responding to practical questions with practical answers. Perhaps this is why such a variety of style and mood is found in her oracles.

One feature of Delphi's operation finds no parallel in modern Western cultures. An entire institution, sheltered by state government, was dedicated to preserving oracular consciousness. Everything was done to protect the pythoness and foster her special abilities. We can imagine how supported she must have felt as she carried out her duties. Daily life was filled with ritual, prayer, and an abiding sense of spiritual presence. Oracular work unfolded in a setting of enchantment that engaged in all the senses. The priestess bathed in spring waters, inhaled pungent incense, tasted bitter leaves, grasped a branch of laurel, and meditated to celestial music. The tripod upon which she sat was an object of such intense meaning that even touching it could transport her into trance. At a personal level, each woman serving as pythoness must have cherished a feeling of having been chosen, even destined, for this vocation. She also drew strength from the ancient site itself and the lineage of powerful feminine deities whose name she invoked each day.

The priestess must also have benefited from the institutional support she received in her work. She could surrender to an exalted state of spiritual communion knowing that she was totally protected. Attendants watched over her body, priests dealt with the outside world, and an entire civilization paid homage to her art. Each time the pythoness stepped into her holy chamber of oracles, she not only ministered to the people but affirmed for all generations the boundlessness of spirit.

Oracular Messages: More than Meets the Eye

I remember feeling disappointed when I first read the actual oracles uttered by Delphi's priestess. I had assumed that most of her statements would be as memorable as the famous "Know thyself" or "No one is wiser than Socrates." But I was wrong. Responses that have come down to us from legend deal mostly with waging war, founding colonies, and scrambling for political position. A supplicant named Battus was instructed to sail without delay to Libya and destroy the "savages wearing sheepskin

*A 19th-century engraving depicts the oracle of Delphi as losing
her wits and becoming terrified at the snakes she holds. This
portrait reflects our modern distrust of oracular practice and
contrasts sharply with ancient images (see page 68).*

coats." One ruler asked the oracle permission to invade the territory of Arcadia. The oracle told him to ravage a neighboring town instead. After reading dozens of such accounts, I felt worn out by the ceaseless themes of conquest and cruelty.

My pleasure in studying oracular sayings took another nosedive after learning that a mere fraction were authentic. When the classicist Joseph Fontenrose analyzed over five hundred Delphic oracles, he determined that only seventy-five had a firm historical foundation.[4] The others appear to be borrowed from folklore or created by ancient writers for their own purposes. For instance, if a war had been won, they would say, "And this event was predicted by the pythoness, who said that 'Victory shall bless the Athenians during the time of harvest.'" Their intent was not to deceive the reader, but to emphasize the underlying order that shapes all human affairs.

Most of the cunning double-edged oracles we read about cannot be authenticated. For instance, a famous story told in classical lore concerns Croesus, a powerful ruler and warlord. Croesus asked the pythoness whether he should cross the river Aly and attack Persia. He was itching to invade that country and hoped the oracle would give a favorable response. "If Croesus crosses the river Aly," the priestess answered, "a mighty kingdom will be destroyed." The ruler shouted in joy to hear such good tidings, and he eagerly went to battle. But later, as the Persians dragged him away in chains through the ruins of his kingdom, he had a terrible realization: The oracle never said *whose* kingdom would be lost! An unforgettable account—but almost certainly literary fiction, according to scholars.

Few interesting predictions may be found among Delphic oracles. The pythoness showed little interest in forecasting global events, and her visions never wandered far beyond her own time and culture. Petitioners rarely asked for glimpses of the future. Most individuals in the ancient world considered it impious to seek foreknowledge of events. They believed that humankind has its being within the matrix of Divine Being, and that personal destinies are not wholly ours to shape and control. The correct spiritual move, from their viewpoint, was to align oneself with the larger destiny and promote its intentions through right action. Then both personal and divine purposes would be served. It was acceptable to ask for guidance, to check out the advisability of an action, or to request a blessing. But foreknowledge belonged to the gods alone. Thus, most oracles instructed people about which deities they should pray to or how they should carry out rituals properly.

After studying as many oracular responses as I could find, I had to admit my discouragement. Did people really travel for weeks through rough and dangerous territories just to hear that they should worship Demeter? Why did they need an oracle to tell them what they already knew?

Then a realization began to take shape gently, as when eyes adjust to the dark. Pilgrims did not journey to Delphi or other sacred shrines in order to receive information. They came because something *happened* to them there. Oracular presence transforms everything it touches, and this presence must have been very powerful in a site where oracles had lived for centuries. Hearing the oracle-speaker's actual words was only a small portion of the gift they received.

I know how affected I am when a personal oracle comes to me through a dream, divination, or mysterious happening. Many things shift in ways I never could have anticipated. How much greater the psychic impact must have been for seekers at Delphi.

When their session was over, seekers were escorted out of the chamber, blinking at the light of day and perhaps trembling from what had just happened. The priestess may have spoken words that were simple and sensible, offering no big surprises. But the world itself seemed strangely altered after leaving her presence. Life's scattered pieces fell into new patterns of meaning, and one's own place in the scheme of things took on new significance. Former problems remained, but they suddenly grew thinner, lost substance, faded into the background. And flowing through the entire experience was a feeling of blessedness, not only for oneself but for all creation. It was for the sake of this deeper message—the one that could be known but never explained—that pilgrims across a thousand years made the journey to Delphi.

Delphi's Last Message

No earthly institution lives forever. By late Roman times, oracle centers of the Mediterranean world had fallen into decline. The importance of religion was fading in light of new social and political conditions. No longer did leaders of nations seek advice from the pythoness about important decisions. Greece was an impoverished country ruled by foreigners, and the temple of Delphi was sacked many times, Among the educated classes, personal values shifted in the direction of modernism. Logical reasoning, critical analysis, goal-directed planning, and other skills born of rational philosophy were prized above the old oracular ways of knowing.

We can see these changes reflected most clearly in the way writers and artists depicted the pythoness. In the fifth century B.C.E. she was portrayed as a figure of dignity. Posed serenely on her sacred tripod, the priestess delivered oracles with an air of mastery. But beginning in the first century of the common era, a new image arose. The priestess was shown as a tragic creature who lost her wits as she became possessed with the god. She tore her hair, crashed into walls, and fell insensibly to the ground as horrible noises shrieked from her throat. Thank heavens that trained priests stood by who could interpret her mad ravings!

Two early church fathers, Origen and Chrysostom, added pornographic imagery to their accounts.[5] As the bride of Apollo sat upon the tripod with her legs spread apart, an evil spirit from the bowels of hell entered her vagina and filled her with madness. Foam gushed from her mouth as evil demons took possession of her throat. Clearly, these images devalue women as well as oracular practice. As we will see in our exploration of sibyls (chapter 6), the association between sexuality and oracles has survived well into the twentieth century.

In the year 362 c.e., a Roman emperor sent his messenger to Delphi to see whether the oracular tradition still survived. Legend recounts that the messenger received a somber answer from the last remaining pythoness. "The beautiful house has fallen," she said. "Apollo has no shelter; the sacred laurel has no resting place. Our fountain is silent. Our voice is stilled."[6]

These words were reported as the last oracle from Delphi. Not long after, the shrine was plundered by Christian troops. Not only were the buildings torn down, but every feature of the temple's interior was demolished with special thoroughness. Its altars, receiving rooms, living quarters, and holy *adyton* were pounded into rubble. The beautiful house did not only fall but was violently dismembered. This is why visitors to Delphi today see only a few broken walls and scattered pieces of marble where a living legend used to stand.

Those of us who love Delphi feel sorrow at recalling these scenes. We ardently wish that the center had been spared, at least in physical form. Then we could trace the footsteps of its pythoness across the courtyard and see where she lived and bathed, chanted and prayed. A wealth of knowledge about Delphi's operation could be learned from studying the kitchen areas, storerooms, and priests' quarters. Finally, we would steal into the holy chamber of oracles itself to catch a glimpse of the ancient magic.

But Delphi's downfall may also be viewed in a more positive light. Could it be that the Fates willed the oracle's destruction for purposes of their own? Knowing what we do about Greek faith in destiny, we must assume that the pythoness accepted events with tranquility. Let us imagine our way into this scenario, for it may reveal her most important message for our time.

It is the fourth century of the common era, and Delphi's curtain is about to fall. The priestess has known for some time that an army of Christian soldiers is galloping toward the sanctuary. Her visions often have forecast the invasion. She has seen their beefy faces redden with glee as the temple door gives way. She has witnessed them snatching the golden tripod with wild hoots as the sacred statues are pulled down. When they finally arrive, it is the same. There is no end to their passion for ruin. Everything soft is torched, everything hard is rammed and smashed. For weeks afterward, spirals of dust circle above the site like death-birds.

If the soldiers had hoped for a slaughter of pagans, they are disappointed. The pythoness and her priests had removed themselves to safety well in advance, taking a few holy objects with them. They also have stuffed their carrying bags with small items from the temple treasury to provide support in the months ahead. The rest they commend to the gods.

Delphi's fall is terrible to behold, but the priestess resists a temptation to mourn. After all, do not the deities alone create, preserve, and destroy all things? They are quite capable of taking care of their shrines when they wish. When Persian armies attacked Delphi in the past century, Apollo not only caused huge boulders to roll down from the hillside to crush the enemy but materialized a giant spirit-warrior who sent the invaders fleeing. The Divinities could easily have chased away this latest band of glory seekers. She can only conclude that the gods have allowed—or even directed—the shrine to be destroyed.

It is not difficult to see why the Great Accomplishers might have allowed Delphi to be erased. The temple's plush treasure room, the costly fees that petitioners are asked to pay, the bloody animal sacrifices, the coterie of priests who pad around the grounds feeling self-satisfied—perhaps the gods have grown weary of these forms and conventions. Even the old symbols of laurel and tripod, libation bowl and omphalos, have lost much of their spiritual power in recent decades.

The pythoness also has to admit that service in the temple has brought her little satisfaction of late. She is kept in strict isolation, almost like a prisoner. No one is allowed to visit, and her only recreation is to wander about the compound. The ideal priestess, according to prevailing ideas, is a woman who possesses no education and knows little of practical affairs. So she is prevented from learning to read or write, and news of the outside world seldom reaches her ears. Long ago, the pythoness had been a woman of intellectual and poetic refinement, thrilling the best minds of the age with her wise sophistication. Standards have certainly declined since then.

Furthermore, the priestess has grown bored with her own oracles. She still values the inspired state of mind she enters, but the questions put before her are drearily mundane. Money, property, legal disputes, demands to find a stolen ring, conflicts with a landlord—these are the types of concerns burning in the hearts of her petitioners. Where are the pious inquiries about the meaning of life or the will of the deities, she wonders. No, she has to admit that the oracle of Delphi no longer inflames the passions of either the gods or mortals.

As the pythoness reflects on these things, she recalls the old legend of the goat herder. She remembers that Delphi originally belong to Ge, primordial creatrix and sustainer of all life. The sacred ground needed no temple in those days. It drew power from rocks and caverns, root and chasms, and all the deep places that shelter soul. In the beginning, oracular inspiration gave itself freely to anyone who would receive it. But over time the gift became subject to increasing regulation and stricture. Now, only a few specially appointed individuals are given the right to speak for Earth, and even they are no longer lent an ear. Suddenly the priestess understands! Delphi's shrine has to be destroyed so that individuals can discover a connection to Ge in fresh, new places.

Thus, Delphi's message for us can be found in its rubble as well as in its glory. Temples rise and fall, but oracular consciousness is imperishable. We will always reach out to sources of psychic vitality beyond the personal self, seeking responses that address the soul directly. Nor is the communication one-sided. Delphi's example suggests that life itself perpetually streams forth its desires and yearnings. The ancient oracular shrines served as holy receiving vessels for some of these messages. Their old containers shattered long ago, but their contents are ever present, urging us to answer them voice to voice.

A Modern Journey to the Oracle

Today we cannot turn our eyes toward a temple on the hill and rest assured that oracle-speakers are sheltered there. But oracular art still thrives in regions of the world where ancient folkways are not yet obliterated. Private enclaves of mediumistic work may also be found in technologically developed countries, especially among ethnic groups who have preserved the traditions of their ancestors. Native American practitioners use altered states of consciousness to access information and guidance from oracular sources. Trance work plays a central role in the Vodon spiritual tradition of Haiti and is cultivated by some Haitian Americans. Oracular traditions from Vietnam, Laos, and Cambodia have found a foothold in the United States thanks to Southeast Asian immigrants. Hispanic *curanderos* and *curanderas* (male and female folk healers) may enter into a deeply receptive state through prayer and speak on behalf of the Virgin and other sacred personages. These are only a few of the groups who keep oracle-speaking alive in contemporary times.

During recent centuries of Western history, oracular pythonesses such as Helena Petrovna Blavatsky (1831-1891) have produced volumes of impressive material. Blavatsky's contemporaries reported that she would include long quotations from rare books in her writing, even though she had never physically seen these volumes. While working on a manuscript, the author would pause and gaze into the empty space in front of her. Then she would write down a quotation, which was later verified as accurate through library research. In describing her own process, Blavatsky related that knowledge came to her "first in dreams and then in pictures presented to the inner eye during meditation." Knowledge obtained in this way impressed itself on her mind in such a clear, convincing, and indelible way that all ordinary sources of information dwindled into insignificance. Blavatsky's prolific writing, which include *Isis Unveiled*, *The Secret Doctrine* and *The Voice of the Silence*, helped to found a major metaphysical movement, Theosophy.[7] This movement has been a catalytic force in religious thought and was a pioneering agency for acquainting Westerners with Eastern spiritual traditions. Today the Theosophical Society has branches in over sixty countries.

Alice Bailey (1880-1949), Edgar Cayce (1877-1945), and Jane Roberts (1929-1984) have also changed the course of modern spirituality with their various forms of oracle-speaking. Bailey's communications spawned many publications, including the influential *Course in Miracles*. Cayce's fifteen thousand sessions, delivered while in a sleeplike state, have provided abundant information on health, soul reincarnation, earth changes, and other topics of abiding interest. Roberts's transmissions from "Seth," as well as her own personal writings, offer reflections of unusual intelligence and grace. Her work helped inspire a resurgence of trans-egoic "channeling" in the 1970s and 80s. Though resulting communications varied widely in quality, many people experienced the benefit and surprise of what may happen when the self conjoins with expanded forms of consciousness.

My consultations with one such practitioner made a lasting impression on me. I didn't realize it at the time, but my experi-

The Oracular Shepherd of Rajasthan

THE ORACULAR ARTS STILL OCCUPY A CENTRAL PLACE in the spiritual life of rural India. American journalist William Dalrymple traveled by jeep to a remote part of Rajasthan near Rohet in order to see a living oracle called the *bhopa*.[8] The oracle is a shepherd who becomes possessed by Papuji the Warrior, an incarnation of the God Shiva. Through the power of this deity, the shepherd is said to have worked many miracles.

Dalrymple arrived to find a very old man squatting on a mat with his armpits cupped over his knees. He poured a ladle of clarified butter over the flames and began chanting a mantra. Rocking from side to side, the bhopa started trembling all over until his whole body was seized with shaking.

After a period of time, the oracle-speaker grew still and waited for petitioners to ask him questions. Dalrymple was taken aback when a wealthy Rajput asked, "Is it acceptable to the gods that I install a swimming pool at my estate?" But the oracle-speaker seemed untroubled and told the suppliant that he must eat only plain rice every day for two months as an offering to Shiva. Then the pool could be constructed.

Devotees of this oracular shepherd tell how he has cast out spirits, healed the sick, given wise counsel, and prophesied the future. Witnessing work such as his links us to folkways many thousands of years old.

ence paralleled that of suppliants to Delphi long ago. This experience provides an excellent example of some of the underlying purposes oracles serve in psychological life today.

One day an acquaintance said to me, "I know a very, very remarkable channeler. His name is Hossca. Wait until you hear the story of this man!" She then told me the following account. Hossca had been living an apparently normal life, running a small business and taking occasional excursions with his wife, whom I will call Patty, to recreational areas in Colorado. One weekend while he was boating on a lake, his craft overturned in the icy water. By the time rescuers came he was blue, had stopped breathing, and registered no pulse. Frantic efforts were made to resuscitate the victim as his terrified wife looked on. Suddenly everyone whooped with joy, for Hossca began coughing and breathing again. He opened his eyes and gazed at one face after another in a calm, almost serene, manner. He showed no particular recognition of Patty, and this fact struck her as a little strange. People assumed that the man was in shock.

Hossca barely spoke for the next day or two. Then one evening as he was lying in bed next to Patty, he told her something that almost made her heart fail on the spot. "The man Hossca whom you knew as your husband has departed the body," he said. "I am Jonah. I will occupy his place so that much needful work can be done in your plane of existence. Be assured that Hossca lives happily on without his physical casing. I am occupying his old place with his full permission."

After taking a deep breath, Patty smiled and told her husband not to worry, for he had been through a very traumatic experience. She thought that his bizarre behavior might be the result of minor brain damage. But deep down, she could not quite believe her own explanation. Everything about this man felt different from Hossca. An aura of wise maturity, almost of majesty, hovered about him, as though he were an old king. His eyes seemed larger and darker than she had remembered, and they shone with a look of. . .brilliance? Engagement? There was a certain penetration in his gaze that she had never seen in Hossca's eyes. And most oddly of all, she could have sworn that the hand lying beside hers on the bed was considerably bigger than that of her husband.

During the next weeks, Jonah talked to Patty about his multidimensional existence in different realities. A part of his being expressed itself through Hossca's body, but a greater part lived in other dimensions that were not bound by our laws of time and space. One of his purposes in conjoining with Hossca's body was to help people expand their limited notions of who they really were; he would encourage them to find their way back to the strata of natural joy that binds all creation together. The soul whom Hossca had called his wife could remain with him and share in the work. Or she was free to go her own way with his most respectful love and blessings.

Patty listened to all of this with deepening wonder. Her former husband could not be called a "spiritual" man. In their years together she had never known him to express undue interest in religious matters nor to read books on metaphysical topics. How could he now speak about occult things with such authority and wisdom? Something was happening that surpassed all understanding. And she was right about his hands. They did not fit into any of his old gloves. His hat size was larger, too, for a new ridge of bone had developed across the lower part of his scalp.

When my friend finished her account, we both lapsed into silence. Then she asked, "Do you want to see Jonah in person?"

"Could anything keep me away?" I answered.

I felt weak and trembly sitting on Patty's couch when the day arrived. My reaction surprised me because I had attended many channeling sessions during the previous year. Much of the material I had heard was quite wise and helpful; some of it was complete nonsense. Merely going into a trance does not make a master. But once in a while, holiness breaks through a message like stars through a fog. One has to keep an open mind and observe with discrimination.

If I knew all of this, why had my knees turned to rubber? I realized that Hossca's story had made a deep impression on me. It churned up an intimation of the Mysterious, and my imagination was kindled. What if I indeed were about to stand before an entity from another dimension? What if this Jonah were truly "other" and not just an ordinary man? These thoughts made me want to rush into the oracle room and flee from the house at the same time.

Patty told me I would have about fifteen minutes of individual time with Jonah. He would also make some general remarks to the small group of us who were visiting him that day. Patty said that after the session was over, most people elected to give a donation to help Jonah continue his work. She mentioned a typical amount of twenty or twenty-five dollars for the session, which usually ran ninety minutes. But anything would be appreciated, she added. I thought the amount sounded reasonable, and after all, the former Hossca certainly would not be returning to his old business office. The family deserved to be supported.

I wondered what I should ask Jonah when my turn came. Perhaps I should use the opportunity to probe one of the big questions of life. "Jonah," I could ask, "what is the nature of time?" No, too abstract. Perhaps, "Jonah, the creatures of this world—humans, animals, insects, and maybe plants, too—suffer horrific pain in physical existence. Could you account for that, please?" No, I thought, I'll save that question for the All-That-Is later.

I drew in a breath and asked myself what I really *wanted* to know at this moment. The answer came immediately. Only a month earlier I had left a position I had held for many years in child custody dispute work. Its punishing demands had been eating me up alive, and I knew I had to leave for the sake of my own mental health. But when the moment of freedom finally came, I fell into a state of panic and depression. My mind was in a spin much of the time; I felt like one who must urgently get home but has no idea where home might be. And my money was running out. Perhaps Jonah could help me. Yes, I would do the same thing that suppliants to the oracle had done for thousands of years: humbly ask for personal guidance.

We sat quiet as mice on the carpet, looking up at the man in the chair. He sat motionless with closed eyes for a long time. A very long time. Just as we began to squirm a little and wonder what this was all about, Jonah's head gave a little sideways twitch, the way horses toss off a fly. Another twitch and another, and then the right shoulder jerked; both shoulders jumped and brought the elbows up with them. It looked as though the man in the chair was being stabbed by pins all over his body; muscles spasmed in a gangly, unregulated way. Out of curiosity I later tried to imitate the effect. I found myself totally unable to make so many parts of my body move in so many different ways at once.

A final shudder, and the body settled comfortably into his chair again. The eyes opened. They were deep pools of black that shone strangely, recalling the unnatural brightness of high fever or romantic passion. "Good day, beloved gods, good day!" Jonah called out in a cheerful, vigorous voice. The pronunciation carried an accent that I couldn't place. He leaned forward and seemed to be beaming his good will into us. It must have worked, for I felt a rush of energy tinged with elation.

"For ye *are* gods," he continued. "Once ye know this, ye will stop punishing ye-selves." He pronounced it "Poh-neeshing." A dissolving sensation washed across my mind. His words flowed into each other so transparently that I wondered whether I was thinking them or listening to them. "Yes, pain does teach. The energy of fear and separation and powerlessness do certainly teach, for the soul uses everything in the service of learning. But joy and abundance also teach, beloved gods! It is your free will to choose how to grow."

I felt astounded by the idea that joy and abundance are equally valid ways to learn. Of course I knew it before, but I didn't know it, not like I received it now. Yes, that was why I had left that job, because I was no longer willing to endure so much suffering in the school of life.

Jonah had read my thoughts, or so it seemed. "Ye are here in this school to experience the results of every decision ye make, consciously or unconsciously. Take responsibility for your decisions with open eyes and a joyful heart; then ye will begin to know ye are truly creators. Then ye will accept your own mastership as gods."

Jonah's words were running past me like a river. Meanwhile, I was drifting in the side eddies, turning round and round in their luxurious thoughts. "Experience the results of every decision." I felt the full implication of its meaning. In my mind I saw silvery streams flowing out in all directions from a woman's body. This body was my own. The streams branched and crossed and turned back on themselves in a most exquisite manner until they formed elaborate structures that resembled domes and buildings. I saw the woman walk forward into one of these structures. I knew that she would have all kinds of experiences in there, and those experiences were formed out of her own soul emanations. I didn't understand how this process could happen, but I felt sure that I was seeing something true.

All too soon, it was my turn to go up before Jonah. But my questions had already been answered by his lecture. I knew that my present fear rose from not owning my decision to quit my job. I felt forced out by the crushing workload, and I criticized myself for being too weak to hang in there. But if I joyfully trusted that decision, it would lead me to a shining structure by and by. "Good day, Beloved!" Jonah was saying.

"Well, Jonah, I want to thank you for being here," I stammered, sounding foolishly like the hostess at a birthday party. "It means a lot to me."

"And to me!" he boomed.

"I've been feeling disoriented lately and can't seem to find my direction. I was going to ask you about that, but at this moment it doesn't really seem like a problem."

"Think of one who has been spinning around and around for a long time," he said. "And now this one suddenly stops. What will be this one's experience?" He said it as, "these wone's experrreence."

"They would be dizzy," I answered.

"The world would seem to keep spinning, is it not so? The ground beneath would seem to sway. Right and the left would be hard to know. This is your experience now. Take time to catch your breath. Ye will soon know where to go."

As Jonah spoke, my interior being confirmed every word. I appreciated for the first time how fast I had been spinning in that intense job. I was being too hard on myself, expecting to gain a new direction overnight. The oracle-speaker's words eased my heart so much that I could not help but bring my other concern to him.

"This next question isn't very spiritual, but I must ask it. I find myself worrying about money. Can you advise me?"

"What makes ye think that abundance and poverty are not spiritual questions, my friend? On the one hand ye wish that money were abundant, but secretly ye wonder, 'Am I worthy of receiving?' Ye think that all money must be won by hard, hard, hard earning. This is a pattern of self-punishment, beloved god."

Jonah's words stunned me. I had expected him to say that money wasn't important and that I should turn my mind to spiritual things. But he came at me from the opposite direction. I was reeling with the accuracy of his statements. I always felt I had to work harder than others to merit even a little reward. When he called me a "beloved god," tears came to my eyes, for the idea of a god punishing herself seemed so sad.

Jonah was still speaking, recommending a visualization I might do. He said that it would strengthen my sense of unity with a generous universe that enjoys giving effortlessly to its creatures. I was glad that my friend was taking notes on the session, for I could hardly follow his words. An ocean was roaring in my ears.

I am sure that I looked quite dazed as I thanked Jonah and returned to my seat. I didn't know it at the time, but a fine teaching position with a good salary would be offered to me nine months later. And the universe must have enjoyed its effortless giving on that occasion because I had never even applied for the job!

Why We Need Oracles

My experience with Jonah helped me to imagine more vividly what it must have been like to stand before the pythoness and other oracle-speakers in the past. I am sure that the imagination of pilgrims was inflamed by wondrous stories circulating about the oracle. They undoubtedly heard the same strange roaring in their ears that I heard, and they felt the speaker's words expanding in all directions at once. I understand now why the actual sentences spoken by an oracle may not seem very interesting to an outside observer. The communications are meant for the suppliant's ears alone, and their commonly shared meaning carries only a fraction of the real message.

Ancient peoples were drawn to oracle centers not by the hope of receiving prophecies, but by the desire to fulfill deep spiritual yearnings. These yearnings are native to the human psyche and still call us today. Among them are the longing to be addressed by a numinous Other, the desire to expand consciousness beyond the boundaries of time and space, and the need to affirm one's unity with the matrix of All-That-Is. Oracles can fulfill these needs in several ways.

The personal self yearns to be touched by something greater than itself. Sensing the restriction of our own boundaries, we long to find a gateway into expanded realms of experience. Many of us have touched the beyond-self by falling in love, going into the wilderness, communing with dreams and visions, being transported by the arts, or following a spiritual practice. Illness, defeat, and tragedy may also pay us a visit and confer their terrible, sublime gifts upon the soul.

Oracle-speakers bring us into the presence of otherness. When Jonah opened his oddly shining eyes, I knew I was looking into the face of mystery. A chill ran through me to think that I might be listening to an entity from another dimension. I did not really know who was speaking, but at that moment its identity did not matter. The "otherness" of the experience was enough to carry me into a different state of awareness.

Not only do oracles allow us to experience a numinous Other, they focus that Other's attention upon the personal self. Imagine how ancient people must have felt when a divine being took interest in their private lives. I myself was comforted when Jonah responded to my questions with such earnest attention. When he probed beneath my surface questions so insightfully, my sense of gratitude increased. One must be addressed personally to be addressed at all. According to the OED, the Latin word for "address" *addrictiare*, originally carried the meaning of "making straight or right." Oracular messages have the power to straighten out or make right areas of psychic entanglement. As depth psychologist Lionel Corbett has noted in his study of the religious function of the psyche, numinous experiences have the effect of correcting your direction.[10] The change may seem minor at the time, but like a missile traveling into space, small corrections in the beginning make a significant difference later.

Oracular art lifts consciousness out of time and space. Oracles belong to a realm where the past, present, and future coexist in the timeless presence of "now". Everything that has

The Tibetan State Oracle Is Alive and Well (and Living in India)

FOR AT LEAST EIGHT HUNDRED YEARS, A STATE-supported oracular institution thrived at the monastery of Nechung ("Small Palace") in Tibet. Since the Chinese annexation of that country in the 1950s, the oracle has functioned in exile at Dharmasala, 250 miles north of Delhi. Author W. Geoffrey Arnott has pointed out that the operation of this oracle bears striking resemblance to those of Delphi.[9] A monk called the *kuden* purifies himself for two days before delivering oracles. He meditates, performs rituals, and abstains from food that is unclean according to his personal spiritual practice. The kuden also undergoes various rites of consecration, such as having holy saffron water poured over his head while mantras are chanted.

The kuden is dressed in elaborate costume, waiting to go into trance. Sounds of horns, drums, and cymbals fill the hall, creating a hypnotic atmosphere. Soon the oracle-speaker leaps from his chair and whirls around the room as a great spirit entity (Dorje Drakden, a protector of Tibet) possesses his senses. After he sits down again, petitioners may approach him with their questions. He answers each in turn. Then he collapses into unconsciousness and is carried from the room. Suppliants return to their daily lives, inspired and full of hope after coming face to face with a spokesperson for the divine.

occurred or will occur is contained there, as well as the infinite rings of possibility that life itself generates. Those of us who have worked with dreams, divination, channeling, or other oracular arts know how time dissolves at the moment we enter psychic space. An hour slips by when we could have sworn that only ten minutes had passed. Or we pass through endless tunnels of images and associations—more than we could process in a week—yet only twenty minutes have gone by on the clock. This, I believe, is the real secret of time travel. We don't move like a streetcar along the track of time. Time itself travels through our psyche as we hover motionless in oracular space.

Time took on peculiar qualities while I was in the presence of Jonah. Each one of his sentences entered my mind and then proliferated in all directions. I could have stopped the clock and meditated for hours on their implications. An image comes to mind of CD-ROMs and the way information is encoded on them. As the reader reads the text, certain words appear highlighted. The reader can press a key and see what additional information lies behind that word. Then the reader may return to the original text. In the same way, I found myself assessing large amounts of information behind Jonah's words. Meanwhile, he was continuing on with his dialogue. It is common to experience reality unfolding in multiple time tracks when oracular consciousness is bright.

Finally, and most importantly, oracular knowing unites us with the matrix of All-That-Is. We long to feel connected with something larger than ourselves. We want to know that a certain order pervades the universe, that events do not happen at random. Viktor Frankl, a psychoanalyst who survived the concentration camps during the Holocaust, said that people can bear anything if they can find a sense of purpose in their experience.[11] But if that purpose is taken away, they may die even while receiving food and shelter. Oracular communications give us information, guidance, and insight. But the most precious gift is to bestow meaning on our lives.

The underlying message of all oracles is this: "The universe is both intelligent and purposeful. We will now show you a little part of its divine intention, a part that pertains directly to you. Be assured that you are not alone. You belong to the Matrix that holds and beholds us all." No matter what other communication is offered in an oracle, this one is primary. It carries the central power to comfort and heal.

My state of mind was transformed when I left the session with Jonah. Why? He did not offer any concrete prophecies about my life (though others sometimes received them, I learned). He did not say, "Dianne, don't worry about a thing. Two months from today you will get your bearings again and realize that you want to return to academic life. You'll apply for teaching positions at several colleges, but you won't be offered any of them. You'll feel quite discouraged. Then someone you knew a long time ago will call you out of the blue and tell you about a teaching opening. Take the job. It will pay well and lead to even better opportunities."

These events happened, but Jonah did not foretell them. And if he had, would I have believed him? Would the desire to teach have felt like "mine" if Jonah had planted the idea in advance? I believe the oracle-speaker was wise to keep my future hidden, even if he did see it in a vision. Perhaps this is why we find so few specific predictions in the records of Delphi. The priestess did not wish to weigh down the minds of her votaries with too many visions of the future.

Jonah's work made a lasting impression on me. Knowing about his personal story awakened a renewed sense of life's mystery. Observing his ability to touch my soul on so many levels demonstrated again the power of oracular work. But most of all, he helped me remember and experience a part of me that can never be separated from the Ever-Present. In fulfilling this mission, Jonah took his place among the great oracle-speakers of old.

Consulting a Psychic Reader:
Thoughts and Suggestions

The following suggestions are meant to guide someone who has little experience with psychic readers but would like to open the door further.

1. *Don't leap blindly.* If you are new to the field, avoid visiting a booth at the psychic fair or stopping at a roadside card reader's house. The work of telephone psychics can be of good quality, but I don't recommend it as a first introduction. Also, the cost can be shockingly high.

Ask acquaintances whether they have heard of any psychic practitioners who do really good work. By asking, "Have you heard of any?" you avoid putting them in the awkward position of admitting their own involvement, should they feel shy about the subject. You will probably be surprised, though, to learn how many people eagerly discuss the subject as soon as you confide in your interest.

2. *When you call the practitioner for an appointment, openly ask how much you can expect to pay for the session.* You may be quoted a per-hour fee. Or you may be told that the practitioner does not charge but will accept a donation. I always inquire, "What is the average donation that people tend to give?" If the practitioner answers, "They give anything they wish," I again request to be told a general range amount to guide me. You should also discuss how long your session will be. Ask whether you will have the option of extending the time if you elect to do so.

3. *Take time to examine your attitudes about oracular communications.* Do you think that any channeled message is from a Divine Authority and must be accepted? This is an incorrect

and dangerous idea, as anyone with experience in the field can tell you. The quality of information you receive can vary widely, and it is your responsibility to use common sense and discrimination. At the other extreme, make sure that you are not so skeptical about psychic work that you will close your mind to genuine oracles meant for you. Try to identify any feelings you may have that could stand in the way of a positive outcome. For example, would it upset you to see the practitioner go into a deep trance? If a reader should tell you that a dead relative or acquaintance is standing near you and wants to communicate with you, would this statement cause distress? If you discover areas of serious fear about oracular work, tell them to the practitioner before you begin the session. You may want to place limits on the session by saying, "I do not wish to make contact with spirits of any kind. Can you avoid this topic in your reading?" If the practitioner says no, consider leaving the session before it begins.

4. *Like pilgrims to the oracle of Delphi, you might write down a few questions in advance.* Perhaps you will elect not to ask them during the session, but they serve to focus your thoughts and provide a starting point for oracular inquiry. Here are some types of questions that work well: "Please give me helpful information or advice about [name the issue]." "I have been dealing with [name the particular issue]. Tell me what you see about this issue from the expanded viewpoint of Spirit." "I am struggling with making a decision. Tell me about the consequences of going in one direction or another." "Please give me a clearer understanding about my purpose and destiny in life. What can I do right now to come into better alignment with this purpose?" Questions like these are likely to yield more productive responses than requests for predictions. But if you feel strongly motivated to ask a particular question, do so.

In my opinion it is a waste of your time and money to demand that the practitioner answer test questions, such as

"Where was I born? How old am I? What is my middle name?" Trick questions are also fruitless. I knew a man who visited one practitioner after another to see how thoroughly he could fool them. Though unmarried, he put on a wedding ring; he asked about his children, who did not exist. Afterward he would gloat that no one had picked up on his charade. I believe that he had an unconscious wish to be "penetrated" by a spiritual experience. But he certainly was working against himself in the effort.

Keep in mind that psychic abilities take many forms. Many practitioners are not good at picking up names, dates, and other concrete facts. But they may be able to reach to the heart of a problem and help you in ways that are very important. The best way to evaluate a practitioner's quality is to ask yourself, "Is this person giving me information, guidance, or illumination that really feels on target and seems useful to me?" Trust your own responses.

5. *As the session unfolds, ask yourself how you feel in the presence of this person.* Remember that your own intuition will be especially keen during an oracular encounter, for like begets like. Carefully notice how your body is reacting. Prolonged sensations of sinking, suffocating, wanting to run, being seized up, or becoming sick may signal that something is very wrong. Stop the interaction and tell the practitioner about your experience. If he or she shows concern and invites you to explore the matter further, this is a good sign. But if you are ignored, dismissed, met with irritation, or blamed for the response, terminate the session immediately. You may be picking up unhealthy energies in the psychic field that are affecting your body and emotions.

Most practitioners are motivated by a desire to serve the Spirit, and they maintain high ethical standards in their work. But a few individuals use oracular abilities destructively. I recently heard about a client who was persuaded to transfer ownership of his (fully paid) home to a very charismatic psychic. Luckily, the client's wife intervened before papers were actually signed. Should any practitioner attempt to extract money, goods, services or sexual favors from you, terminate the session immediately. Consider reporting the incident to the police.

6. *Take an active role in the session, asking questions, providing information, and carrying on a dialogue with the reader or channeler.* Remember that the most important insights come not only from the practitioner but from your own oracular knowing. I realized this clearly during my time with Jonah. His words were valuable in themselves, but their meaning expanded ten times within me, providing knowledge of great subtlety. High-quality oracular work has a life of its own. It happens to the reader and to the client simultaneously. While the practitioner is speaking, you may feel inspired to interrupt with a thought of your own. By all means follow this prompting, for it may well lead you both into territories beyond your imagining.

7. *When your session is over, thank the practitioner and the Presences who made the work possible.* I like to hand my readers their fee or donation directly while looking into their eyes. They gave me something, and I wish to give something back in a fully conscious way. I dislike arrangements where one slips a donation into a box hidden in the lobby, for they rob us of the chance to complete our interaction with the practitioner. The exchange of money is the exchange of psychic energy. (See chapter 5 for a more detailed discussion of money and oracular practice.) When giving it, I mentally say, "May this money bless you, and may abundance return to me." I think it is important never to feel pinched or reluctant while giving others their due. I release the money from my hand freely, even when my bank account is thin. If writing a check, I sign my name a little larger than usual. This affirms to the universe that I endorse my own giving.

8. *Take notes on the experience as soon as you are able.* Sometimes I run to the nearest coffee shop and scribble down

my thoughts while they still hold their golden lining. Tape recording a reading is useful, but it does not substitute for your recollections. Keep in mind that the practitioner's words carry only 10 percent of the total message. The rest lives in your own oracular consciousness. Proof of this will come later when you tell a friend about the reading. As you relate what the practitioner said, additional insights and hunches about the future may pop into awareness. You may also wonder whether you actually heard certain things spoken or whether you merely thought them at the time. Don't worry about solving this puzzle, for there are realities that exist somewhere between external events and imaginal life, drawing power from both realms. Oracular events are not bounded by the clock. They continue to expand in ever-widening circles through the expanses of time.

We have seen that oracle-speakers throughout history have offered guidance and encouragement to those who sought their counsel. But there is another source of illumination close at hand. More intimate than our own names, more inventive than imagination itself, it accompanies our lives from the moment of birth. Let us now enter the chamber of dreams.

Chapter 4

Dreams as Oracles
Awakening to the Dark

Dreams offer themselves to all.
They are oracles, always ready to serve
as our quiet and unerring counselors.
SYNESIUS OF CYRENE AROUND 400 C.E.[1]

What would it be like to have a "quiet and unerring counselor" at our side each night? How might our relationship with dreams change if we trusted their ability to guide, warn, inspire, and heal? Questions such as these naturally arise when we listen to ancient authors such as Synesius or explore the wisdom of native cultures. Ancient peoples regarded dreaming as an important experience worthy of our attention and reverence. In their view, sleep opens a portal between the human soul and sacred realities. Perhaps this is why Egyptians chose the hieroglyph of an *open* eye to represent dreaming! What is invisible to daylight eyes may become clear in the illuminated darkness of sleep.

Premodern cultures assigned the dream an important place in daily life. Individuals expected to receive dream advice on how to treat a health problem or prepare for a journey. Kings and rulers anxiously sought the counsel of wise interpreters whenever they awoke with a stirring dream. Throughout Egypt, Mesopotamia, Greece, and other regions of the ancient world, pilgrims journeyed to sacred dreaming sites in hopes of receiving a numinous visitation during sleep.

Oracles speak through our dreams today with as much meaning as they did in legendary times. But we often remain asleep to their communications due to the habit of long inattention. In this chapter we will peer at a hidden dimension of dreams by examining true accounts from many different time periods. This particular kind of peering has been expressed beautifully in a phrase used by the Yansi people of Zaire in West Africa. Anthropologist Mubuy Mpier tells us that the Yansi term *bumi ndoey* means "to turn a dream," just as one turns an object to see a hidden or obscured side. The Yansi feel that we have to turn dreams very carefully, for often the obscure portions prove more important than all the rest.[2] Let us become better acquainted with the oracular side of dreams by seeing how guidance may be found in "visions of the night."

Dream Oracles Impart Creativity and Insight

Perhaps the most celebrated type of dream oracle is the kind that visits artists, writers, inventors, and other individuals involved in creative tasks. Dream states and creative states resemble each other because they both access domains of psychic life beyond rational consciousness. Many individuals, such as Chinese American author Amy Tan (best known for *The Joy Luck Club*), say that they enter into a type of dream realm as they connect with their imaginative material. Tan notes that in dreams she can change a scene by looking down at her feet and then looking up again. Applying the same technique to writings she closes her eyes, glances downward, and then notices what scenes open to her vision. Soon whole new worlds appear and begin to tell their stories.[3]

Another way dreams may assist creative life is by providing solutions to very difficult problems. One of the most dramatic examples of this experience was recounted by Elias Howe, who is credited with inventing the sewing machine. Howe worked for years trying to perfect a machine that could stitch thread into cloth automatically. Everything seemed to work well except for one flaw: The thread kept getting tangled around the needle as it moved up and down. No matter what design adjustment Howe made, he could not prevent the thread from wrapping itself up in knots within a few moments. After a long fruitless effort, he was ready to give up his plans altogether.

One night Howe had a frightening dream. He had been captured by aboriginals and dragged before a great assembly. "Unless you can produce a working machine within twenty-four hours," the king said, "you will die by the spear." Howe worked furiously but met with the same problems that had plagued him in waking life. Now the aboriginals closed in to carry out the execution, lowering their spears in unison toward the prisoner. When the tips were only inches from his face, Howe woke in terror, covered in sweat. Then he realized something odd. Each spear point had a small hole drilled in the tip. The hole seemed to glow in his memory. With a start the inventor knew that his problem had just been solved. He immediately designed a sewing needle with its hole near the point rather than at the top. When he placed it in the machine, the whole thing worked like magic.[4]

As Howe discovered, dream oracles often present themselves with one particular image or message highlighted. We have no difficulty recognizing the oracular portion, for it glows with special import or rings clearly in our ears. As with Howe's hole-tipped spears, the image may strike us as unusual. Indeed, we've seen how oracles like to yell at us, grab our attention, and turn our thinking in a different direction. We therefore should pay special attention to those dreams that jolt our consciousness. Then we ask, "What gift do you bring?"

To receive a creative breakthrough through dreaming is impressive enough, but to be handed a full completed work during sleep is astounding. Artists in many fields have reported having this experience. One of the strangest accounts was related by the eighteenth-century Italian musician and composer Giuseppe Tartini.[5] Tartini's virtuosity on the violin was legendary, even in his own day. His bow cut the strings so fast that onlookers saw six bows instead of one. When Tartini played, witnesses said, his eyes rolled back and his fair flew in all directions like someone possessed.

Perhaps there was a bit of possession in Tartini's art, for when he was twenty-one he had an extraordinary dream. The devil appeared before him and asked what he desired. "Play for me," the young man said. Tartini was astonished to see the strange figure take up the violin and play a piece of such exquisite beauty that it surpassed the boldest flights of imagination. "I felt enraptured, transported, enchanted," Tartini later wrote. "My breath was taken away, and I awoke."

Springing from the bed in a heat, Tartini tried to write down the music he had heard. The resulting sonata is now known as "the Devil's Trill," and everyone, including the composer himself, has judged it to be the best work to issue from his pen. "But it is far below the music I heard in my dream," Tartini sadly noted.

Dreams may give us creative treasures, but we must act quickly to preserve them. The English poet Samuel Coleridge had an experience that provides a warning for all creative people.[6] In the year 1791, Coleridge moved to a lonely farmhouse in an effort to recover from serious health problems. One night he felt too tired for work, and so he settled in his armchair to peruse a travelogue. Soon he felt sleep overtaking his senses. The last passage he remembered read, "Here the Khan Kubla commanded a palace to be built, and a stately garden thereunto." Coleridge then slipped into a dream that seemed more real than life. Panoramas of magnificent scenes rose up before his eyes, showing him ancient wonders upon wonders. Meanwhile, a voice recited a long poem describing everything he saw in the most cunning rhymes and rhythms imaginable. The entire presentation created itself seamlessly, effortlessly, without one moment of strain or conscious effort. Coleridge awoke three hours later. He could still hear every word of the poem. Rushing to his desk, he wrote furiously, recording as many lines as he could. But then a loud knocking sounded at the door. With annoyance, the poet remembered that he had made an appointment to conduct some minor business at his home. He dutifully attended to his business obligation and returned to his writing desk an hour later. But alas, the verses had vanished. From the scattered images and words that remained, Coleridge finished the poem that was to become his hallmark—*Kubla Khan*. Those who have read *Kubla Khan* are usually struck by its haunting, otherworldly quality. The internal cadence seems to stir deep rhythms in the body and mind, similar to how native drums pull consciousness into hypnotic patterns. Its images hint at both the beauty and the awe-fulness of drawing close to the numinous Ancient Ones. Let us review the opening and closing lines of the poem, just to appreciate once again the creative power of our "theater of the night."

> In Xanadu did Kubla Khan
> A stately pleasure dome decree:
> Where Alph, the sacred river, ran
> Through caverns measureless to man
> Down to a sunless sea.

[The poet expresses his wish to revive the music he heard in Xanadu and bring back a vision of Khan and the dome.]

That sunny dome! those caves of ice!
And all who heard should see them there,
And all should cry, Beware! Beware!
His flashing eyes, his floating hair!
Weave a circle round him thrice,
And close your eyes with holy dread,
For he on honeydew hath fed,
And drunk the milk of Paradise.

To the end of his days, Coleridge lamented that he lost most of *Kubla Khan* when his transcription was interrupted. The poet's experience reminds us that each dream-creation has its own life span. Some images hold steady in the waking world for many years, but others shimmer only a few moments before vanishing into a separate reality. We risk a lot by saying, "I'll attend to this dream later. It's so vivid that I won't forget it." One knock on the door, and Coleridge lost a kingdom. When an important dream appears, we must sweep aside the clutter of outside distractions and make room for the sacred guest. Writing down the experience in full detail builds a little chamber where the dream may dwell for a time. When we later return to that chamber, our guest will be waiting with new wonders to tell.

Dream Oracles May Presage the Future

Nothing grips the imagination like a precognitive dream. When we see events during sleep that then come true in waking life, we can only blink in amazement. Sometimes the images in question are so unusual that they never could have developed by coincidence.[7] Frederick Greenwood, a British writer, once dreamed that he was standing in the drawing room of a fine house, resting his arm on the mantelpiece above the fireplace. He became aware of something cold under his hand. Turning to see what the object was, he recoiled in horror, for his fingers lay upon the dead hand of a woman, newly cut from the wrist. He awoke with a creepy feeling spreading through his body, then tried to put the dream out of his mind.

On the following day, Greenwood visited the home of a little-known acquaintance on business. While waiting in the large drawing room, he wandered over to the fireplace and absent-mindedly lounged against it. What should he see but the hand of a mummy lying there with other artifacts. It was a very little hand, cut at the wrist, and it wore a small ring with the gemstone missing. Greenwood snatched his hand away from the mantel, his heart pounding.

Greenwood's psyche seems to have anticipated the details of his waking experience. But one image was different. His dream called attention to the humanity of that little hand, bringing into remembrance the flesh-and-blood reality of one woman's life. Greenwood did not report that anything unusual happened as a consequence of the dream. But surely he never again regarded mummies as mere objects for display. Even we, who share in his experience years later, may feel a deeper sensitivity to how ancient corpses are treated.

Most precognitive dreams foreshadow less startling events than a mummy encounter; they usually portray more ordinary situations from everyday life. We should not discount these seemingly small images, for they may prove to be details of a larger scene from the future. Keeping track of our dreams is important, for they may reveal their true importance only after a certain amount of time has passed. I always feel reassured on this point when I think about the experience of a woman named Barbara.

In the early seventies, Barbara told me the following dream. "I have a job in a peculiar building. The place has an empty, barren feeling, and the ceiling is very high, as in a warehouse. I am sitting at a desk in a corner, facing a strange machine I have never seen before. It's like a television set, but there are no pic-

tures on the screen, only printed words. I am supposed to control these words but cannot. They keep sliding sideways out of
view." After Barbara related this dream, she mentioned that it
had a different quality from most others. The experience seemed
solid and matter-of-fact, like a slice from everyday life. The
events had no story line, and images did not mutate and transform as they often do in dreams.

Several months later, the organization for which Barbara
had been working moved to another state. She was distressed by
this and wondered whether she could find other employment in
the tight job market. But soon an acquaintance called who had
just established a geological consulting firm. He hoped that
Barbara would accept a position with them analyzing data,
preparing reports, and managing office operations. Barbara felt
very heartened and agreed to meet him the next day. The directions she followed took her to the far edge of town, where an old
warehouse stood. It was a cavernous place with high metal ceil-
ings and no aesthetic grace. Barbara was escorted to a curious-
looking machine perched on a desk in the corner. "This is something few people have ever seen," the owner said with pride.
"It's called a word processor."

I have always been impressed with this dream experience,
for it paralleled subsequent events in waking life with stunning
accuracy. Most intriguing was Barbara's vision of a machine she
had never seen or imagined. Her mind could not quite digest the
vision at the time, but she later discovered that it was a detailed
forecast of a future reality. For instance, Barbara met with frus-
tration in her first attempts to master word processing because
her text kept sliding sideways off the screen—a common problem for users of early software. She also felt cold much of the
time because the building was not insulated. Checking her
dream journal later, she found the words, "I am cold sitting in
front of the machine"—a detail she had not told me at the time.

This experience carried profound meaning for Barbara. We

can imagine her feelings when she walked into the warehouse and was shown the work station so similar to the dream image. She felt reassured that events were somehow falling into proper order. It seemed that a mysterious force was keeping an eye on her affairs and knew quite a bit about the future. As it turned out, the geological job sustained her for several years in an interesting and cooperative setting. Though Barbara encountered various hardships as life unfolded, she never could feel entirely unmoored, for an oracle had shown her that life follows certain patterns beyond our comprehension.

Dream Oracles May Guide, Warn, and Reveal

Accounts are found in all times and cultures of how dreams have saved lives. The psi researcher Louisa Rhine related an unforgettable experience told to her by a Los Angeles streetcar conductor.[8] One night the man dreamed of a terrible accident. He was driving the streetcar on its accustomed route, when another streetcar came by and blocked his view of the intersection ahead. At the next moment he plowed broadside into a large red truck that had turned illegally into his path. The impact killed two men instantly and hurled their bodies onto the street. The dreamer then ran over to the place where a woman was screaming in pain. She turned to him and shouted, "You could have avoided this!" The conductor noticed that she had the most intensely blue eyes he had ever seen. He awoke drenched in perspiration.

Putting the nightmare out of his mind, the conductor went to work and drove his familiar route the next morning. But when he came to the intersection pictured in his dream, he suddenly felt sick. Instead of proceeding through the crossing, he hit the brakes and turned off the motor. At that instant a big truck shot directly into his path. It was not red, but its side panel had a large advertising space painted in red. The three occupants of the truck—two men and a woman—gaped in fear at the streetcar when they saw how close they were to being hit. As they passed, the driver clearly saw what large and strikingly blue eyes the woman had.

Experiences such as these excite many questions about destiny, free will, and the nature of predictive dreams. This dream portrayed a tragedy with gruesome specificity. On the next day, actual events paralleled these details so closely that we would call the dream "precognitive." But the driver himself changed the ending of the story by his actions. We therefore wonder what kind of reality the driver was picking up during sleep. If he saw something that was destined to happen in the future, why did the future not match the dream? And if the events were not slated to occur the next day, how do we account for the reckless truck, the three occupants, and those blue, blue eyes?

The Stoics of ancient Rome devoted considerable thought to questions of this nature. Dreams can divine the future, they believed, because sleep connects the human soul with the pervasive governing principles of existence. These governing principles might be called "Fate." But, as the historian Patricia Miller has pointed out, the Stoics did not believe that fate was a relentless, deterministic force imprisoning human lives.[9] They used the words *praesensio* and *praesentio* when speaking about foreseeing the future. Neither of these terms means "predicting" in a fixed sense. A *praesensio* is a foreboding or a presentiment. *Praesentio* is "to feel or perceive beforehand." Since the future is not yet uncoiled in time, there is no way to unravel it fully in the present. We can only get a feeling for its shape through dreams, revelation, divination, and other oracular means. From the Stoic viewpoint, the streetcar driver sensed the configuration of terrible events through his dream. But as it turned out, Fate used the driver and his dream to give those events their final configuration—a much happier one.

Dramatic dream warnings provide fascinating subjects for study. But most oracles guide us through life's smaller turning points. One woman, Juanita, told me how she learned to protect her own interests more assertively through a small but important dream. A month earlier, Juanita's husband of many years had moved out of the house, announcing that he was in love with another woman and wanted a divorce. Juanita felt devastated by this cruel news. To make matters worse, her husband withdrew nearly all of the funds from their joint bank account. He said something vague about giving her more money later. Juanita dared not protest the withdrawal too strongly, fearing that her spouse would get angry and cut her off completely. From the day of their marriage, she had felt intimidated by his aggressive personality. And deep down, she believed it was pointless to insist on an equal share of anything in their marriage, for he regarded all of their assets as belonging to him alone.

Funds were running very low, and Juanita's job as a store clerk was insufficient to pay the bills. One day an envelope came in the mail. Inside was an insurance check compensating them for damages incurred many months ago when their house had flooded during severe rainstorms. It was made out to both of them jointly. For a moment she was tempted to forge her spouse's signature and take half the money. But she did not want to be underhanded. So Juanita called her husband, who immediately came over and snatched up the check before she had even signed it, and said, "Good, I need this right now." When she asked about getting her share of the settlement, he snapped, "Later, later." That night Juanita had a dream. She was walking through dark corridors and had no idea where they were leading. Then suddenly, a tiny light appeared ahead, blinking weakly. It was just a pinpoint at first, but as Juanita drew nearer, she saw the light was really a little sign made of neon letters. The letters flashed "equal funds, equal funds, equal funds" over and over again. She awoke, feeling at peace without knowing why.

The next morning, another letter arrived from the insurance company. It explained that the enclosed check provided "balance of payment" for the damage claim. The amount matched the other check to the penny. Remembering the flashing message, Juanita knew with certainty that this money was meant for her. She cashed it without hesitation, and the money

An Inuit Eskimo artist depicts her experience of soul flight in this stonecut and stencil work entitled, "Flying near the Rainbow." (Natachie Pootoogook, Cape Dorset, 1980. From Inuit Women Artists, *Chronicle Books, 1996. Collection: Canadian Museum of Civilization)*

got her through a very rough time. Strangely, her husband never inquired about the existence of a second payment.

Juanita told me that this dream marked a change in her attitude. She believed that the little flashing sign must have come from a holy source, for it accurately predicted the arrival of matching funds. But more importantly, Juanita now began to feel that she deserved "equal funds" in the divorce settlement, even if it infuriated her husband. At the advice of friends, she hired a lawyer to represent her interests—a move that would have been unthinkable to her previously.

Hundreds of dream images present themselves during any given night. But some dreams carry special power to influence our attitudes and direction. We can identify oracular visions during sleep by noticing our response to them. Very often, we cannot get the image out of our mind. It glows in a certain way, or the shock of its strangeness disturbs our peace. We may feel a resolution or clarity that was missing before. Or, as in the case of the streetcar driver, a mood of nervous watchfulness may prevail. It is not quite accurate to say that we merely "react" to an oracular dream. Rather, the dream infuses us with its own qualities. It injects a certain mood or thought or desire into our psyche so that the action may be carried forward.

Another sign by which we know oracular dreams is their power to evoke wonder and awe. Whenever we think about them or recount them to another person, a little tremor may pass through us. We find it easy to reenter the dream and experience its spell all over again. Because oracles are living transmissions from Elsewhere, they continue to work their magic across past, present, and future dimensions. In fact, a dream may offer new illuminations when reviewed years later. We serve oracular consciousness well by keeping good records of our dreams, for they need only a small rooting in this world to spring into life anew.

Healing and Restoration
in the Temple of Dreams

Dreams can serve as agents of healing. From the earliest times, cultures around the world have regarded the dreaming state as a portal to their domains, where transhuman forces may be contacted. It was believed that these forces could heal a person directly or provide key information about how a cure could be obtained. Among many native groups, shamans or folk healers depended on dreams to supply the right prescriptions or procedures for their patients. Even Galen, the famous Roman physician honored for his scientific approach to medicine, reported that his dreams showed him how to perform certain forms of surgery he had never imagined before.

In all of Western history, no institution has brought dreams and healing together in a more powerful way than the temples dedicated to Asclepius, the Greek god of medicine. These temples thrived for nearly a thousand years, closing their doors for good during the fifth century of the common era. At the time of Alexander the Great, more than three hundred sanctuaries were spread across the Mediterranean world. Pilgrims could find sacred dreaming sites in Athens, Epaudarus, Cos, Pergamon, Syracuse, Carthage, Lesbos, Rome, and many other localities. The structures were built in secluded areas of great beauty, usually near natural springs. Anyone was welcome, free of charge. The only patients forbidden entrance to an *Asclepieion* were pregnant women (for birth was not considered a disease) and those who were about to die. Combining features of a temple and a sanatorium, the sanctuaries provided therapies for the body and the spirit. A retinue of priests, attendants, athletic trainers, massage therapists, and other skilled practitioners fostered a therapeutic atmosphere so that healing could be promoted. But these treatments were only preparations for the most exalted treatment of all.

After preparing themselves through baths, fasting, ritual, and prayer, patients descended into a lower chamber and went to sleep on goat skins. There they awaited a dream visitation from Asclepius or one of his companion deities. Miraculous cures came to thousands of pilgrims in this way, and many of their stories were inscribed on tablets at the temple.

Asclepius did not work alone in the sanctuaries. Goddesses such as Hygieia (health), Panaceia (all healing), and Iaso (recovery) were powerful sources of miracles. Many of these figures derived from female deities worshipped in earlier times. Hygieia, for example, has been considered a transmutation of the Egyptian Isis, who had always healed disease. Divine forces within the sanctuary also took the shape of serpents, whose connection with the healing arts is as old as humankind. Dogs abounded everywhere, particularly at Epaudarus, and they were revered as touchstones of health.

During the past century, a great deal of archaeological research has been devoted to these sites. Many features of the sanctuaries remain obscure, but we can piece together enough information to gain a good working picture of their operation. As a way of entering this picture more fully, I would like to take an imaginative journey back to the year 350 B.C.E. and describe what we know about the Epaudarus sanctuary through the fictional experiences of a young Greek woman named Rhea. Rhea's story represents what could have happened when one woman journeyed to the sacred house of dreams.

Rhea has been suffering pains in her abdomen for a half a year. Each monthly flow is heavier than before, and at times it seems that all of her life blood will drain away into the cloths she washes and washes again. Physicians examine her urine and count her pulse, administer herbal hot packs to her stomach, and insist that she eat only bland, moisture-reducing foods. But her flow always returns with renewed fury and terrible cramping.

"There is a time for the doctors and a time for the gods." Rhea hears these words in her head as she gradually awakens one morning. She cannot remember her dream, but the image of a man lingers somewhere in her memory: a mild, untroubled face and the kindest eyes she has ever seen. Wrapped around his arm like a comfortable sleeve is a great serpent. Asclepius! Yes, it must be the god, for Rhea has seen holy statues of him many times. And she understands the dream's communication. Her time of doctors is over, and she must now go to the abode of healing itself.

Epaudarus is even more beautiful than she has imagined. Cradled by soft hills and opening out to the western sun, the temple glows with quiet sanctity. As she enters the grounds, a very tall man with skin like polished wood touches her shoulder. "I am Asius the Ethiopian," he says. "I will watch over you during your stay here." His easy tone makes Rhea feel like a relative whom everyone has expected for weeks. "First you will go to the women's bathhouse," Asius explains. "The water will be cold and salty like the night sea. But it is necessary for your purification. The attendants will give you a loose white dress to wear. When the gods see you in white they will think, 'Ah, what a pure and perfect pilgrim this is! Let us hurry to this pilgrim's side!'" Asius says these words without smiling, but his eyes twinkle.

Rhea is not prepared for the richness awaiting her senses when she enters the main hall. Vapors of incense waft through the air. Every wall is covered with murals painted in hues of delicate gold and warm carnelian, chalky blue and sea green. Statues of deities and heroines tower higher than a building. And where is the heavenly music coming from? Now she sees them, an ensemble of flutists and harpists swaying under the spell of their stately melodies.

Just as she is ready to proceed again, Rhea registers a spongy pressure at her ankles, like the stroke of fat fingers. A pale serpent lounges on her sandal, flashing its tongue. "Don't be afraid," Asius chuckles. "These serpents are companions to Asclepius and Hygieia. We care for hundreds of them in the temple. Lucky you, to have been *blessed by their attention." Seeing no relief in Rhea's face, the guide goes on to say, "There is no poison in them. Your bite would hurt more than theirs." Then the snake glides off and disappears behind a statue.*

"I'm tired," Rhea whispers.

That night she stays in one of the dormitories reserved for women. There is something moving about the sight of eight pilgrims dressed in white like herself, stretched out on simple pads. What brings each one here? Will they find a cure? And the miracles that everyone talks about—are they true? Yesterday, it was told, a young man had come to the sanctuary with a horrible festering sore on his toe, his flesh eaten away almost to the bone. Dozing on a bench in the garden, he had dreamed that a handsome young lad had approached him and put salve on the wound. When he awoke, the toe was completely restored, healed without a scar. "If only I could witness something like that with my own eyes," she reflects before falling asleep. "Than I could have faith in my own cure."

The next morning, Rhea wonders how she should use the day. One could go to the gymnasium, see dramas in the great outdoor theater, bathe in the springs, or be massaged by experts. Because laughter is good medicine, patients might also attend a comic play and watch satyrs with donkey-sized penises chase maenads [female followers of Dionysus] around the room. But it is the sacred groves that beckon Rhea most strongly. Walking under their canopy is like entering a cavern of green light. Small offerings dangle from the branches like jewels. Each tree breathes forth a silent greeting as she passes, and time dissolves into an eternal moment of "now."

Rhea has no idea how long she stays in the grove, but when she finally leaves its magic kingdom, Asius appears beside her. "Your face looks peaceful," he says, "I think you will be ready to fast and make sacrifice tomorrow. Then if the gods given consent, you will go to the abaton."

The abaton—its name is always spoken in hushed tones, for this is the holy of holies, the place where deities make contact with human beings. But no mortal may enter the abaton unbidden. To obtain divine permission, Rhea will have to reach into a skin pouch and draw out a disc of wood. If the disc says "Come," she will sleep in the abaton that night. If it says "Wait, she will try again on the next day, and the next. Some people fail to get permission for weeks and weeks on end.

That night, Rhea's thoughts turn inward as she wanders alone through the sanctuary. "Will pain always be my only companion?" she wonders. Certainly her husband of three years has not been much of a companion to her, since he is always in one foreign country or another fighting enemies. The total number of days he has actually lived at home and shared their bed would scarcely make a month. Nor has she found any comfort in their cramped, sunless house, living with her mother-in-law. Even so, the emptiness was somewhat bearable until the pain came. Then every hour became a punishment. And what makes her think that Rhea, child of the plain face, wife uncherished, daughter-in-law without merit, can win the favor of a god or goddess? Before coming to the sanctuary, she spoke with passion of her belief in miracles. But now, wandering alone in a hallway of lifeless statues, she feels that even the deities will abandon her in the end.

Ritual is a comfort to those bereft of hope. Beginning at dawn, Rhea allows herself to be ushered through each step of the day-long purifications. She fasts, bathes in hot and cold tubs of water, and drinks from a holy spring that is said to open up second sight. At the end of the day, Asius finds her sitting alone on a stone bench.

"Come," he urges. "It is time to draw lots. Do you have your sacrificial cakes ready?"

Several people stand piously with heads bowed while two priests chant a prayer in fine, practiced voice. "Awake, Asclepius, gentleminded son of Apollo and noble Coronis," they intone. "Hear the prayers of thy worshipers. Once again, and never in vain, we ask the blessings of your beneficent powers."[10]

Now a priest raises a flask of wine toward the sun and puts its *contents upon a stone altar. The first patient approaches the altar and places upon it a round, thin cake pierced with holes. Then he draws a lot from the pouch. Negative. The poor man's face collapses in misery, and he is led away by an attendant who murmurs reassuringly.*

Rhea's heart pounds so hard that her hand jerks as she thrusts it into the bag. "Allow me to enter your chamber, Sweet Comforter," she whispers as her fingers close around a slip of wood.

"Come," the disc says. "Come, come."

Rhea is led to the abaton, where she cradles herself in a hollow on the floor, but how does one sleep with every vein in flames? Rhea has never felt this kind of heat before. She knows the blaze of Athens in summer, the pressured hotness of racing up a hill, the crackling of passion in her belly. The way she burns now is like all of these combined, yet different. It is alive, this throbbing thing that claims her body, destroying and creating her at the same time.

Sleep closes in without warning. Rhea finds herself lying in a shallow pool at the women's bathhouse. Blue flames play across the water's surface and smolder in its deeper layers. An old woman approaches. She passes a hand back and forth across the flames in a stroking, caressing gesture. Rhea sees that her right arm is covered with a thick spiral bracelet crafted of tiny overlapping scale. Wait, it is no bracelet, but a live serpent!

Plunging her hand underwater, the old woman traces a line down Rhea's abdomen from waist to pubic bone. The cavity slits opens like the belly of a fish. Blood gushes out and spreads through the water in flat bands. Casually, almost lazily, the reptile uncoils itself and glides straight into the crack. A quick tug, a ripping pang, then the snake emerges, carrying away a small spongy mass. For a moment, its luminous eyes meet hers. They seem kind, so very kind.

"Are you awake?" a voice asks. Rhea focuses slowly on the inquiring faces of Asius and a priest unknown to her. Does she want to tell about the dream? they ask. A serpentine movement swishes in her stomach. No, she shakes her head. The dream is still with her, too alive for binding into words. Later, perhaps, she will recount

it image by image to a priest who possesses special knowledge of such matters.

Rhea is content to lay for a long time in her crumpled dress, inhaling the smell of goat musk. Only after raising herself to a sitting position does she notice something unusual. The region between her hip bones and groin, home of so much misery in the past, feels totally clear of pain. She springs from the couch to test out the sensation, twisting her pelvis this way and that, pressing a fist into her womb, bending over and straightening again. No pain, not a twinge.

"So you have taken up dancing!" Asius says, laughing.

"I think I'm healed, Asius," Rhea says with wonder. "I feel so different inside, like I'm made of clear crystal. If only I could believe this."

"Results first, belief later," he advises. "If the healing stays with you this month and the next and the next, then you'll know the truth. The Great Ones show before they tell. I doubt they will disappoint you."

Rhea is not disappointed. After returning home, she waits five full months, and when each cycle of the moon brings a sweet and mild menses, she crosses both arms upon her chest and thanks the Mysteries. The sense of having a clear, light-filled abdomen never leaves her. More than that, Rhea feels the constant presence of an indefinable "other" stationed nearby. Since imagining that a god has become her companion would be immodest, she addresses the presence as "Friend."

But one step remains to complete the circle. Like countless pilgrims before her, Rhea desires to return to Epaudarus and give a thank-offering to the gods. It takes a long time to decide what the gift should be. Sometimes they present casks filled with precious jewels, incense, or unguents. It is also a common practice to dedicate an effigy of the body part that has been healed. Rhea almost asks the family jeweler to cast a small womb of gold as her offering. But another image tugs at her mind.

Early Roots of Greek Dream Incubation

ASCLEPIAN DREAM TEMPLES WERE BUILT UPON OLDER traditions inherited from regional peoples: Egyptian reverence for dreams is legendary, and incubation sites were found everywhere in its kingdoms. The Mesopotamians and Babylonians sought oracles during sleep, as did early Semitic peoples. Scholars pointed to several passages in Hebrew scriptures that bear the mark of Near Eastern dream incubation pro-cedures. For example, Abraham made a sacrifice and slept on hallowed ground before having a vision of the night, and Jacob was resting at an ancient holy site when the ladder dream opened to him.

But these ancient practices were founded upon even earlier traditions. In Gaia-centered cultures, dreams were imagined to waft up from the Deep Below and enter the mind/soul of the dreamer. Underworld realms were associated with the dead, whose bodies were planted in the ground like seeds. Snakes were also revered as agents of healing and magic because they came from powerful underground realms.

Influences of Earth worship can be seen in Asclepian practices. Altars were often built low and fashioned with a hole in the middle so that libations could be poured into the ground. Patients seeking a dream oracle slept in a hollow, drawing as close to the underworld as possible. It would seem that even Apollo agreed with the playwright Euripides, who said, "Earth is the mother of all dreams."

Then one day, she knows exactly what to do. Wrapping the tiny package in three coverings of white linen, Rhea begins the long journey back to Epaudarus. How differently her legs move up the hills this time; how strong she feels dancing under a cove of trees at moonrise. She cannot wait to see Asius and tell him he was right about her miracle. And she already knows how Asclepius and Hygieia will smile down upon her when she lays at their feet the small golden serpent.

Seeking a Dream Oracle in Modern Times

Throughout the centuries, dreams have brought comfort, guidance, and healing to those in need. But how can we seek dream oracles in our modern world? No sacred shrines await us at the edge of the wilderness; no priests and priestesses of dreaming pass down their art to successive generations; no temples of Karnak or Asclepius provide ritual frameworks for invoking dream-visitations. We are obliged to find our way alone.

Trying to reproduce ancient institutions is not the answer, for they arose within unique historical conditions that could never be replicated in our time. Many of those conditions, such as widespread slavery and warfare, are abhorrent to us. We would not wish to call them back, even if the temples were thrown in for free. But studying dream practices in other societies can help us identify the more general features of their method, for these features tap into archetypal realities of psychic life. Once an archetypal pattern is activated, new exciting forms of practice create themselves spontaneously. What was the general approach, then, used to invoke dream oracles in the past?

This ancient process has come to be known as "dream incubation" (deriving from *incubare*—"to sleep in the sacred precinct"). Though incubation was often surrounded by elaborate rituals, it always involved the same basic elements. A petitioner had a problem that could not be solved through ordinary means. He or she decided to seek oracular assistance through the medium of dreams. Preparation was made for receiving the dream. Sacrifice, contemplation, and purification brought the seeker into a proper relationship with the Source of oracular dreams. Before retiring the seeker asked for the dream clearly and directly, then fell asleep in a hallowed place. Upon waking, dreams were carefully noted. Further insight sometimes was gained through consultation with a wise person who had spiritual insight. After the seeker received an oracle, a thank-offering was given. If an oracle was not granted, the incubation was repeated at a later time.

Let us explore the forms these procedures might take today.

Decision

As in any oracular work, you should have a clear need or question in mind before seeking a dream oracle. Here are some frequent kinds of questions submitted to incubation. "I ask for healing in regard to [name the particular illness, problem, or situation]." "I wish to be shown the right decision concerning. . . ." "I ask for illumination about. . . ." "I wish to know whether my plan of action is the right one, and if not, what else should I do?"

Make sure that you have done everything possible to address the issue through reason and worldly means before turning to dream oracles for instructions. For example, if you need to make an important decision, have you researched all the facts? Have you consulted with knowledgeable people and explored your own various feelings on the matter? A woman once told me she was going to do a dream incubation to help her decide which art school to attend. After discussing the matter with her, I learned that she had not even obtained catalogues from prospective schools! I told her to wait until she had gotten further along in the process before consulting an oracle.

Several months later I saw her again. She had been accepted to a school that seemed perfect for her. Now we planned a dream incubation to ask the Invisibles either to give their blessing on the decision or to warn her clearly if she was making the wrong choice. That night, the woman dreamed that someone gave her a book from medieval times full of small, exquisite drawings. She awoke feeling very happy. "Oh," the woman exclaimed when recounting the dream, "that's called an *illuminated* book! I think my school experience will illuminate a lot of things for me—in a beautiful way." Then she went off to her studies with complete confidence. It is our job to do the human legwork in life; then deities will send a wind to our sails once we are underway.

Preparation

To enter the realm of dreams is to cross over into another reality. Therefore it is not surprising that practices similar to initiatory rites of passage usually play a part in dream incubation. The petitioner first must be separated from his or her normal routine and way of feeling. As we saw at Epaudarus, supplicants went to a special place removed from everyday life; they took purifying baths, changed into special clothing, meditated, and fasted. These steps helped them shift out of old patterns and enter a more open, receptive state of being.

Modern petitioners can follow the ancient example. If you plan to seek a dream oracle on a particular evening, it is important to step away from your customary routine and go to a different place—at least psychologically. If you are fortunate enough to have access to a spiritual retreat center for a few days, this is an ideal setting for dream incubation. Wilderness areas are extremely conducive to oracular dreaming, for here we are in contact with the original ground of sanctity. But you can also create very favorable incubation conditions at home.

Cease your daily activities at least twelve hours before going to sleep. Unless a medical condition prevents it, you should fast during this twelve-hour period, ingesting only water and perhaps a little juice. Preparation will begin with immersion in water. In classical antiquity, salt water was always used as a purifying agent, for it recalled our connection with the sea. Pouring a little sea salt or Epsom salts in a tub of water will replicate the practice nicely. After drying the body, a clean, simple garb should be put on. The color white was favored in Greece, but most colors have been associated with spirituality in one culture or another.

You should surround yourself with as much natural and artistic beauty as possible before the incubation. The major dream-oracle sites of antiquity were situated near springs, rivers, caves, clefts in the earth, or other points of geographical wonder. Numinous dreaming also took place near great monuments like the pyramids and sphinx. If a temple was built at the site, it was invariably a work of art. Asclepian sanctuaries, as we have seen, surround the pilgrim with music, art, drama, baths, exercise, massage, and wonderful fragrances. Similarly, shamanic practitioners used every sensory channel to inspire revelation and healing.

These models can inform our own incubation. Time spent outdoors should include many hours in nature's company; trees, animals, and water have always been powerful allies in oracular work. Indoor environments should be adorned with images, music, incense, and objects that carry spiritual meaning. Reading poetry or literature (or being read to by another) on the day of incubation will bring good results, for the literary arts are closely aligned with oracular consciousness.

It is preferable not to sleep in your own bed during incubation. Pilgrims of antiquity nearly always left their own chambers and went elsewhere to dream an oracle. Remember that *incubate* is "to sleep in the sacred precinct." If you elect to sleep outdoors, choose a place that seems to emanate unusual presence or "suchness," as Buddhist traditions phrase it. You will sense this quality immediately because it flows from the land itself. If you sleep indoors, consecrate a hallowed place for dreaming. You might utilize a very old custom and trace a circle on an area of the floor while asking for assistance and protection. Bedding can be formed of materials that have spiritual meaning or that give you aesthetic pleasure. A token left to you by a departed relative, teacher, or friend might be placed in or near your bed, for it will connect your dreaming-place with others outside yourself.

Sacrifice

We may say that sacrifice is performed as a means of establishing reciprocity with the Unseen. We receive so much from life—existence itself is handed to us from a mysterious Source—and we wish to give something back. When one asks for a special gift such as a dream oracle, the need to reciprocate is even greater. But what could the All-That-Is possibly want from us? The thing that we alone can personally give: a moment of conscious attention, a gesture to the I-Thou bond.

On the day of dream incubation, you might devote some thought to what you will offer as a sacrifice. To sacrifice does not mean to deprive yourself painfully. Today we often use the word in that sense, as in,"I've made a lot of sacrifices for her college education!" But Latin origins of the term reveal that to sacrifice is "to make sacred." Ask yourself, what can I make sacred by my offering? What would be a fitting gesture of appreciation as I request a dream oracle? This inquiry will help you decide what shape your sacrifice might take.

Placing a flower, fruit, feather, crystal, stone or other creation of nature on an altar carries a simple beauty that extends back to the earliest times. You may also consider offering something intangible. I know a man named Brian who asked for a dream oracle to help him find a satisfying love relationship. I suggested that he sacrifice something to the Invisibles that would show his good faith in asking for love. After thinking for a moment, he arrived at a surprising answer. "My damned sarcasm," he said. "I stick little sarcastic knives into every friend I have. I'll stop it. That will be my sacrifice." I was impressed by the elegance of Brian's choice. By relinquishing his sarcasm, he both affirmed the value of that native gift and acknowledged that he was willing to exchange it for a better one—love.

Brian did, in fact, have a beautiful erotic dream that night in which he took the part of an unusually tender lover. The dream did not give him specific advice on how to find a partner, but its warming mood stayed with him for weeks. Then, unexpectedly, he met someone at a friend's dinner party and began a fine, compatible relationship. But something Brian told me four months later struck me as even more interesting. "My sarcasm has taken on a new life," he said. "Since I stopped aiming it at my friends (okay, I slip now and then), it has all landed in my writing. My movie reviews are sharp enough to perforate the page!" The local newspaper editors liked his witty reviews of films so much that they hired him as a regular contributor. The sarcasm that Brian offered up as a sacrifice did indeed become transformed into something that pleased both gods and mortals.

Asking

Though your desire has already been formulated, it must now be given clear articulation. Speaking out the request was so important in earlier times that it often took quite dramatic forms. A four-thousand-year-old text from Ugarit in the Near East described how the seeker of a dream oracle first made sacrifice and then cried to the gods in a loud voice, weeping bowls of tears on the bed.[11] In many parts of the world loud cries and weeping were considered effective ways of getting one's point across to the deities. The intense cathartic effect also cleared the way for oracular receptivity.

You need not weep bowls of tears—though anyone who has sobbed with utter abandon knows how purifying the experience can be. But your request should be spoken aloud. If you are unaccustomed to hearing your own voice while alone in a room, the experience may seem strange. But the power of "giving voice" has been affirmed through the centuries. When I first speak out my request, my tone is often a bit weak and wavering. Few of us feel we have permission to state our needs clearly and directly. But then I repeat the words, and I can hear strength coming into my voice. A third or fourth repetition may be necessary. You will know when you have hit the mark. The sound resonates all through your body; the meaning is full and real; you can feel a deeper layer of the psyche affirming your intention. "Yes, this is my desire," it says. "This *is* my desire."

Dreaming

"We do not have the dream," Jung said; "the dream has us." How true his statement is. One cannot anticipate, shape, or control what kind of dream may come during an incubation. Nothing at all may happen. The dreamer might awaken in as much doubt and confusion as prevailed the night before. Or pale impressions of a dream now lost may linger for just a few seconds before blinking out of memory. Even reaching for the pen to take notes may shatter an image and send its atoms flying. Perhaps this is why dreams have won the admiration of humanity from the beginning of time. They are wholly "other," paying visit on their own terms at their own choosing.

You can expect one of four results from an incubation. At the lower end of desirability, you may remember nothing from your sleep and feel no change in mood or thought. If your impression that "nothing happened" persists for twenty-four hours, you must accept the verdict. The oracle may be classified as a "no show." Such an experience was very common in the past, even during those spiritually charged eras when supernal messages were raining from the skies. Petitioners often were obliged to continue fasting and weeping bowls of tears for a long time before the dream spoke. Native American initiates who undertook spirit quests often endured painful hardships for thirty days or more before a vision graced them. So we should not become too discouraged if a dream does not appear on the first night of incubation.

The second possibility is that you don't remember having a dream, or you remember it only vaguely, but you feel strongly that "something did happen." You may find yourself thinking quite differently about the matter at issue, or you may awaken filled with certain emotions that were not there before. If the impression of "something did happen" persists after twenty-four hours, you can be sure that it did. Remember that oracles are known by their results. They effect a change in awareness, feeling, action, or life circumstance. Some oracles are received first at the deepest levels of the unconscious and then percolate up to the surface later. You will soon be able to identify the result of the dream-message, even if you can't remember its content. You might even find that a dream starts forming in your mind, and you can't be sure whether you are remembering it or creating it. This is a valid experience. The dream is a living entity that keeps unfolding and creating itself anew within us. We keep dreaming long after we awake.

In a third scenario, you remember having a dream (or more than one), but you are unsure whether it communicated an oracle. The first step will be to put aside the dream for a moment and think about your original issue. Do you feel different about it now? Does the way seem clearer? Is an answer there that was not there before? Has the issue seemed to evaporate or lose its power to trouble you? If the answer to any of these questions is yes, it is likely that you received an oracle. Reviewing each image and feeling of the dream will help you identify exactly what the message was communicating. You might enlist a friend or counselor to participate with you in this work. Excellent guides to in-depth dream work are also available. But if, after exploring the dream thoroughly, you still experience no major change in your relationship with the original issue, you must conclude that an oracle did not pay visit that night. Watch carefully, though, for the desired communication may come spontaneously through a later dream that is not incubated. This often happens once we begin cultivating oracular consciousness.

The most sought-after result of incubation is waking up with a clear "hit." The dream is vivid and charged. Its texture and feel linger in memory. And you know with certainty what it is telling you. The "telling" happens on many levels at once. While the intellect registers insight, the emotions change like colors in an alchemist's flask. While the spirit touches realities that can't yet be put into words, the body flushes with new vitality; meanwhile, the action-self is already making plans.

A direct-hit oracle dream does not have to be interpreted because, in a curious way, the dream is the message. The visitor has already done its work in us. I agree with the Jungian psychologist C.A. Meier, who maintained that dreams were not interpreted at the Asclepieia.[12] There would have been no need to extract symbolic meaning from a dream that instantaneously healed a man's horribly festering toe. The meaning was self-evident. But it is likely that suppliants took pleasure in discussing their numinous experiences, just as we do. Dream oracles received during incubation should be tenderly written down, pondered over, and celebrated. When possible, they should be honored with a poem, artwork, monument, or charitable act.

These productions might serve as thank-offerings to the Sweet Comforters who respond to our needs.

Thank Offering

The thank-offering is of extreme antiquity, and for good reason. It is our nature to return thanks when something has been given; the disposition to reciprocate may have tipped the balance in favor of human survival, many theorists argue. Reciprocation is very important in oracular work as well. Once we know that our oracle has been of genuine benefit, a thank-offering can be planned. We should postpone the offering until we are sure the advice we were given has brought good results or that a promise of healing was duly fulfilled. Empty faith and empty thanks never do anyone much good, especially the gods.

Offerings mean the most when we devote our own time or resources to them. A creative work of music, writing, or art dedicated to the oracle will shine both in this world and the Otherworld. Gifts of service, such as helping a person in need or volunteering your time to a worthy cause, also make fitting thank-offerings. When possible, the offering's theme should reflect the oracle received. Rhea's gift of a serpent paid homage both to the archetypal forces of healing and to the specific image of her dream. We can muse upon the ancient connections between various elements of nature and aspects of human experience. Birds, snakes, dogs, cats, trees, rivers, springs—the archetypal associations are so vast that we never tire of contemplating them.

I had a breakthrough one day while trying to figure out how to incorporate an animal into my thank-offering. Specifically, I wanted to offer a rooster, traditional symbol of a new day dawning, for an important piece of guidance I had received. Having no talent for art, I doubted that the deities would enjoy any roosterish image I might create. In olden times, the poor creature would have been carried to the block in sacrifice—obviously not an option for me. Then the idea struck. To sacrifice is to make sacred. I knew of an organization that fought against the inhumane conditions of factory farming. They protested the way chickens lived miserable lives squeezed in cages, their beaks cut off. I joined that organization and sent them a donation, silently dedicating my actions to the oracle. It represented a kind of animal sacrifice in reverse, and a very fitting one for our times. I realized then that any entity of nature could be honored in this way.

When we make the right thank-offering, there is a satisfying feeling of, "Now it's completed." A need was spoken, an answer was given, a thanks was offered, and the circle is closed. We then realize again that nothing is more mysterious that our relationship with dreams. I think that Henri Cocteau, the French filmmaker, expressed this relationship best. Dreamers and poets "are at the disposal of the night," he said. "Our role is humble. We must clean house and await its due visitation."[13]

Chapter 5

The Shadow Side
of Oracles

E ven to say the word "shadow" darkens our inner landscape. No bright images relieve the gloom. We recall
the inky double of our form poured out upon the ground, mute
and faceless. It portends the dark melting of our bodies in the
grave. Does the soul become a "shade" after death, as the
ancient Greeks believed, drifting thin and hungry through the
underworld? Or perhaps life's crushing blows have already flat-
tened us into a "shadow of our former self."

Omens were called "shadows" in old Britain, and ghosts
were also known by that name. To grow old is to "cast a long
shadow," according to a common saying. Friends and sweet-
hearts dread that chilling moment when a "shadow falls"
between them and changes their love. Shadowy figures of crime
haunt the underworld of every modern culture. And if you
should hear stealthy footsteps a pace behind, watch out.
Someone may be "shadowing" your every move.

We are not what we seem, according to depth psychologists,
for behind the surface self a hidden "shadow" lies. It holds all

those things we cannot bear to be: the ungood child, the attention hogger, the wanton heartbreaker. Each of us casts a different shadow, the reverse image of our public face. That which
might have been, but never had a chance to develop, also
belongs to the house of shadows. Neglected abilities and different ways of thinking live just below the threshold of consciousness. Though pushed out of awareness, shadow material pops up
over and over through dreams, fantasies, projections, impulsive
behavior, and unintended actions. Not necessarily evil but
never wholly good, the shadow is always with us.

The oracular arts carry many shadows, large and small. We
must peer into their uncomfortable corners if our work is to
become more mature and integrated. Looking only at the pleasant surface of psychic life sets us up for devastation when things
start to go wrong. A naive attitude also leaves us more vulnerable to corrupt characters who would manipulate us in the name
of spirituality.

As Jung said, "One does not become enlightened by imagining figures of light, but by making the darkness conscious."[1]
This work has no end, for as soon as we shine the light of recognition into one area, another falls into darkness. But every new
discovery hones our discrimination and stabilizes our practice.

I will be using the word "shadow" in two ways. It will first
refer to elements of oracular practice that may lead us into pain,
fear, or horror. These include having one's trust shattered
through betrayal, feeling engulfed or possessed by alien psychic
forces, or being physically harmed by encounters with the otherworld. The word "shadow" may also refer to elements that are
hidden from view. Because they have not been incorporated
into our picture of the oracular world, we overlook their existence. Issues of this kind include the relationship of money and
spirituality, cheating and the pres-sure to perform, and personal
projections in psychic work. In each of these matters, the shadow may appear in unexpected places when we seek the oracle.

Charlatans Lying in Wait

My first encounter with a charlatan in psychic clothing took place when I was eighteen years old. Even though I suffered no real harm from the experience, I could never again believe that all oracular practitioners were devoted to the common good. The experience taught me to exercise critical judgment before opening my heart and mind to a stranger, human or transhuman. I have learned many times over how important this lesson is whenever you commune with oracles.

While driving along a country road in north Florida one day, I saw a palmist's sign hanging from two chains by an old house. It swayed to and fro, to and fro, with the breeze. I already felt a little fuzzy from long hours of driving, and the rocking hand exerted a sweetly hypnotic pull. Besides, all forms of oracular practice enticed my interest. How could I pass by this opportunity? So I turned off my ignition and walked toward the paint-blistered door.

A pinched face greeted me. The woman was about forty-five and smelled like cigarettes. I introduced myself and walked into a living room of astounding clutter. Teetering pillars of magazines and newspapers rose from each corner, reaching almost to the ceiling. Boxes, books, cardboard, remnants of sewing material, and stacks of mail were layered like geological strata upon every flat surface. All that remained of the floor was the narrow aisle where I walked. It led to a small table lit by a green banker's lamp. But I was not bothered by this spectacle. Some gifted psychics invest more energy in the unseen world than the material plane, I reasoned, and their habitats are bound to reflect a bit of cosmic chaos. "This person must really stay 'out there' a lot of time," I reflected, stepping over a bag of groceries.

We faced each other in the green glow. A feeling of warm happiness suffused through me as I prepared to be touched by psychic presence once again. I loved this work. And I loved practitioners who could journey with me through its domain. How fortunate I was to find this little oracular outpost on a country road where few traveled. I wondered who this palmist was and how her life story had unfolded.

I closed my eyes and waited to hear the opening invocation or prayer. Then damp fingers closed around my hand and pulled it forward. I looked up to see the reader scowling at my palm in silence. "You have enemies!" she declared. "Serious enemies. They seek to harm you." Her opening statement jarred me, for it was the last thing I expected to hear. Still, I mentally catalogued all the people I could think of, in case I was missing something. No candidates came to mind. Some people didn't care much for me. In fact, they cared too little even to become my enemy. "Who has time for enemies these days?" I wondered to myself.

"We must quickly break the spell before it's too late!" the woman breathed, gripping my hand in urgency. Confused by the strange direction this reading was taking, I nodded faintly. "Now here's what I want you to do," she continued. "A mile down the road there's a grocery store. Drive there as fast as you can. Buy me a five-pound bag of sugar and a large can of coffee. We'll mix a pinch of them together, mix the bitter and the sweet. This will stop your enemies dead. But only for a little while."

"In all honesty, I don't think I have enemies of the kind you are talking about," I protested.

"That proves my point!" she exclaimed. "They've pulled the wool over your eyes. You're in terrible danger. But I can do more than just protect you. I can destroy these people."

The palmist went on to say that it would only cost me fifteen dollars a head to destroy my enemies. Of course, I had to purchase some candles at the grocery store along with the coffee and sugar. She would then light a candle for each of them, invoke certain dark powers, and snuff out the candles one by one. Poof. It would be all over for them. I wasn't told what "all over" meant, but she glinted at me meaningfully.

Suddenly I felt as though I were in the middle of a weird dream. Who was this distasteful woman with the yellow teeth? Why was my psychic encounter taking such a dark turn? Then a veil lifted. Of course. She was a farce, a petty con, a charlatan. My realization churned up waves of anger. Didn't this fool see how much damage she was doing? Her behavior polluted the sacred arts and hurt the reputation of sincere practitioners. Hundreds of people would never again trust psychic work because their faith was shattered by a crook.

I glared at the palmist, wishing I could give voice to all that raged in my mind. But as often happens in overwhelming moments, my throat turned to cement and no words came out. I answered the best I could with my body, springing up from the chair in a gesture of outrage. I tried to march toward the door but instead had to mince my way down the cluttered aisle.

"Hey, what's the matter?" she shouted.

Recalling my answer will always be a point of embarrassment.

Had I whirled out the door in silence, I might have made an eloquent statement. Had I confronted her with being a fraud, all the better. But I heard my own voice sputter, "Five pounds of sugar? A bit excessive, wouldn't you say?"

All experiences contain a hidden gift if we search for it. In time, I realized that my reader (despite her selfish intentions) really did give me something of value. The word "enemy" derives from the Latin *in-amicus*, a not-friend. I needed to become more aware of the not-friend forces in life so that I could rise to meet them in a stronger way. I had offered my tender spiritual yearnings to a stranger and was hit with a spray of poisonous ink. Consequences had been mild this time, but what if I should encounter a genuinely malevolent individual? Never again did I enter an unknown oracular setting impulsively. I

made it my practice to ask for protection, to anchor my awareness fully in my body, and to check out the situation before getting involved. If a serious *in-amicus* crossed my path, I claimed
the right to draw my own weapons in response. I have not yet
tried mixing sugar and coffee to stop a foe. But perhaps I should
keep an open mind.

Corrupt practitioners may be found in every field.
Medicine, psychology, religion, politics, and business all have
their sad tales to tell. But we must remain particularly aware of
the potential for abuse in oracular practice. Most people seek
consultations because they feel a need for guidance. Even the
tug of mere curiosity often signals a desire for spiritual deepening. Psychic work takes place in profoundly intimate settings.
Lights are dimmed, the senses are hushed, and rituals are enacted to escort consciousness into alternate states. Participants usually sit close together and sometimes touch each other's hands.
In short, everything in the consultation room promotes an
opening of the soul. It resembles the psychotherapy setting in
fostering conditions of trust and rapport. When this trust is violated, a person may experience wounds that heal only slowly.

Charlatans of the oracle may take a person's money and give
nothing of value in return. But this is the least of their crimes.
By posing as an agency of spiritual counsel, they invite us to
open the most private chambers of inner life. In polluting these
chambers, they sin against both the human and the divine.

Do Money and Spirit Go Together?

Most oracular practitioners carry out their work from a deep
sense of calling. Yet their very desire to serve brings them face
to face with difficult questions. Should they charge a set fee for
services, or should they merely accept a donation if one is
offered? Should anyone be paid for ministering to the spirit?
Questions such as these sag with shadow. Research suggests that

personal money matters are among the most cloaked topics in Western culture. They carry the same taboos as sexuality carried in Victorian times. Today, many people will disclose information about their sexual life to friends, or even to strangers, but few would think of revealing their exact yearly income or net worth. A large percentage of Americans have not told their parents or children how much money they make, according to surveys on the subject. Some individuals even keep their spouses or life partners in the dark about how much they earn. In research on self-disclosure, subjects were found to talk less about the details of their finances than about any other topic except intimate bodily functions.[2] Wealth is tinged with a godlike aura today. It has been pointed out that our banks resemble temples (often Greek in design), and that patrons lower their voices to a hush when performing the holy rites of withdrawal and deposit.[3] Yet negative feelings also surround money. Terms such as "filthy rich," "stinking rich," and "rolling in dough" underscore the age-old association between money and excrement.

With these values in the background, it is not surprising that conflicting emotions arise around oracular practice and money. Mediums, diviners, and psychic readers often find it difficult to see how they can charge a fee and still function as purveyors of good. If I feel that I am taking something away from you by asking for a fee, this conviction may fill me with guilt and interfere with my psychic acuity. I may even fear that my abilities will disappear as a kind of divine punishment for my selfishness.

Furthermore, oracular practitioners have always suffered harsh condemnation from society whenever they have dared to charge fees for their services. As long as they remain on the fringes of society eking out a scanty living, they are grudgingly tolerated. But as soon as their economic power increases, citizens from more "respectable" professions become incensed and try to close down their operation.

Examples of this pattern may be found everywhere. In England during the 1800s, many spiritualists also served as folk healers in their small communities.[4] They used psychic gifts, mesmerism (hypnosis), and homeopathy to treat illnesses and restore balance to body, mind, and spirit. According to accounts of the time, they often obtained outstanding results and were patronized by many citizens. One psychic, Bessie Williams, reported that she could see into a body as though it were made of glass. Many of her diagnoses, such as internal cysts and tumors, were later confirmed by medical surgery.

Physicians of the time viewed mediumistic healers as an affront and a threat to their (still-infant) science of medicine. They exerted fierce pressure on legislators, and in 1858, an amendment was passed making it illegal for unorthodox healers to receive any compensation for their work. This act dealt a severe economic blow to large numbers of spiritualists in the country, most of whom were women. It will be recalled that Englishwomen at this time had no legal rights, were barred from most professions, and were required to turn over any wages they earned to their husbands or guardians. Thus, the amendment dealt a double blow. It attacked the spiritualist community (which actively promoted growing feminist movements), and it cut off many women from their only source of economic support. Suppressing oracular practice and women's power have gone hand in hand throughout many periods of history.

Money's shadow will be impossible to detect unless we bring to light broader social and political realities. Anyone involved in oracular work should examine his or her own attitudes toward money; it is quite likely that some of these attitudes have been picked up unknowingly from the culture. Here are some questions to ask yourself.

- Do I feel that psychic work should be conducted on a free or donation-only basis? Or do I feel that a provider should charge a fee like any other professional? What is the basis of my conviction?

- Am I suspicious of practitioners who earn a good income for their work, thinking perhaps that "something must be wrong" if they are making so much money? Or do I respect people who earn fine incomes from their skills? In my mind, what is the connection between spirituality and worldly success?

- Do I believe that prosperity could ruin a sensitive oracular reader? In what ways? Or do I believe that economic security can support and enhance a psychic gift? In my view, how do prosperity and poverty affect the soul? How has money or the lack thereof affected my own spiritual life?

I have interviewed many people about their views on charging or not charging fees for psychic work. I have noticed that those who have given serious thought to the issue allow themselves freedom to change their positions over time. One man began his career by commanding very high fees and attracting many affluent clients. But after a few years, he began to feel uncomfortable. Something nagged at him, telling him he was doing the wrong thing. His sources of spiritual guidance encouraged him to give more freely and generously of his time. So he adopted a sliding-scale fee; prosperous clients paid top prices, but more needy clients paid only a fraction of the cost.

At the opposite pole, a woman reader named Susan worked on a donation basis for many years. She told clients, "Give me whatever you wish to give." In her experience, some people gave a reasonable donation to express their appreciation for the work. But many of her clients (usually the more immature, self-centered ones) gave ridiculously low donations and seemed reluctant to given even that much. Some people handed her a dollar or two at the end of a long session and then kept coming back to take advantage of her time. Susan's resentment began to interfere with her ability to give good readings. Finally, she decided to charge a regular fee for her work. If a client could not pay the fee but seemed sincere about wanting assistance, Susan willingly accepted less. This arrangement worked beautifully for her. She found that the "users" dropped out of sight, leaving her with a much more enjoyable clientele.

Regardless of what financial arrangements are made between client and practitioner, the exchange of money should be respected as an important dimension of the work. It must be noticed, talked about, and blessed in the relationship. If money is honored mindfully, it will not have to torment us with shadow-tricks in order to gain our attention.

Trying, Cheating, and the Pressure to Perform

Anyone who has ever tried to gain oracular results by a force of effort knows what failure means. The act of "trying" mobilizes personal will, narrows the focus, and directs our thoughts in a concentrated ray toward a particular goal. These attitudes of mind work against the intuitive function, whose nature is more indirect and subtle. Exerting the will fills up our entire field of consciousness and leaves no space for anything to enter from the periphery. Oracles love the periphery, the unfocused places, the diffuse light. Most of us know that our attunement is best when we relax into a state of trusting receptivity. But when the stakes are high and we must obtain results, it is difficult to relax.

Many practitioners find themselves in situations where they have to produce oracular displays on demand. Sometimes their livelihoods depend on impressing the public favorably. Under these conditions of pressure and strain, inspiration is stifled. Then a dark temptation stirs: Why not cheat a little? Why not fake psychic phenomena with the help of a few tricks?

Genuinely gifted people have destroyed their reputations when they have succumbed to this temptation and were caught.

Since modern cultures are intolerant of oracular practice in the first place, they never forget or forgive practitioners who cheat even once. In nearly every account of Delphi on record, mention is made of one pythoness who apparently accepted a bribe to give a favorable oracle. A single incident of deception came to light in a thousand years of successful operation. But this story has been told and retold throughout history, usually as a way of expressing skepticism about the whole Delphi operation. The fear of being deceived casts a heavy shadow over all oracular practice.

The following case provides a sad but instructive example of how the pressure to perform can ruin good work and throw a talented psychic far off track. My account is based primarily on the research carried out by Alex Owen in his book *The Darkened Room*.

Florence Cook was celebrated as one of the most skilled mediums in Victorian Britain.[5] Born in 1856, she began falling into strange trancelike episodes at the age of fourteen. Her alarmed family often could not rouse her from these states. As she drifted in and out of consciousness, Cook saw glowing lights, heard beautiful angelic voices, and received strong impressions about people and events that later turned out to be true. The girl feared she was going crazy until she made the acquaintance of a spiritualist circle who recognized her psychic abilities. Under their tutelage, she quickly mastered a variety of mediumistic arts, including telepathy, psychokinesis, seeing spirit forms, and communicating with departed souls.

Cook described her training experience as similar to "catching a fever." Her enthusiasm for the field was boundless, and she went away from every séance with new, exciting skills. By the age of sixteen, she had mastered everything known in the area of mediumship. When a channeled message came through predicting that she would become a world-renowned medium, no one doubted its validity. This was a good period for Florence Cook. Receiving guidance and encouragement from her kindly mentors each week had a stabilizing effect on her life. Even the girl's parents approved of her psychic training when they saw how she was maturing under its influence.

Cook's most spectacular achievement was to materialize portions of spirit forms for all to see. Unlike other mediums, she worked in fully lighted conditions and preferred to remain as conscious as possible during sessions. At first only faces would appear. These were described by witnesses as rather awful to see. They stared ahead with frozen eyes as though still in the grip of death. But eventually, complete three-dimensional heads and shoulders became visible, as well as portions of hands and arms. Cook recounted that she felt a little frightened at times to see a head with no body floating in the air inches from her own face. But she pressed on, wanting to develop her art to its furthest reaches.

Though other gifted mediums in England had produced partial materializations, no one had yet been able to summon a full figure into the room. When Cook was seventeen years old, she accomplished the feat before numerous onlookers. A tall female figure appeared before them draped classically in a white gown. She spoke a few words (which were not recorded) before leaving again. The materialization was attested to by a visitor who reported his experience in the *Daily Telegraph* newspaper.

Most mediums reclined behind a drape or lounged in a small, tented enclosure while going into trance and producing spirit forms. They argued that darkness and freedom from sensory distraction helped them enter the proper state of mind. It is noteworthy that Cook herself originally preferred to sit in the open while summoning materializations. She was later persuaded by teachers that exposure to the audience's commotion would be harmful to her, especially because skeptics occasionally became rowdy or abusive. But cloaked chambers raised suspicion. Many people believed that the medium left her chamber and paraded around the room in costume, imitating a spirit. Why didn't the materialization and medium appear side by side and erase all doubts, they asked?

Since fakery was always a concern in mediumistic demonstrations, elaborate measures were taken to guard against fraud. It became standard procedure to Cook and other practitioners to be stripped and searched by women monitors before beginning a session. Once inside her chamber, she was tied to her cot by the neck, ankles, and wrists. All knots were sealed with wax. One end of the rope was passed outside to the audience and tied to a chair for everyone to see. If the medium tried to get up during a séance, her movements could easily be detected. One practitioner had a threaded needle passed through the pierced hole in her earlobe and attached to a chair outside of the chamber. Others were locked in elaborate cages. No precautionary measures were considered too extreme in the battle against deception.

Cook's fame spread rapidly through England. The spirit she materialized, named Katie King, began to walk around and talk to guests, sometimes playing friendly jokes, such as causing mounds of flower petals to rain upon them. When a visiting princess mentioned her interest in cactus plants, twenty of the plants suddenly fell upon the table. On one occasion Katie took a pair of scissors and cut holes from her white dress, giving the pieces to several visitors in the room. Someone inquired whether the spirit could mend her garment again. She held up the holes for everyone to see and with a flap of her hand, the dress was perfectly restored. Another man asked Katie whether she was "real." In response she invited him to caress her hair. What a shock he received to find that the back of her head was missing. She laughed and said that she had neglected to finish herself completely that day.

Dozens of incidents as astonishing as these were reported in numerous magazines and journals. Psychical researchers clamored to study Cook's remarkable abilities, and she always consented to be tested under very stringent conditions. One researcher hooked her body up to a galvanometer so that her slightest movement would complete an electrical circuit and register on the needle. Cook passed this test with flying colors. While she lay behind the curtain, Katie King materialized clearly and walked around the room. The galvanometer needle never even twitched.

With fame came more tests, more challenges to the authenticity of her work, more detractors who disrupted séances. Those who organized Cook's business charged increasingly higher fees for admittance, and sessions were now held several times a week. Since materializing a spirit was considered the most taxing of all psychic work, strain was mounting on all sides. Cook now left each session pale and exhausted.

In 1880, two researchers from Oxford University were busy conducting another test séance on Cook. The medium was supposedly lying behind her curtain while a spirit named Marie appeared to the scientists. One of them grabbed "Marie," wrestled her down, and tore off her veil. They found that the figure was Cook herself dressed up in robes. The researchers wrote scathing letters to the newspapers denouncing all spiritualism as trickery. Although Cook continued giving séances after that, her reputation was forever ruined. Even today, she is remembered as "the medium who faked materializations." Other aspects of her work are largely ignored.

During this same period, several other famous mediums were caught impersonating spirits. The great age of seances in England collapsed all at once. This decline coincided with a period of considerable gains in women's social empowerment, including a more promising job market and the passage of legislation granting them the right to earn wages, own property, and function as legal entities. With new avenues of expression opening, fewer young women were attracted to the shadowy world of spiritualism.

What conclusions are we to draw from the experience of Florence Cook and others like her? Several come to mind. First, oracular art grows twisted when it is used primarily for entertainment. Enjoyment has a role in the art, for the otherworld is filled with playful energies. But when the work shifts into pure theater, it becomes something other than itself. An actor cultivates the art of deception. Theater is designed to fool our senses to the point that we suspend disbelief and become emotionally involved with the drama as though it were real life. If Florence Cook had joined the theater and given everyone goose bumps from the impersonation of a spirit, she would have earned wild applause. But a convincing performance in the seance room only shattered faith and incurred contempt.

Secondly, Cook and her colleagues lost sight of their original purpose. They began as a little group of seekers holding hands around a table and asking the spirits for guidance. They ended up in a gallery of hooting patrons, desperately trying to create more flamboyant displays. Cook must have lain in bed after those depleting evenings and wondered how she had gotten into such a mess. Her divine "fever" of earlier years probably seemed like a dim memory from long ago. Things go very wrong when one forgets the central mission of oracular work: to join people more closely with numinous sources of guidance. Seances, materializations, and bushels of phantom cacti may promote this mission along with all other psi phenomena, but when they become ends in themselves, nothing prospers.

Finally, Florence Cook's story offers an important lesson about the effects of social pressure on psychic undertakings. No one who studies this case can deny that Cook must have been an extraordinary gifted medium. She was also fortunate to be born into a time and place where spiritualism flourished (the era lasted only a few decades). Cook's early desire was to explore all forms of oracular practice and learn as much as she could from her teachers. She reminds us of those young shamans who, after receiving their first call to service, burn with desire to master every detail of the craft. Eventually they acquired many skills and discover specialty areas in which they truly excel. Who knows where Cook's path might have led if she had followed the natural prompting of her gifts?

Though few of us aspire to be renowned practitioners, we are all vulnerable to social pressure in spiritual work. Whenever we feel that we *must* produce certain results, a warning bell should ring. Whom are we really serving? What are the deepest intentions of our work? How can we proceed in good faith and surrender the results to a higher power? If these questions are answered honestly, we will never find ourselves foolishly marching around in costume, pretending to be what we already are.

Horror Beyond the Pale

As we descend further into the realms of shadow, a silence falls. We have entered a place that has no name. Certain terrors overreach the boundaries of words, for the soul cannot hold them, cannot hold up under them, cannot hold together. I am referring to encounters that lie beyond the usual range of human experience. They include feelings of being possessed, going psychotic, disintegrating into fragments, and losing one's soul. Ordeals such as these also belong to the world of oracles.

By opening our psychic portals to expanded realities, we also open to potentially destructive forces. Whether these forces are imagined to originate from the personal unconscious or from sources outside ourselves, their effects are equally devastating. Depth psychologists are trained to recognize patients who should not venture too deeply into themselves during the course of analysis. Their fragile ego structures cannot tolerate the intrusion of primitive rage, envy, terror, and thoughts that seem foreign to them. Psychosis will result if the ego fragments too much in the face of these experiences. Dreams, associations, drifting imagination, intuitive perceptions, and oracular practices all serve to "loosen the joints" of psychic life. The looser we become, the more strangeness we can hold. But the more strangeness we hold, the less familiar we feel to ourselves.

Each of us differs in our ability to metabolize radical "otherness." Shamanic practitioners have always recognized that the visible and invisible worlds are populated with things that cannot be endured by most minds. Madness or death may result from the encounter. For this reason, shamans undergo years of training before risking major encounters with alien forces. They tell frightening stories of practitioners who dared too much too soon and actually died in the middle of a trance-journey.

Even to come in contact with a powerful deity can have a shattering effect on mortals. In one Greek myth, a beautiful woman, Semele, is lover to the god Zeus. He comes to her in the form of an ordinary man so that they can relate as one human to another. But one day Semele is persuaded (by Zeus's jealous wife) that she should make the god reveal himself in his true form. Reluctantly, he agrees, transforming into a massive explosion of thunder and lightning. Semele ignites into flames and is killed instantly. The story reminds us that human beings cannot survive exposure to unshielded supernal power.

What might it look like to "go too far" during an oracular session? One of the most memorable accounts I have ever read was related by Bruce T. Grindal in the *Journal of Anthropological Research*.[6] His experience during a West African "death divination" stretches the frontiers of what most people consider possible—or desirable.

During the 1960s, Grindal lived for eighteen months with the Sisala people of northwest Ghana in Africa. He immersed himself in their daily activities and spiritual practices, endeavoring to understand their perspectives as deeply as possible. Grindal learned that the Sisala regard death as an extremely important event in the life of the soul, and they carry out complex funeral rites to facilitate the passage from one state of being to another. After someone dies but before the burial takes place, a "death divination" is performed to learn more about the deceased's spiritual condition before, during, and after death. These revelations form the basis of further rituals that will properly protect the deceased and the community from harm. Grindal observed many aspects of the death divination while he was there, but he was not prepared for what happened on one particular night, that of October 27.

Preparations were being made to bury the man who had served as the chief's drummer. The corpse was propped up in a sitting position against the compound wall; a cloth covered his head. Directly above the wall lay the drums on which the man had played for so many years. A group of funerary singers called the *goka* now approached the corpse. They danced forward, drawing close to its shrouded form as though whispering in its ear. Then with a backward jerk of their heads they retreated again. Back and forth, back and forth, their undulating motions against the firelight cast a spell on everyone present.

Grindal watched the dancers, transfixed. He already was woozy from having eaten very little during the preceding days, and a number of disturbing events had robbed him of sleep, setting his nerves on edge. Now it seemed to him that the corpse jerked and pulsated a little whenever the *goka* drew near. Was Grindal's mind playing tricks? As though the question answered itself, Grindal suddenly was seized by anticipation and terror. He knew that the unthinkable was about to happen. The events that followed are best recounted in his own words:

> I felt my body become rigid. My jaws tightened and at
> the base of my skull I felt a jolt as though my head had

been snapped off my spinal column. A terrible and beautiful sight burst upon me. Stretching from the amazingly delicate fingers and mouths of the *goka*, strands of fibrous light played upon the head, fingers, and toes of the dead man. The corpse, shaken by spasms, then rose to its feet, spinning and dancing in a frenzy. As I watched, convulsions in the pit of my stomach tied not only my eyes but also my whole being into this vortex of power. It seemed that the very floor and walls of the compound had come to life, radiating light and power, drawing the dancers in one direction and then another. Then a most wonderful thing happened. The talking drums on the roof of the dead man's house began to glow with a light so strong that it drew the dancers to the rooftop. The corpse picked up the drumsticks and began to play.

Grindal could not say how long the experience lasted. But when the light finally faded, he saw that the corpse had returned to its old position propped against the wall. The dancers were panting and dripping in sweat. In a state of shock, Grindal somehow stumbled home and fell into a deep sleep.

The anthropologist awoke the next morning feeling strangely disoriented and out of sorts. He attributed his symptoms to exhaustion from the night before and assumed that he would recover within a day or two. But during the ensuing weeks it became clear that he was not himself. Though not actually ill, he suffered from heart palpitations, shortness of breath, and sick sensations in the abdomen. Bouts of giddiness made him laugh inappropriately during serious conversations. Perhaps the strain of working so hard was finally taking its toll, Grindal thought. Surely he'd snap out of the condition soon.

One day, a Sisala villager named Kojo called Grindal aside. What had happened at the funeral that night was a very serious matter, Kojo told him. Witnessing certain kinds of things can kill an uninitiated person. According to Sisala beliefs, we should only participate in events that do not exceed the strength of our own heart. Death is such an event, for it catalyzes mystical power and danger. If we push too far beyond our personal strength, life ebbs away. Kojo recognized the signs of deterioration in his friend and knew that unless something was done soon, he could die.

A few days later, Grindal unexpectedly received an invitation to visit Kojo's house. Upon arriving he was instructed to sit on a short stool and say nothing. Kojo set before him a little mound of black pasty porridge, explaining that it was medicine for the heart. For some reason, Grindal did not resist putting the ugly substance in his mouth. It tasted so vile that his stomach convulsed and he wrenched away. But then he felt a touch upon his shoulders, calming him. Kneeling close, Kojo moved his hands slowly over the sick man's chest, stroking back and forth in a soothing way. His soft voice whispered, "Don't lose your heart here, Sir. This is not your home." Grindal began to weep from the central core of his being. And from that day forward he rapidly improved.

Grindal's moving account reminds us that some realms of experience cannot safely be held by the personal self. These realms carry us into the darkest shadows of oracular practice. Nor do the same rules apply for every individual. African villagers who had participated in many death divinations had developed a capacity to witness the unearthly things taking place that night. But the non-African guest, regardless of how open-minded he tried to be, suffered a violent psychic injury in their presence. Each of us must carefully consider where our limits lie before rushing into alien realities. As the Sisala teach, we must match events with the strength of our own hearts. Then our spiritual range will safely and steadily expand.

Protecting the Soul

As we explore ways of protecting ourselves in oracular work, it is important to remember that encounters with the shadow are usually helpful and strengthening. Jungian psychologists point out that the shadow consists of positive qualities as well as negative ones. For instance, a woman may not recognize her own capacity for influencing others in a powerful way; her ability might remain hidden from consciousness even though it expresses itself in her love for mighty female deities. When she begins to notice that the traits she reveres in Kali and Athena also bear resemblance to her own character, her spiritual practice will brighten like a nova and enter into a whole new dimension. Attending to the oracles we receive is an immensely potent means of integrating the positive shadows of our being.

Painful shadow encounters—if they do not tear the psychic fabric—weave threads of a deeper hue into the self's design. Patterns of light and dark become more complex, resulting in a process that James Hillman calls "soul making."[7] Sometimes the soul willingly attracts difficult encounters in order to reveal what is hidden or to release what is no longer necessary. And as analyst Lionel Corbett has noted in *The Religious Function of the Psyche*, "personal suffering has a hollowing effect; it allows us the internal space to be able to contain the suffering of others."[8] Practitioners who use their talents in service of humankind must be able to tolerate the suffering of others. Otherwise they will continually defend against painful realities and cling only to surface issues. Courageously facing the shadow side or oracular work, while respecting our own limits, hollows out a place where wisdom can dwell.

Once we feel prepared to face the darkness along with the light, what means can we use to protect ourselves? I offer four suggestions, which are synthesized from both psychology and ancient traditions.

Uncanny realms of experience draw us to their mystery while evoking awe or fear. Acknowledging the shadow side of oracles helps us venture with courage yet stay grounded in common sense. ("Where Ravens Rule," Jose Tisnikar; oil, tempera, canvas, 1975)

Keep Your Eyes Open in the Dark

We are most likely to bump into troubling shadow forces when we fail to watch where we are going. Drifting unaware into random experiences is a risky practice. My visit to the coffee-and-sugar psychic would have turned out better had I stayed alert to warning signals along the way. Instead, I glided along in a spacey state of mind until rudely thumped. Similarly, the anthropologist Grindal took no precautions before exposing his consciousness to extreme occult practices. According to his African friend, the price he nearly paid was death.

When approaching an oracular situation that is new, unusual, or eerie in any way, maintain a stance of relaxed vigilance. You need not tie yourself up in knots or fear the worst; just keep your senses open and stay "present" to everything around you. We employ this attitude often in everyday life. For example, as parents chat by the swimming pool, they never stop watching the children splashing nearby. Their eyes continually scan the pool for signs of trouble. At a dinner party, the host will talk to all guests with spontaneous enjoyment, but another portion of his or her awareness sweeps back and forth across the room all evening to monitor how things are going. In oracular work, one part of consciousness should immerse itself in the experience while the other part stands back a little and asks, "Is everything okay here?"

You are the best judge of when a situation is becoming too strange. If you receive signals that "all is not well," pull back and decide whether or not to continue. On one occasion I ignored persistent physical warnings and suffered permanent consequences. It happened when two friends and I wanted to see for ourselves whether an old cabin in the foothills of Denver was indeed haunted. Its occupant had reported hearing footsteps and labored breathing in the night. He also frequently felt a peculiar chilly hollowness in the living room area.

Our merry little party of ghost-seekers settled own in the cabin one night and waited with only a candle flame for lighting. After about an hour we all heard a muffled dragging sound, as though someone were shuffling with impaired legs. Then we heard a labored sigh, as though someone were exhausted. My friends and I whispered excitedly among ourselves, agreeing that we felt the presence of a bulky old man, perhaps a miner from the gold rush days. "Lord, the place really *is* haunted!" we exclaimed.

Despite my fascination at being there, I began to feel very unwell. My limbs were turning to lead, and a weight pressed on my chest. I could not shake the irrational belief that my face was swelling to an enormous size. "Does my face look all right?" I asked a companion. She assured me that I looked fine. After twenty minutes of struggling with these sensations, I wanted to flee from the cabin. But everyone else was so pleased to be witnessing an occult phenomenon that I said nothing. Then without warning my left eye began to swell. Fluids actually poured down my cheek like a waterfall. This time I knew I wasn't imagining things. I pointed to my eye and whispered urgently, "We must go. Now!"

By the time I got home after an hour's drive, my blood-red eye was bulging from its socket like an ill-fated experiment in a monster movie. As it did not improve by the next morning, I rushed to the clinic. Apparently, I had suffered a severe allergic reaction of unknown origin, and all the tissues had filled with water. Even with strong medication, recovery took over a week, and my left eye is still very prone to inflammation.

I feel certain that I brushed a force in that cabin that was harmful to me. My body told me to get out of its range, but I did not comply until things got urgent. Since that time I have found these same symptoms discussed often in writings on paranormal phenomena. Sensations of heavy weight upon the chest or limbs, difficulty in breathing, oppression, and feelings that the body is becoming distorted—these are classic signs of "psychic attack." The attack may result from being in the wrong place at the wrong time (similar to being shocked by a defective toaster) rather than from malevolence, but its consequences are nonetheless dangerous. Other signs of psychic attack, according to the pioneer occultist Dion Fortune, include smelling rotten odors and finding thin slime on your body or surroundings.[9] Unexplained bruises have also been reported.

The psyche loves a good scare once in a while. Heart palpitations and goose bumps are not necessarily signs that you are at risk. But pay attention the moment you begin to feel sick, become extremely weak, think you might pass out, or have very bizarre imaginings. Common sense will tell you to leave the area or to snap into a more worldly state of mind if you experience severe distress of any kind. The oracular realms will always welcome your return another day.

If You See Something Weird, Look Quickly in the Mirror

The shadow side of life, both negative and positive, thrives in hidden places. We may sense someone lurking behind us and become paralyzed with fear, only to turn around and find a stray dog meandering by. An apparition of angelic beauty may glimmer in the corner of our vision, but when viewed straight on, it reveals itself to be just a glint of light dancing through the branches. Perceptions shift because our interior dreaming self flows into the world and mixes with it. The resulting creation is partly "self" and partly "other."

As we know, the process of disowning qualities in oneself (whether good or bad) and then seeing them reflected in others is called "projection" by depth psychologists (see sidebar, page 156). Identifying this process at work in our oracular practice is very important. If we find ourselves having similar kinds of experiences over and over again, and if we react intensely to them each time, we should suspect that some element of projection is at work. Seeing personal shadow material take form before our eyes always elicits strong emotions. The following example illustrates how projection can shape the result of oracular practice.

A woman named April had received an unusual number of sarcastic and critical oracles. Scornful figures in dreams told her that she had a fat ass or hips like a hippo. She would open books during bibliomancy sessions and blindly put her finger on words like "slob," "slug," and "tub." In fact, she was the only person I ever knew who received a negative comment in a Chinese fortune cookie. It said, "You eat with all your might and have a lot to show for your work."

Each time April got a negative oracular message, she dissolved in tears. How could her guides be so cruel? We talked about these events in detail. It was clear to both of us that she was influenced by our culture's disdainful attitudes toward women who are not thin; she was now turning this criticism upon herself. But less clear to April was her capacity for being sarcastic and critical toward others. To bring out this repressed shadow material, I suggested that she practice saying utterly vicious things about her friends (and me) in the privacy of my office. The sessions were liberating and often ended in peals of laughter. Within two months, most of the negative oracles ceased. New communications of a more supportive nature began appearing.

By highlighting the role of projection in oracular work, I do not mean to imply that oracles are illusions spun out from our own psychological problems. I am suggesting that a relationship exists between the inner and the outer, the personal and the transpersonal. Oracles and those messengers whom we call guides, spirits, ghosts and the like are composite creations, neither wholly "them" nor wholly "us." They are not mere figures of our imagination, nor can they be said to have an entirely independent existence *in the form that we know them*. British author Patrick Harpur proposes that phenomena such as apparitions, fairies, elementals, crop circles, Big Foot, and otherworldly encounters belong to an order of reality that he calls "daimonic."[10] Not to be confused with demons, *daimons* were known from classical times as denizens from another realm who intersect with our world in a variety of ways. They assume the forms of giant animals, delicate elves, grotesque monsters, or strange objects, only to disappear from view at a moment's notice. Because daimons are not physical beings in the ordinary sense, they can never be captured. This is why, Harpur suggests, we can have sightings of the Loch Ness monster or the Yeti, but we will never track them to their lairs. However, daimons are very "real." They can leave footprints, snap trees in two, leave marks upon our bodies, and give us material gifts (which often vanish later). If they have any purpose in being here at all, it is to shake loose our grip on literal reality. They bring soul, mystery, and new dimensions to the over rationalized ego of modern life. In this sense, they initiate us back into a part of ourselves that we long to know again.

Reflecting on the daimonic nature of reality helps us cope with those times when oracles take on a frightening appearance. An interesting recommendation of Harpur's is that we should make a small offering to a daimon when it appears. Daimons wish their existence to be recognized and honored; they wish to have their place restored in our psychic field. Knowing this principle helps us understand why, from ancient times, people of wisdom have left gifts for the fairies, spirits, ghost-animals, and other invisibles. We can find protection in following this tradition.

If forging a relationship with the shadow figure does not work, you may try withdrawing your attention from what is "out

Projection and Oracular Practice

PROJECTION IS AN UNCONSCIOUS DEFENSE USED TO protect our self-identity. When thoughts or impulses arise that conflict with our ego-ideal, we cast them off like hateful insects, denying that they belong to us. Then we see them crop up in people around us. Positive qualities can also be projected, leading to idealization of others whom we regard as superior to ourselves.

Modern depth psychologists have further developed the notion of projection. Rather than thinking of the process as a simple one-way action, they emphasize the shared field of influence existing between persons who associate together. This field includes dreams, fantasies, thoughts, and other imaginal realities.

Projection, in its most expanded sense, is an important idea for oracular practice. We should remain aware of the many influences that shape each moment of work. Our underlying desires and fears always leave their mark on how we interpret an oracle. Currents drifting in from other people wash into our minds. The ecological field of plants, animals, and landscapes shapes our experience. "Invisibles" from many worlds brush us, soul to soul. Attending to these realities helps us appreciate that no psyche is an island.

there" and focusing on what is "in here." You might ask, "What aspect of my own being has mingled in this situation? What feelings and qualities in myself are being mirrored back to me?" Making this move will not instantly transform the experience into a positive one. But it will accomplish two things. The psychic traction beam that pulls you into the force field of the "other" will be disrupted. No one can feel totally engulfed while he or she is busy analyzing the experience. Second, your fear or loathing will ease as soon as you recognize a little part of yourself in the thing confronting you. That which seemed entirely alien will begin to look more familiar.

Acknowledge the Experience but Distance Yourself

Still another technique for breaking the spell of a bad oracular experience is to look at it squarely and say, "You are a dream that I am having. I grant you your own reality. But you are not the only reality." You may have to say those sentences over and over like a mantra until the force dissipates or you calm down. By granting the experience its own reality, you stay in relationship with it. This move is more effective than trying to make the encounter disappear. Chances are, the specter had paid a visit for a reason (just like an important dream) and will not go away until you come to grips with it in some way.

Approaching an experience as a vivid dream helps you keep things in perspective. Remember that all dreams end by themselves, and we tend to wake up when the alarm becomes too intense. But if the spell will not seem to break on its own, try doing a very physical activity such a eating, drinking, or jumping around. Apparitions hate loud noises, so bellowing from the bottom of your gut will shatter many energetic configurations. When your ordeal is over, make sure that you benefit from the experience by processing it in words or images.

Use Ritual to Bind the Forces of Heaven and Hell

As a final suggestion for protecting the self against negative shadow in oracular work, I turn to the most archaic practice in human history: performing ritual. I am always moved to think about a particular archaeological find dating sixty thousand years ago. A Neanderthal man, found buried in a northern Iraqi cave had been covered with a triangular mound of flowers by his companions.[11] Over six species of blossoms had apparently been woven into pine boughs for the grave. This is the first ritual act known to us. At this state of evolution, our species' intellectual development had much further to go, but a yearning for ritual expression already ran deep.

Rituals must have a beginning, middle, and end. Even brief actions such as placing flowers on a grave, have a clear starting and ending point. Rituals help us step into a certain place of experiencing and then step out again. Those who have cultivated "ritual consciousness" know what mysterious transformative power it carries.

In all native cultures, ritual is seen as a force that influences events and corrects things that have gone wrong. Malidoma Somé, a scholar from West Africa, notes that in traditional thinking, visible wrongs have their roots in the world of the spirit. "To deal only with their visibility is like trimming the leaves of a weed when you mean to uproot it," he says. "Ritual is the mechanism that uproots these dysfunctions."[12] Because ritual works directly on the unseen realms, it gains additional potency when used in oracular practices. Each of us who earnestly seeks the guidance of oracles in everyday life will profit by cultivating personal rituals to frame our work. If rituals of protection are enacted on a regular basis, we will find ourselves better able to handle strange or disturbing events when they manifest.

Some individuals are fortunate to have inherited rich ceremonial practices from their own ethnic culture. If you feel close
to the traditional ceremonies of your family and community,
you will always have a strong ally at your side. Nothing protects
you better than invoking the familiar words, prayers, songs,
dances, gestures, or ritual practices used by the ancestors to
commune with sacred forces. You might select two or three
of these practices to employ during oracular work. One of
them should be identified as your "serious protection" measure
to be used in very difficult situations. Chances are that your
cultural tradition has already developed protection rituals
against dangerous forces.

Or, like many people today, you may never have been educated in ceremonial matters. Perhaps the religious rituals you
witnessed in childhood carry little meaning for you now. If you
are among those who feel disappointed or betrayed by organized
religion, then you will not be attracted to using its forms or
vocabulary. Many of us must learn to create our own rituals of
protection. The following suggestions may be helpful in beginning this inspiring task.

Take a moment to consider whether you are most deeply
connected with the auditory, visual, or sensate channel of experiencing. Auditory people are more affected by sounds, words,
and music than by anything else. They close their eyes and open
their ears to perceive better. Those who love the visual channel
find that images, patterns, and colors reach them the most
profoundly. A magnificent work of art or the glister of light
upon a river is worth more than a thousand words. Some individuals experience their body as a finely tuned receiving
station. Important communications are often felt rather than
seen or heard. A single gesture of the hand may carry more
power than many words or pictures. All channels are important,
but you probably have noticed a special kinship with one or
two of them.

Your ritual of protection will be built upon material from your favored channel(s). Auditory persons are advised to use a chant or mantra as the center point of their action. They may also consider using a small trumpet, a flute, a drum, finger cymbals, a singing bowl, or another instrument to emit a sound of protection. The visually oriented will select (or create) objects or images in their rite. Pictures with special meaning, sacred mandalas, or statues of animals or holy persons will generate a beneficial field. Those who are blessed with bodily knowing will profit most from ritual gestures, movements, and enactments. Tracing a sign of the circle, cross, six-pointed star, ankh, or pentagram will do more for them than uttering long litanies of words.

Inspiration for rituals may come from many sources. You may borrow freely from your early spiritual training or cross over to another tradition, for ancient civilizations and native traditions offer astonishing elements of ritual for you to adopt. The world of creative arts also provides many gifts, for creativity and the sacred are closely aligned. Dreams, fantasies, sudden intuitions, and oracular messages are splendid sources of ritual elements because they issue directly from archetypal levels of reality.

To convey an idea of what the final product of your endeavor might look like, there are examples of three simple rituals of protection. The first is auditory, the second visual, and the third sensate.

Invoking the Sacred Tones. Settle into a meditative position, take a deep breath that reaches to the abdomen, and let it out as you intone a mantra—a sacred name, word, or phrase. The mantra should evoke feelings of awe and comfort in you. Let the sounds roll out slowly and savor their full tonality. For example, if you were to choose the ancient mantra "Aum" (Om), your utterance might sound like this: "AAAAhhhhh-hhhh-hooooooooooommmmmmmmm." Experience the sound wrapping around you like a snug cocoon. Repeat the mantra in three sets of three, pausing between sets. Then take a short breath and open your eyes, feeling purified and protected. In fearful situations, you should repeat the word as long as necessary, building a sacred barrier of sound.

Guarded by the Animals. Collect three images of animals. You may draw, paint, or sculpt them, or you can use pictures created by artists or photographers. Select animals with which you feel a strong bond. Your chosen images may depict species from earth, but they can also be mythical animals or figures appearing in dreams. Sitting before a small altar, place all three images before you. Gaze intently at them one by one, absorbing the beauty of their contours and the strength of their animal nature. You do not have to say the words "protect me," for animals communicate wordlessly with each other, soul to soul. They know what you need. Soon the images may begin to shimmer as though alive. The animals will seem to be looking at you with special intention. This is a sign that protection is now in force. Silently convey your gratitude for their help.

Becoming the Pentagram. Stand barefoot on the floor, poised and balanced. Taking in a deep breath and releasing it, prepare to trace a five-point star of protection, a symbol known to banish evil.[13] Extend the first and second fingers of your right hand while the thumb and other fingers touch at the tips. Point your hand down near your left hip. Now sweep your hand upward to a point directly in front of you at head level, tracing a line in the air. Bring your hand down to the level of the right hip, then up again to the left shoulder. Cross in a straight line to the right shoulder, then lower your hand back to the origin point at your left hip. As you trace the figure, feel every stroke deep in your body. You almost become the pentagram—strong, stable, interlocking, impenetrable. Breathing deeply once again, feel the security of your protection. You may perform this ritual using other sacred symbols as well.

Rituals gain power from repetition. One can only appreciate this statement after putting it to the test. Each time you carry out your ritual of protection you will feel something begin to anchor into your being more deeply. At first your actions may seem pointless or even silly as you do them. But if you have designed a rite that matches your temperament, the rite will start working with you. It will contribute its own meaning and vitality to your efforts. The ritual takes on a life of its own beyond your personal self. Then, like a good ally, it works on your behalf when the time of darkness draws near.

Those who form a wise relationship with the world's shadow become increasingly attuned to the world's suffering. We begin to sense that some of the pain we feel arises not from personal issues alone but from the larger life field in which we have our being. Then we may feel a stronger and stronger pull towards compassionate action on behalf of social and ecological sorrows. In the next chapter, we will find support for our voice in the work of a very special oracle-speaker—the sibyl.

Chapter 6

Sibyls
When the World-Psyche Speaks

One morning long ago, two armies clashed on a hillside. They tore into each other with swords, axes, and blood-soaked hands. As their cries filled the surrounding valleys, something strange happened. A woman draped in white appeared from nowhere and stood motionless on the slope above them. Her form was so regal, so utterly commanding, that both sides stopped fighting and let their weapons drop to the ground. "Fools!" she shouted in a voice too big for her size. "What will you gain from this madness? A polluted grave awaits you all!" Her words penetrated like a death-chill. Arms and legs could fight no more. Wincing against the light, the soldiers caught a glimpse of the face staring down at them. Leathery skin a thousand years old, eyes that could slay, an unsmiling mouth: It was the sibyl.

In the classical world, many stories were told of the sibyl and her stark warnings. She would often appear suddenly and make prophecies about the fate of cities and nations. Again and again she called attention to the tragic consequences of violating sacred principles. The earth itself will rise up against humankind if we transgress too far against its laws, she admonished. Famine, epidemics, and violent convulsions of nature will be our reward for pushing our arrogance too far.

I find sibyl to be a riveting figure in the history of oracles. Her vision swept beyond personal concerns and encompassed broad, collective issues. She possessed a special talent for revealing things that had not yet come into mass awareness. In depth psychology terms, one might say that she became a spokesperson for parts of the world unconscious that demanded to be known. The world unconscious, as described by archetypalist Stephen Aizenstat, is a wider dimension of reality in which all creatures and things are interrelated.[1] They form a broader psychic ecology, a dreamscape where there is room for many beings to "walk around." Communications from the world unconscious often reach human beings through dreams, waking visions, and oracular experiences. The sibyl could hear into these communications more deeply than others, often bringing back messages that no one wanted to hear.

Sibylline prophecy is worthy of study for another reason. It demonstrates how one may receive inspired oracles while holding on to a sense of personal identity. Unlike the oracle of Delphi and other trance-mediums, the sibyl did not "lose herself" in the powerful forces sweeping through her. Our own oracular practice can gain strength by following this example and learning to bridge the "I" with the larger "not-I." Anyone who works with dreams, intuition, imagery, or other imaginal realities also needs to become a medial person—a bridge between different worlds of consciousness.

This chapter will review fascinating legends of the sibyl and reflect upon her method of prophecy. It will also look at a modern ecological activist and explore the sibylline features of her work. We will conclude with meditations and practices that invite larger collected prophecies through our own voices.

Who Was Sibylla?

We see her name in ancient legends. Plato spoke of the sibyl with awe. Virgil told hair-raising stories of how she called out oracles from a misty cave. St. Augustine and over twenty church fathers intoned the sibyl's name with reverence. How did a pagan seeress manage to find a place of honor in Christian lore, we wonder?

We see her image in old churches across Europe. Sibyls gaze down from the Sistine Chapel, some of them young and innocent, others heavy with the authority of age. In the Cathedral of Siena, a black sibyl from Libya stands beside her sisters. How did the original prophetess turn into so many personalities, we ask?

Today, the sibyl's memory glides by darkly, like a shadow under water. We distrust it but have no idea why. Sibylline is portrayed as slippery, serpentine, vaguely unholy. Can her original spirit be restored to modern culture? Questions like these arise as soon as we begin to notice the sibyl's presence in mythology, literature, and religion. Our time will not be wasted by following her footsteps through history.

The first woman to be called "Sibylla" probably lived sometime during the seventh century B.C.E. in Asia Minor, a location well known for its tradition of ecstatic prophecy and divination. Her name may have come from Aeolian words signifying "one who utters divine counsel." Historian H.W. Parke, a foremost authority on the subject, finds it plausible that the original Sibylla was an actual individual who gained distinction for her astonishing oracles.[2] Her name later became attached to an ongoing tradition of sacred prophetic verse. Not given to gentle words, Sibylla often shocked her listeners by condemning their complacency. She told the people of one province that they were a "herd of bottomless bellies thinking only of food," and she warned another nation that their blind pursuit of wealth

*The pagan sibyls found their way into Christianity through
Jewish scholars of the first century. This black sibyl from
Libya stands among her sisters in a Renaissance church
in Siena, Italy. (Guidoccio Cozzaretti, 16th-century
marble inlay on floor of cathedral)*

would lead them to disaster. Many violent earth changes were predicted by the sibyl, including a volcano that closely resembled the eruption of Mount Vesuvius in 79 B.C.E.

But the sibyl was not a fatalist. Like other seers of the ancient world, she emphasized that many disasters could be averted by coming back into harmony with the divine forces of creation. Harmony could best be restored by communicating with the deities through prayer, sacrifice, ritual, and responsible action. Many early sibylline oracles included precise instructions for how to avoid the consequences of a negative prophecy. If a massive famine were predicted, citizens might be advised to build a lavish shrine to the grain goddess Demeter and offer sacrifices to her each morning for a year. Storing up grain in a special chamber of the shrine might also be recommended. By turning the mind, body, and spirit toward the source of all sustenance, the specter of famine perhaps could be banished.

Early legends said that the sibyl's mother was an immortal nymph of the springs. Nymphs were nature-entities who could pass back and forth between material form and invisible essence. They especially loved to clothe themselves with water and assume the shape of springs, lakes, and rivers. Since springs bubbled up from the sacred underworld, they were sources of prophecy and inspired knowing.

Sibylla was not entirely divine, for her father was a human being. He gave her the ability to understand human affairs and see piercingly into the affairs of nations. But the combination of clairvoyance and political awareness must have been a heavy burden to carry. The Greek philosopher Heraclitus noted that Sibylla uttered her prophecies through "unsmiling lips."

Poised between the mortal and immortal worlds, Sibylla was able to extend her life span far beyond that of ordinary persons. It was commonly believed that she could live to the age of a thousand years. This is why accounts depicted her variously as a young woman, a mature woman, and an exceedingly ancient crone. We might say that she carried all the stages of a woman's development within her and drew upon these resources as needed in her long career.

An intriguing glimpse of the sibyl in her old age is found in a legend reported by Roman historians.[3] During the reign of Tarquinius Superbus (534–510 B.C.E.), they say, an exceedingly old woman appeared before the ruler. She displayed nine manuscript scrolls and offered to sell them for a colossal sum of money. "What books are these that ask such a ludicrous price?" Tarquinius scoffed. "The oracles of Sibylla," she answered. Impatiently, the ruler told her to go away. The old woman then knelt down and ignited a small fire in front of Tarquinius. She calmly burned three of the rolls to ashes. "Now I have six books to offer you at the same price," she said. "Will you take them?" Tarquinius did not know whether to laugh or explode into rage. "Be gone with you!" he shouted. The crone knelt down again and placed three more rolls into the flames. "I offer you the remaining oracles for the same price," she said. Tarquinius suddenly felt uneasy. He sent for his augurs—those who received oracular communications from birds—and asked them what he should do. When the augurs heard about the scrolls, they gasped, for their signs had predicted that a god-sent blessing would be offered to the state. If the blessing were rejected, great misfortune would befall. "Buy the scrolls at all costs!" they urged. Tarquinius hastily paid the woman what she asked. She then walked away and was never seen again. It is said that the good fortune deriving from these books lasted throughout the whole history of Rome, and that many disasters were averted because of the sibyl's remarkable prophecies.

The story of Tarquinius and the old sibyl spread throughout the ancient world. It illuminated the wondrous origins of those sibylline oracles kept safeguarded in the capitol. A spiritual lesson also could be gleaned from the tale: messages offered from a divine source have value beyond reckoning. Sometimes they arrive by way of strange carriers, and sometimes we are asked to pay a price that seems high, but their blessings last a lifetime.

With the passing centuries, a profound change began creeping over Sibylla's image. She was still honored as a source of prophecy, but her art now carried a tragic, tormented look. The Roman poet Virgil describes a sibyl who dashes around her cave like a wild animal, trying to drive a great god off her breast.[4] But the god rides her like a horse, plying the spurs to her skin until her raving mouth is tamed and she speaks in oracles.

Virgil portrays the sibyl's prophetic experience as fitful, violent, and cruel. Apollo (the source of her illumination) seems to heap more abuse than inspiration upon his faithful priestess. Other writers later pick up these themes painting the sibyl as a mad figure who shrieks and pulls out her hair as rabid babble pours from her foaming lips. Surely these images speak to a growing fear of oracular art, as well as to the devalued position of women in late pagan times.

Who would ever want to become an oracle-speaker after seeing models like these? And perhaps this was the point. By the early Christian era, oracular knowing was viewed with suspicion by educated people. It was imagined as a heedless force that crashed through the gates of rationality and reduced the mind to sputtering babble. Like the heart-crushing Apollo, divinatory encounter could destroy a person. Oracles were therefore cordoned off from everyday life and handed over to a few specialists whom many consulted but nobody envied.

While pagan intellectuals were pushing Sibylla to the fringes of society, a small group of Jewish and Christian authors were welcoming her with open arms. During the second century B.C.E., Hellenistic Jews living in Alexandria began composing prophetic verses and circulating them as sibylline oracles. Paraphrasing from Jewish sacred texts, the oracles recounted the creation of the world, attached heathen practices, and predicted the coming of a messiah who would rescue the world from its

The words of sibyls, according to ancient accounts, flowed out
"purposeful and perfect." In this painting, musical notes
emphasize the lyrical quality of sibylline utterances.
(Engraving, 1798, after a painting by
Domenichino Zampieri, circa 1600)

pitiful state. Christian authors were impressed by the words of the Jewish sibyl (as she came to be called), and hailed her as a spokesperson for the true religion. Over twenty of the early church fathers, including Jerome, Augustine, and Thomas Aquinas, spoke of sibylline oracles with respect. Their endorsement gave the prophetess a place in Christianity for centuries to come.

Today a sibyl is a distant memory, a word evoking mystery tinged with uneasiness. Oracular women are often sexualized in modern literature. For example, in Par Lagerkvist's novel *The Sibyl*, an old woman relates her experience of once having been the priestess of Delphi. (The sibyl and the Delphic oracles were quite different figures in antiquity, but they are often blended together in modern writing.) Escorted to the sacred tripod in the cavern, she encountered the god. The experience was at first ecstatic. "He was filling me," she recalled, "he was annihilating me and filling me utterly with himself, with his happiness, his joy, his rapture." But soon the sibyl's experience mounted into awful violence.

> It broke all bounds—it broke me, hurt me, it was immeasurable, demented, and I felt my body beginning to writhe, to writhe in agony and torment; being tossed to and fro and strangled, as if I were to be suffocated. But I was not suffocated, and instead I began to hiss forth dreadful, anguished sounds, utterly strange to me, and my lips moved without my will; it was not I who was doing this. And I heard shrieks, loud shrieks.[5]

Month after month, the priestess was taken into the oracular chamber where, as she says, the god "hurled himself upon me again like a storm of savage heat, rapture, bliss." Eventually the prophetess bears a son whose father might be the god. She is driven from the temple in disgrace and retreats to a barren mountain hovel for the rest of her life. As for the child, a strange otherworldly quality shines from his eyes, but he is mute and profoundly retarded.

This novel tells us a great deal about modern attitudes toward oracular knowing. We yearn for a close relationship with a Divine Something. But when the Something finally makes contact with us, the story teaches, watch out! It prefers rape to lovemaking. Bliss will turn to agony. The self will writhe and hiss and shriek. What will the union beget? Not the inspired oracles of classical times but a strange offspring incapable of thought or speech.

This vision warns that we have nothing to gain—not even creative inspiration—by opening to numinous forces beyond the personal self. The most likely outcome will be emotional devastation and loss of mind. Nothing will be left of personal identity but the shriek. With these fears always in the background, is it any wonder that the farther reaches of psychic life have not been explored more extensively in our era?

"My Words Pour Out . . ."

What was the sibyl's own experience of oracular inspiration? We have only a few historical fragments to guide our answers, but from them we can surmise a great deal. One text quotes the sibyl as saying, "The great Divine commands me to speak, and my words pour out, perfect and purposeful, once they are put into my mind."[6] We do not know who wrote this statement in the sibyl's name, but scholars feel sure that it was written at least two thousand years ago. It tells us how prophecy was experienced by certain individuals at that time.

The first thing we notice is that the prophetess does not think of herself as working alone. A numinous "Presence" makes itself known, for she says that the "great Divine commands me to speak." Recipients of oracles in both ancient and modern times nearly always have reported being accompanied, companioned, guided, or inspired by a greater presence than themselves.

Sibylla states that the words she is given flow out "perfect and purposeful." As we have seen from studying dreams, divination, and other oracular phenomena, these messages often carry a quality of inspired perfection. They are designed to reach their mark. The fit is so perfect, so meaningful, that we pull in a sudden breath of air. This is the in-spiration, the Divine In-breathing that ancient peoples revered.

Despite her feeling of being "commanded" to speak, she remains quite independent in her relationship to the Divine. Words are put into her mouth, but her mouth is not taken over by force. The word "I" appears in sibylline prophecies often, and it refers to the sibyl herself, not to a god who is speaking through her. It is clear that the sibyl works *conjointly* with her source of oracular knowing. When two things conjoin they do not merge, but neither do they remain entirely separate. The word "conjoin" comes from a Sanskrit root that means "to pull from the same yoke." Thus, the sibyl interacts side by side with powerful forces. In the relationship she describes, both the ego-consciousness and the source of inspired knowledge seem to find equal footing. Like the sibyl, certain people today are keenly attuned to "what is in the air." They pick up ideas, feelings, trends, and future events before others become aware of them. Often they may find themselves saying things that run counter to the popular ideas of the time. Individuals such as these might be called "medials," according to Toni Wolff, an early analyst in Jung's circle.[7] A medial is an agent, a bridge person, a mediator. His or her psychic structure is very easily penetrated by the unconscious contents of the "collective"—of humanity as a whole. In past ages, medials were heralded as visionaries, dismissed as fools, or burned at the stake, depending on how severely their words threatened society.

Serving as a bridge between worlds can be risky. Medials are always in danger of being engulfed by overwhelming forces. They must therefore stay anchored in a solid ego consciousness and make a good adaptation to reality if they are to survive emotionally. Medials must avoid becoming mere mediums who channel anything and everything flowing through them. By taking responsibility for their unique role as a go-between, they may serve those around them and help the collective psyche gain broader awareness of itself. Common sense must always balance psychic surrender. Those who allow their lives to be taken over completely by external forces pay a tragic price. They may fall prey to political or religious leaders who tap into powerful collective energies and use them for their own purposes. Throughout history, groups of otherwise sensible people have been swept into mass violence, murder, or suicide because they abdicated their own personal judgment. The sibyl teaches us to keep hold of the personal "I" as we commune with the greater "other."

Discrimination is needed to sort out what should be shared with others and what should remain sealed. The medial may pick up many things from the collective unconscious, but not all of them need to be said at all times. In fact, ancient sibyls probably preserved their reputation for wisdom by *closing* their lips as often as they opened them! Oracular practice does not demand that we put ourselves at risk or hurt others with our messages. Providing the ego with a sensible base of safety will encourage it to surrender a portion of its hold on the familiar and venture farther into unknown territory.

Sibyls Among Us

Where are the sibyls today? Does anyone see below the surface of things and speak the unspoken, uttering prophecies "through unsmiling lips"? Their spirit is very much alive in our times. Both men and women are calling out to the world in a sibylline fashion, and yet they rarely identify themselves as seers. Environmentalists, ecofeminists, spokespersons for the poor, guardians of animals, and many other passionate voices warn that we have fallen out of alignment with sacred earth principles. They make ghastly predictions about what will happen when ozone drops to lethal levels or epidemics sweep through the world's ghettos. Soberly, they point to hacked corpses of rain forests, silted-up rivers, crippled frogs. Like Sibylla shouting at the soldiers, they demand to know what we will gain from acting like mad fools.

Perhaps the most unforgettable "sibyl of the earth" in twentieth-century America was the biologist Rachel Carson, author of *Silent Spring*. Carson shocked the world with her vision of a time when death's shadow lies upon the land.[8] Unexplainable illnesses claim children and adults. Farm animals sicken and die in their pens. No bees drone among the blossoms, and so each year we see fewer plants. Anglers stop coming to the lifeless streams. The birds, where did they go? A throbbing chorus of robins, doves, jays, wrens, and scores of others used to call their greeting to the morning. But now spring arrives in ghastly silence. It is no sorcerer or enemy force who has put a curse upon the rebirth of life, Carson said. We have done it to ourselves.

Having proclaimed this desolate vision, Carson proceeded to show us what we did not wish to see: the future was already becoming a reality. Carson stripped away our illusions about the safety of pesticides and herbicides commonly in use at that time. She told how aerial sprayings of the chemical dieldrin had killed nearly every bird, squirrel, and rabbit in a small Illinois town. Ninety percent of all farm cats lay dead in their own backyards. She related how countless thousands of birds had dropped from trees and died in convulsions each year after eating worms and insects saturated with DDT. Those animals who survived were often sterile. We learned how common weed killers contained

powerful cancer-inducing agents and caused grotesque muta-
tions in plants and animals. Whereas childhood cancer was a
rarity in the 1940s, it had become the number-one disease killer
of school-age youngsters two decades later. What was happening
to our world?

Silent Spring was released in 1962, when most people were
ignorant about ecological hazards. It created an earthquake in
public consciousness. Angry citizens demanded to know why
industry and government leaders had not revealed these facts
earlier. Legislators scrambled to launch new studies into the
safety of pesticides against the protest of chemical companies,
who condemned Silent Spring as the ravings of a "priestess of
nature." Opposition to the book also came from farm organiza-
tions, the American Medical Association, and a committee of
the National Academy of Science. But President John Kennedy
personally demanded that the entire matter be investigated, and
he ordered a special advisory committee to begin work. Though
very ill with breast cancer by this time, Carson spoke before
groups around the country, warning that toxic chemicals were
destroying life as we know it. In 1963, the biologist was asked to
testify before congressional committees on the need for environmental laws. Seven years later, the Environmental
Protection Agency was established, and a nationwide ban
on the use of DDT followed. Silent Spring was translated into
at least fourteen languages while prestigious honors from
all over the world were heaped upon the author. But Carson
did not see most of these victories, for she died two years
after the publication of her book, at the age of fifty-six. She was
post-humously awarded the Presidential Medal of Freedom,
inscribed with these lines: "Never silent in the face of destructive trends, Rachel Carson fed a spring of awareness across
America and beyond."

Those who heard Carson speak reported being impressed by
her sober, dignified presence and the sense of authority her

words carried. Even on the printed page, this commanding spirit holds us enthralled. What was the basis of Carson's authority? Certainly she was respected as a competent biologist who built a solid foundation of facts beneath her assertions. But many scientists have produced equally good work without impacting the world. She was an excellent writer, but authors with even greater talent have come and gone without changing the course of events. I believe that we must look to Rachel Carson's sibylline qualities to explain her role in history. As we noted, the sibyl is immersed in the larger collective (transpersonal) forces of her place and time. Because these forces operate below the surface of conscious awareness, they go unnoticed by most of the population. But the sibyl brings them into concrete form through her power of expression. She consecrates herself to animating the new, concealed spirit of her age. When people heard Carson speak, they sensed the power of something larger than one individual. The psychic space around them expanded. New understanding sparked from mind to mind as people began to realize the connections between biosystems on earth. The age of ecological awareness was dawning.

I recall my own experience reading *Silent Spring* for the first time when I was in college. After sampling only a few pages, I knew instinctively that I was in the company of a sibyl. Carson's blunt, declarative sentences pressed me to the wall. I wanted to run away from the appalling facts she exposed, but a helpless compulsion made me read on and on. My feelings were not unusual. When we see hidden realities suddenly being mirrored back to us in concrete form, we cannot help but react strongly. Feelings of passionate approval or violent outrage may course through us, depending on how threatened we feel by the new revelations. Sibyls (and their male counterparts, the prophets) are vulnerable to crucifixion because some people would rather kill them than to accept an idea they unconsciously know to be true.

I devoured Carson's book in one evening. It left me feeling sick within, but strangely relieved. So many things made sense that had been obscure before. I remembered the mosquito-control truck, which passed twice a week down my childhood street in south Florida, puffing out clouds of DDT. We kids danced and whirled in the white smoke. Everyone was told that insecticide "only hurt the pesky bugs," and no one gave the matter much thought. They praised the city for its modern approach to an age-old problem.

Yet many of us sensed that something sinister and unwholesome was going on because, after each spraying, hundreds of butterflies and dragonflies would fall dead at our feet. Witnessing the helpless tremors of their wings tore at my heart, and a muffled signal of alarm went off deep inside. But neither I nor anyone I knew could interpret what the alarm was saying. We could not step outside the communal ideas shaping our own judgments about those clouds of DDT. Only sibyls and prophets can see the hidden patterns of collective life and give them a name. They stand upon an authority separate from laws, government, and powerful interest groups.

Though she probably did not intend to do so, Carson spoke out in the tone and cadence of ancient sibyls. "Who has made the decision that sets in motion these chains of poisoning, this ever widening wave of death?" Carson demanded to know. "Who has placed in one pan of the scales the leaves that might have been eaten by the beetles, and in the other the pitiful heaps of many-hued feathers, the lifeless remains of birds?" Who has the right to destroy life indiscriminately? Who has the right?

Studying Rachel Carson extends our understanding of sibylline figures in modern life. Like the sibyls of old, Carson did not speak on behalf of an organized religion or special interest group. No one owned her allegiance. Carson possessed a personal authority grounded in competent skills and dedicated work. But the activist's real authority came from the sacred forces animating her work and amplifying her voice. The closest we can come to naming these forces is to call them *Anima Mundi*, Ensouled World. It is ironic that Carson's critics condemned her as a "nature priestess," for that is exactly what she was. Her litany was fashioned from research studies. Her gospel exhorted us to protect the earth with all our might. Millions of people (even world leaders) heard the call to service because it echoed their own soul's whisperings.

To survive as a prophetess today requires a very special psychic discipline. Analyst Toni Wolff was right when she said the medials face the danger of drowning in the collective unconscious.[9] Once Carson began to comprehend the horror of widespread chemical poisoning, her mind and emotions must have reeled. Not only did she understand the implications of a poisoned ecosystem from a scientific point of view, but her sensitive, nature-attuned soul directly experienced the anguish of insects, birds, fish, and other living things as they died unnatural deaths. Many people could not have withstood the pain of this connection. The sibyl's task is to separate a part of herself out of the collective force and take an objective view toward it.

I draw inspiration from thinking about Carson as a sibyl in an age that has forgotten prophetesses. Reflecting on her courage in those last years of life should strengthen us all. Carson already knew that she was dying of cancer as she wrote *Silent Spring*. Perhaps the very pollutants she wrote about had triggered her disease. Yet not a trace of personal bitterness can be detected in the book. She only focuses on her unrelenting efforts to help the earth. Like the first Sibylla, Carson truly spoke "divine counsel" to humankind. Her words flowed out, perfect and purposeful, leading us in the direction of a more blessed future.

Are We Willing?

Voices from the world psyche mingle with our everyday conversations. Images from the dreaming earth play across our

mind like a silent movie running in the background. We live
with these messages morning and night without really noticing
them. But the instant we shift our awareness and bring hidden
elements to the foreground, we begin to find the sibyl or
prophet in ourselves.

But are we willing to hear and see? I cannot think of one
sibylline figure who avoided suffering. Ancient Sibylla derived
no pleasure shouting at young men while they sliced one another's hearts out. Followers of Jesus had no choice but to break
with the past and proclaim their new passionate vision, even as
they themselves were broken. Abolitionists in the Old South,
women's rights marchers in Victorian times, nonviolent protest-
ers in colonial India, student dissenters in oppressive regimes,
ecological activists across the globe—individuals like these had
had no choice but to speak out in grim, sibylline voices, regardless of personal consequences.

Experiencing the "underside" of things burdens the heart.
Accustomed pleasures may lose their shine after we see them in
a larger context. Most of us look forward to settling down at a
nice restaurant and opening the smooth, inviting menu. Hands
appear out of nowhere to fill water glasses. A cup of hot coffee
or tea is set before us with quiet dignity. All is well in the world.
But then a shadow falls. All is not well in the world. From the
restaurant window we clearly see their bleak faces as they beg
quarters on the sidewalk. A half dozen more homeless people
languish on the next block. And the next. In poorer countries,
every single street overflows with want and pain. Here comes
the exquisite entrée, held high like an offering to the god. We
eat it carelessly and cancel the dessert.

Once our inner vision opens to collective realities, it can
never close again. Rachel Carson said that she never wanted to
write an exposé like *Silent Spring*. But she had no choice, once
the facts revealed themselves to her. The world presses us to

take more and more of itself into our being. It longs to be known, to gain a cherished place in human awareness.

Becoming world-conscious destroys our former ease. Suddenly we cannot find peace unless we speak and act on behalf of those issues that personally tap us on the shoulder. One morning, we find that images of the dying wetlands haunt us like a personal problem. Visions of children sleeping under cardboard in the city streets rob us of our own sleep. Those who are called to a life of service find that the "me" component of identity starts to merge with something beyond itself. When Mother Teresa was asked how she could devote every ounce of her energy to caring for the poorest of the poor, she answered, "Their heart is my heart. Their flesh is my flesh. How could I not care for them?"

Not all background voices from the world unconscious are mournful. Even in these troubled times there is a "song in the air." Nature continues to pulse out joyful praise-poems to all who live. The genius of humankind never stops conceiving new worlds, and we join in the spirited exchange each time we give ourselves freedom to imagine. People who allow the collective psyche to speak through them find abundant creative inspiration for their work. It is easy to give up portions of the self to a larger calling when energy starts to flow in from I-don't-know-where. Being willing to host collective realities may evoke suffering, but it also brings profound satisfaction and reward.

If we should say yes to serving as a "medial" for the larger forces of community and earth, how do we proceed? I offer the following meditations and practices as departure points.

Meditation:
Reaching Out to the World-Psyche

Say this meditation to yourself upon arising in the morning, and repeat it once or twice during the day: *In this moment and throughout the day, I am willing to know the world more deeply. I will accept each new revelation, whether joyous or sad, as a personal gift and blessing.*

Practice:
Receiving Messages from the World-Psyche

After you have said the "reaching out" meditation a number of times, you may be surprised at how quickly the world responds. Messages about "what's so" filter in from all directions. Events you witness in the street contain important teachings; new broadcasts take on new meaning; strangers make statements that open up insights; books come your way by chance; movies and television programs look different than they did before. The hidden side of things will become more and more apparent to you. Keep a journal of your experiences for at least two weeks. You might call it "Teachings from the World-Psyche." Describe events and situations that reveal something new about the world unconscious. You can identify these experiences rather easily because they possess a certain psychic charge and stand out from the thousands of other happenings that fly by during the day. In your journal, jot down where you were and what you were doing when the teaching came to you. Explore what it means for your own perspective on the world. Below is a sample of what such an entry might look like. It was written by a thirty-year-old Caucasian woman.

October 29, 1:45, department store. Was in a rush, needed to pay for the stockings and then quickly leave.

A man and woman of color were waiting ahead of me with their items in hand. The clerk (Caucasian) looked at them, then turned straight to me and started ringing up my purchase. I glanced at the couple, and they looked back with sad, resigned expressions on their faces. I don't know why, but that expression really got to me. I can still see it in my mind. I said, "That couple was here first." But the clerk ignored me and rang up my stockings. I wish I had complained, but I didn't. Felt bad.

I know the World Psyche was telling me something today. The expression I saw comes from being treated as "less than" all through life. It comes from being dealt thousands of little blows, like the one in the store. I never noticed this fully before. Next time I will speak out, I promise!

By keeping a diary of both painful and joyful experiences, we can bring into clearer focus those elements of life that are trying to make themselves more fully known. Oracles come from many places besides dreams and divination. They stream in from the everyday world all around us. Not only did the sibyl and prophet see deeply into collective forces, they shouted a wake-up call for all to hear. Some of us feel a growing need to speak out on behalf of convictions we regard as sacred. As we see and hear more of the underside of things, the pressure mounts to do something constructive. But we need help in finding our voice. As children we were often told to "be quiet" rather than to broadcast our thoughts. School settings inhibit personal expression and encourage conformity. Industrial life confers no blessing on dissenting voices. So we must rely on spiritual help to bring forth the sibyl or prophet. I have found the following prayer to give me courage.

Teach my sibyl [prophet] voice to speak. Let my words flow out purposeful and perfect, guided by sacred intention. Protect me as I dedicate myself to service in the world.

Practice:
Following the Arrow of Service

The world is vast. Each of us can make only small offerings to collective good, and these offerings must be gathered from our own essential nature to be passionately communicated. Many needs and problems bid for our attention in the world. When we feel overwhelmed, we ask ourselves, "How may I choose among them?" Psychologist Mary Watkins who combines an imaginal perspective with the vigor of social activism, helps individuals and groups form answers to this question.[10] The interesting and reassuring thing, Watkins says, is that each of us is not called equally by all the world's sufferings. We are individually attuned to different kinds of suffering, and these are the domains in which we can make a unique contribution. But if we think, "There is so much to do! I wouldn't know where to begin!" we become distracted from the personal, specific ways in which the world is calling us.

Hearing our personal call to service begins when we notice that we are leading a "double life." One part of us longs for safety, security, and pleasure, while the other part feels prompted to take risks for our own convictions. These two selves compete for our loyalty, and the safety-seeker usually wins. But when the sibylline or prophet voice is closed down within, we forfeit a measure of aliveness.

The following exercise is based on Watkin's work with many groups around the country who wish to hear more clearly how the world is calling them.[11] It makes use of observation, reflection, and active imagination to help us identify deep desires we have not named before.

First, keep a notebook of the social, ecological, and spiritual issues that affect you most keenly. Observe events in your community to identify issues close to home. Listen to media broadcasts with the special purpose of writing down world problems that concern *you*. Look back over the years and claim those awarenesses that have visited and revisited you many times before. Now divide these items into three columns labeled "Intensely Important to Me," "Very Important to Me," "Important to Me." Remember that you should base your judgment on what you personally feel, not on what the larger society deems more or less urgent. All the issues are important, all are worthy of attention. But which ones directly and intimately call you?

Sit with the issues in the "intensely important" column and feel which one claims you the most and is closest to your heart. Ask yourself the following questions and jot down the answers or relate your response to a friend:

- What would it look like if I were to imagine myself serving this cause? What might be said or done through my words or actions, in small and large ways?

- What part of my current life would support involvement in this cause? What part of my current life would work against my involvement?

- If I devoted a portion of my time to following this call to service, how would my present life change?

- Is there a figure within me who opposes my getting involved in this issue? Who is that figure? What does he, she, or it say? What does the figure fear?

- Who within me is aware of this problem and desires to act and speak on its behalf? (Allow this one to present itself to you as a thought, a figure in a dream, or a character in a novel.) What is this one like? What is life like for this one when its awareness is not heeded, not given room, pushed to the side?

Now carry on a dialogue with the various figures you have encountered. Let them speak together. For example, a person who desired to work with animal rights causes reported that her dialogue went something like this:

> The figure who opposes my involvement is a practical, down-to-earth housewife who reminds me of my mother. "If you work for animal rights causes," she warns, "people will think you are a radical. You'll have to picket fur stores and get arrested. You'll have to become a vegetarian and throw away all your leather. Are you ready for that?" The figure who wants to serve this cause is strong and lean with brown skin. She reminds me of a female Mowgli from *The Jungle Book*. "Many respectable professionals support animal rights," she says. "They aren't radicals. No one will force you to do anything you don't want to do. Sitting by and doing nothing isn't the answer. You still will feel the pain of these animals, and that pain will eat at you deep down."

Take your time and carry on the dialogue as long as necessary. Unless all voices have their fair airtime, you will remain in conflict over your desire to serve.

All important decisions begin in the imagination. By giving the idea of world service a broad imaginal space in which to develop, we discover the direction of our personal calling. As Watkins says, "In dreams begins responsibility."

Sibylline figures live among us today. They are the men and women who raise their strident voices to warn that the green of earth is turning gray, that the nymph-infused waters are drying up (and with them our life's wellsprings). They are found among

Was Martin Luther King a Prophet?

THE LATE MARTIN LUTHER KING IS VENERATED FOR
his courageous and inspired leadership in civil rights.
We remember how King led thousands of protestors
through city after city and demanded an end to segre-
gation. We recall him accepting the Nobel Peace Prize
on behalf of all people who believe in nonviolent
solutions. Few speeches in American history linger
in the mind more hauntingly than King's "I have
a dream" address.[12]

But could King be called a "prophet"? A strong
case could be made in the affirmative. Like sibyls and
prophets of old, he drew upon sources of guidance from
beyond the personal self. A minister by profession, he
found it natural to seek guidance through prayer before
making major decisions. And when the answer came,
he acted without hesitation. His words flowed out
"purposeful and perfect" like those of great spiritual
leaders. Those who heard King speak in person never
forgot the experience. He drew power from larger collective realities, yet stayed firmly anchored in his personal identity.

By calling attention to the indignity suffered by
Americans of color, King brought potent shadow material into the light of day. He paid the ultimate price for
his service. Yet we will always remember him best not
for his death, but for his dream.

indigenous peoples around the world who provide sanctuary for ancient ways of knowing. Medials exist (usually at the fringes) in all cultures, welcoming the numinous Others into their personal chambers without fear. If we can preserve the spirit of these remarkable people in our new millennium, then the sibyl will live for another thousand years. And this time she may offer a small smile with her prophecies.

Chapter 7

Restoring Divination to the Divine

Ancient Thoughts for Modern Practice

W hen I was fifteen, an old woman offered to "read the cards" for me. Her invitation scared me a little. I associated the occult with roadside shacks and palmistry signs, creepy-looking moons with human faces, and weird oversized cards (one of them showing a hanged man!). Yet Mrs. Cavallero seemed like a kindly soul. Not knowing what to do, I shrugged a half-hearted "yes" and sank into her gold armchair.

Mrs. Cavallero lifted out a deck of cards from a beautiful enameled box. To my relief I saw hearts and clubs and queens flashing by as she shuffled them. It was an ordinary playing deck. She said a little prayer and then told me to choose seven cards. I knew that no wish could possibly form in my churning mind, but I dutifully followed instructions. After peering at the row for a long time, Mrs. Cavallero took a deep breath. "Well," she exhaled, as though something very important were about to happen. "Let's see what we have here."

Not one word of that reading from long ago remains in my memory. I don't think that the information I received made a deep impression on me, even at the time. But I recall vividly how the atmosphere in the room seemed to change as soon as my hand closed around the smooth deck of cards. A feeling of presence and portent filled the spaces around me. I could smell the musty Persian carpet beneath my feet, the leather books behind my head, the cool night fog. The old woman's voice slipped into my body like a wren into her nest. I was being instructed, not in words, but in larger patterns of knowing. My own being took on a new and precious value because it belonged to something larger than itself. Every detail of the present moment seemed exquisitely perfect. I felt as though time had stopped, fixing those bright cards upon the table for all eternity.

After the reading was over, I blinked and stammered, got up from the chair, and then sat down again. I felt happily disoriented, as though I had just been told something unbelievably wonderful. Mrs. Cavallero chuckled in a warm, knowing way, telling me to stay seated for a while. Then she brought out a platter of dates stuffed with cream cheese and walnuts. Never had I tasted anything so sublime!

Many years passed before I fully understood or appreciated what happened to me that evening. The reading did not predict my future destiny or uncover smoldering secrets. But it initiated me into a different way of knowing. Through the ritual process of divination, I took my first step into oracular space. "Oracular space" is a realm of experiencing where the senses open wide, time hovers in suspension, and the soul is brushed by a mysterious Something that offers knowledge or direction. All successful divination carries us into this domain. We need not be distracted by the thousands of different materials and interpretive systems found in divinatory arts around the world. Their underlying aims are the same, and they all work when approached with integrity.

What can we learn from studying divination in different times and cultures? How can modern practitioners work most effectively with their own methods? By what means does divination usher consciousness into oracular space? How can our theories of reality account for the success of divinatory practices? These questions lie at the heart of my interest in divination. None of them can be explored fully in a single lifetime; this is why the same queries turn up again and again in writings throughout the ages. But it is worthwhile to follow their lead, for each step of the way leads to new unexpected wonders.

The history of divination has no starting point and no destination. It is woven so tightly into the spiritual life of humankind that we cannot imagine a time when some form of divining was not used. The practice has always held a place of honor in archaic shamanic traditions. Even today, native peoples around the world utilize ancient methods of invoking divine guidance. The Bible recounts many stories of divination. Who can read about the mysterious Urim and Thummim, the sprouting rods of Moses, or the late-night necromancy (consultation with the dead) of King Saul without feeling an excited chill? Folk practices such as reading tea leaves and pulling petals off a daisy survive in households across Europe and the United States. An anthropologist summarized the matter well when he concluded that divination "is a practice of the greatest antiquity, performed everywhere in the world, by peoples in every cultural status, and utilizing almost every conceivable instrument or phenomenon as an indicator."[1]

The word "divination" derives from the Latin *divi*—a deity. Therefore, to divine a thing is to discover the intention or the configuration of the Sacred in relation to that matter. Depending on the belief system in which divination is situated, the Sacred may be regarded as a unitary force or as a multiplicity of forces, which might include spirits, animal powers, and a host of otherworldly entities. Even secular forms of divination

*Romans seek an answer to their inquiry by observing the behavior
of birds. Augury, or understanding "bird-speak," gives us the
word auspicious, meaning "the blessing of a bird."*
(19th-century lithograph)

are based on the conviction that an inscrutable "unknown"
beyond the personal self (such as the unconscious) may be consulted to provide guidance and illumination. Without the *divi* in
divination, cards are only squares of paper, and rune stones are
mere decorated rocks.

Divination should not be equated only with predicting the
future, for it serves many other purposes as well. One may
inquire into mysteries of the past, such as finding out what happened to a missing person years ago, or trying to learn what
grandmother was whispering as she died. Diviners ask for clarification of present events, particularly when an important decision has to be made. I have found that the most successful

inquires often lead with the question, "What perspective should I take on this issue in order to proceed in the best way?" Thus, divination is concerned with the past, present, and future, in addition to providing spiritual and psychological guidance on life issues.

Learning about divination practices in various times and places can inform our own work profoundly. Even if we do not adopt the specific methods of other practitioners, we may gain inspiration from drawing near to their magic. The best way to entering oracular space is to keep the company of those who are already there. Let us therefore look into the experiences of three very different types of diviners: an ancient Israelite, a shaman from Nepal, and a modern American man who receives oracular messages from his computer.

"Lights and Perfections" — An Israelite Mystery

When Moses anointed Aaron as high priest of the newly liberated Israelites, he bestowed on him a special instrument of divination. We know it by the name "Urim and Thummim."[2] According to Hebrew scholars, *urim* carries the image of a light that makes things clear or manifest. *Thummim* translates as "perfect" or "a perfection." We are told in Exodus 28:30 that Aaron was to wear this *mispat* (oracle) upon his breast whenever he went before the presence of the Lord.

Many biblical passages affirm how important the Urim and Thummim (abbreviated UT below) was to the early Israelites. Moses, Aaron, Eleazar, and Samuel were among those who consulted it to make decisions. For example, we find a brief but fascinating account related in the book of Ezra (2:61-63). During a terrible war, many Israelites were taken into slavery by King Nebuchadnezzar of Babylon. But the political landscape changed after a time, and great numbers of individuals were able to return again to Jerusalem and Judah. Everyone who returned was required to re-register in the tribal role so that rights and property could be secured for successive generations and foreign interlopers into the nation could be detected. But a certain group of priests ran into trouble when no trace of their family lineage could be found in the records. It was decreed that these individuals must instantly step down from their positions and relinquish all privileges until it could be proven that they had descended from the original Israelite tribes. In the absence of records, such a fact could only be proven by consulting the Urim and Thummim. The oracle would reveal the true situation with perfect truth and clarity. A decision on the matter was therefore delayed until a priest could be found who read the UT. Regrettably, we are never told what the oracle revealed.

What were the Urim and Thummim, and how did they bestow the light of perfect revelation on issues? Combining clues from various sources, scholars believe that the UT were luminous stones attached to (or tucked within) the priestly breastplate. A minority opinion holds that the UT were discs of metal or wood engraved with letters of the Hebrew alphabet or the name of YHWH. But the gem theory has gained wider acceptance. We know that precious and semiprecious stones played an important role in the religious life of Hebraic peoples. The book of Exodus tells us that twelve gems, including a topaz, emerald, sapphire, diamond, and amethyst, were sewn in rows across Aaron's beautifully woven breastplate. Every stone bore the name of a tribe of Israel. Two large onyx, each engraved with six tribe names, adorned the priest's shoulders.

Several ancient writers offered their opinion on how the Urim and Thummim actually operated. Augustine (354 to 430 C.E.) suggested that the UT was a stone that changed from one color to another in response to questions. An affirmative answer would be given by the appearance of one hue, while a negative response would be reflected in a different hue. Because the stone was oracular, Augustine said, it was written that

"Aaron shall bear the decisions of the children of Israel on his heart" (Ex.28:30).

In the early first century C.E., the Greco-Jewish philosopher Philo Judaeus of Alexandria provided a dramatic account of the UT. During an important ancient battle, Philo wrote, priests consulted the Urim and Thummim to see how their troops would fare. No sooner did they ask the question when a brilliant light flashed from the stones. Its splendor was so great that no one had any doubt God had come to their aid. Victory was theirs that night. In commenting on this event, Philo made it clear that neither the breastplate nor the stones were unique in themselves. Solomon, he said, possessed many similar vestments. It was divine intervention alone that caused the UT to pour out light in a miraculous manner. Philo also noted sadly that the oracle had stopped functioning two hundred years prior to his writing. No lights could be evoked from it, despite the most ardent efforts and prayers.

We do not know whether Philo obtained his information from texts that were later lost or whether his account was an exercise in religious imagination. In either case, the image of oracular stones flooding the room with radiance is one we cannot easily forget. I treasure the image on two levels: as a literal possibility and as a metaphor for oracular consciousness. The ancient Hebrews must have obtained fairly spectacular results with the UT, or they would not have brought the oracle with them from Egypt and given it a central place in their holiest tabernacle. No intelligent individuals would make life-and-death decisions based on guidance that was vague or irrelevant. We must assume that the UT consistently responded to inquiries in a helpful, unambiguous way. Unless the UT merely consisted of lots drawn from a pouch (a theory most scholars doubt), it seems likely that its materials *did* something fairly dramatic to indicate answers. Stones that swell with rapture when the Divine draws near—is the notion so impossible?

As a metaphor, the idea of oracular "lights and perfections" is one of the most beautiful in all of history. Those of us who have experienced divinatory guidance at its best know about the clear spaciousness that opens during this work. It is as though someone has changed the lighting within and without. The mind's eye sees differently, thoughts gain new contours, and both past and future seem closer at hand. In the rarefied light of oracular presence, each moment takes on a kind of perfection. Messages arrive at the right moment and in the right form. One feels that the universe has coherence after all. Though we may never know how the Israelites actually carried out their practice of lights and perfections, a glimmer from the ancient art still remains in our collective memory.

A Nepalese Shaman Divines the Cause of Illness

Divination and healing practices used today by Nepalese shamans have been passed down from teacher to student for thousands of years. Each time they are enacted, the distant past comes to life again. I am fortunate to have learned a great deal about these traditions through the anthropologist Peter Skafte, who has carried out extensive fieldwork among shamans in Nepal. Peter has brought shamanic practitioners from the Himalayas to live at our home, and they have generously shared their knowledge with us.

The following account is based on Peter's work with Maili, a forty-two-year-old shaman from the Tamang ethnic group.

As Maili finishes washing plates and pots from the family's evening meal, and her husband and four-year-old son stack clean dishes on the shelf, an urgent banging suddenly shakes the house. Opening the door she finds a frightened-looking man drooping from exhaustion.

"Tell me what has happened," Maili asks, leading him to the fire. She learns that the man's wife has been acting strange for a long time.

When people try to rouse her from bed in the morning, she pulls the covers over her face and tells them to go away. In the past she has always had a hearty appetite, along with a hearty laugh, but she now rejects food and has grown thin.

"She is dying," the man sobs. "Please, kind Jankri [healer shaman], will you come right away?"

Maili answers with a single nod. They will depart immediately. With smooth efficiency, she gathers together her sacred tools: a jama (ritual tunic), a drum, a brass pan for diagnostic divination, and a leather bag filled with altar materials. Wrapping herself in a woolen cloak for the long, wind-swept trek ahead, Maili kisses her son goodbye and strides out into the dark. She can hear his brokenhearted wails for a long time as she trudges forward.

Arriving at the hut an hour later, Maili is escorted inside. The patient stares darkly ahead and acknowledges no one. "What is her name?" Maili asks. "Amriti," somebody answers. "Amriti," Maili echoes, brushing her hand across the woman's forehead and cheeks. After a moment's pause, Maili says, "The deities will tell us how healing can come to Amriti."

An altar must be built. Maili sets up twenty small figurines made of dried flour dough, each one representing a particular helping spirit or deity. The figurines are not merely symbolic. They provide anchorpoints in this world where the Invisibles can dwell. "Come, sit with me at this altar," the shaman chants to them. "Take your place on the thrones I have made in your honor."

Having consecrated her altar, the shaman withdraws behind a partition to put on her sacred garb. It is designed to protect the wearer and to serve as a bridge to the unseen worlds. Peacock feathers in the headdress give wing to her soul for spiritual flights. Necklaces of snake vertebrae draw up ancient powers from the earth. Rita beads invoke the protection of Shiva, and rudrakshi beads inspire the great underworld serpent, Sesnag, to stand guard over her work. A long flowing headdress and tunic protect the healer's entire body from invasion by alien forces. And perhaps most importantly, the resonant tones of her shamanic drum open the portal between ordinary reality and the supernatural realms.

Maili sits before her altar and begins to drum a slow, deliberate rhythm. Rocking to and fro, she chants an invocation asking for guidance and protection. The goddess Saraswati, an honored deity who first brought speech, writing, music, and oracular inspiration to humankind, is asked to guide her tongue so that everything she speaks will be accurate and helpful. Maili's own personal spirit-teachers are called, for their assistance will be essential.

Then it is time to carry out a special form of divination called the Tara Jokana. "Bring me a flower blossom, a coin, and a handful of uncooked rice," the shaman says. Several family members jump up simultaneously to procure the needed items. "Amriti", her lulling voice continues, "take this coin and place it here." She indicates the divination plate. At first the patient doesn't respond, but Maili turns and looks her fully in the face. The shaman's eyes are large and unnaturally dark, like tunnels that draw the soul down, downward. Amriti does as she is told.

Holding her plate in one hand and the rice in the other, Maili utters a melodious chain of words, some of which have no translatable meaning in any language. The invocation is a sacred mantra given to her in a dream by her spirit-teacher. Its purpose is to activate the plate and the rice with spiritual power so that they become a channel of communication with sacred forces. "We ask assistance for Amriti," the shaman chants in a sweet voice. "Tell us, what is the nature of her affliction? Most powerful Sesnag, healer of all creatures, help us in this effort." Maili's eyes are closed in deep communion as her body rocks to and fro. After a few moments she pinches a small amount of rice between her fingers and drops it onto the brass surface.

Tipping her plate toward the firelight, Maili begins to shuffle through the grains of rice, separating them into pairs. Two by two, two by two, she patiently organizes the scattered array. Each pattern yields meaning to her trained eye. "I see," the shaman says after a time. "It is mouch [the ghost of a dead child]. The patient is being sucked on by a mouch. The ghost must be persuaded to leave or she may die."

Murmurs of surprise echo around the room, for everyone knows something the shaman could not have known. A half year earlier, Amriti suffered a miscarriage during the seventh month of pregnancy. Expelling the fetus was a long, agonizing ordeal. But after it was over, the matter was never spoken of again. Amriti went about her business as though nothing had happened. Then the decline set in a few weeks later.

Maili hears this account and instantly comprehends the situation. Yes, the ghost of that little expelled child has been lingering around its mother, trying to suck the milk and the life it never had. The shaman knows exactly what to do. She will return the next week and help the mouch move on to a better place in the spirit world, perhaps to be born again. The mother will be treated with sacred herbs and rituals of restoration to help her return to a normal life in this world.

When the Tara Jokana is completed, Maili rests her eyes upon the patient.

"Do you consent to be treated seven days from tonight?" she asks soberly. Amriti nods. Her face now seems alive, receptive, wonderstruck. Maili sets aside her divination plate and begins drumming a slow beat. She brings forth round, hollow tones that reverberate through the whole family. Their small room suddenly feels larger than the starry spaces outside. They know that something awesome has happened tonight, and for the first time in months, a new hope enters their hearts.

After thanking the deities and helpers, Maili takes off her sacred clothes and dismantles the altar, promising to return in seven days. The long trek home turns her body to ice. But she feels good, for signs point to a good outcome for the patient. In an hour she will be cradling a cup of tea prepared by her kind husband. Then she will bend down to kiss a little boy upon his sleeping lips.

Amriti's prospects prove to be favorable, as Maili has predicted.

Shortly after the second visit by the shaman, she spontaneously sits up in bed as though awakening from a coma. Then she smiles at her husband and says, "I could eat a mountain." But the family does not rejoice prematurely. They are careful to offer flowers and fruits to the little mouch spirit each day for a month, as Maili has instructed, lest it grow hungry again. Their efforts are rewarded by the full recovery of Amriti's strength and zest for life.

Experiences similar to Maili's are shared by many shamans in Nepal. Summoned at any time of the night or day by those in need, they tirelessly work to heal affliction, provide spiritual guidance, help people through transitions, and stabilize the community through cycles of ritual enactment. Divination forms a centerpiece to all of these activities. It enables shamans to obtain guidance from otherworld forces who are "in the know" about deeper realities behind human affairs. Practitioners gain strength and comfort from realizing that they do not have to work alone. An oracle is always willing to speak through grains of rice and a hundred other means, offering the counsel that only a "divi" can give.

Words of Wisdom from the Computer

I have a friend named Tom who possesses a preternatural ability to communicate with all things mechanical. At four years old he received a message from the old family radio offering to show him its inner workings. Sneaking into the dark living room at 3 a.m., he dismantled the system down to its last vacuum tube. Then, to his own amazement, he put the whole thing back together again and found that it worked perfectly. This was the beginning of his brilliant career as an ambassador between the world of humans and the world of machines.

In the early 1980's, Tom told me that he had designed a simple computer program to do divinations. The program generated at random a page number of the dictionary, a column

The Wise-Woman's Divination Ax

A VIKING NAMED GUDMUND THE MIGHTY WAS
so worried about getting killed that he consulted a
local wise-woman known for her second sight. She
told him to meet her at the ocean. When Gudmund
arrived, he was filled with awe to see her dressed as
a male warrior, complete with metal helmet and a
battle-ax. She marched into the surf and plunged her
ax into the waves. "No harm will come to you," she
assured him. Gudmund then asked about the safety
of his family. The diviner again sliced her ax into the
waves. This time, blood poured from the blade. "One
of your sons will suffer a severe injury. But he will
live." The Viking was about to ask another question
when he was interrupted. "Do not inquire further," the
woman said, turning to leave. "You have no idea what
pain this divination cost me." All that she predicted
came to pass.

This description of a divination procedure comes
from *Ljovetninga Saga*, a medieval Scandinavian
narrative.[3] The sagas bear witness to an era
when divinatory arts played an important
role in human affairs.

A contemporary Nepalese shaman seeks guidance through a Jokana divination, an ancient method utilizing grains of rice tossed on a brass plate. (Photo by Peter Skafte)

indicator (right or left), and a number counting either from the top or bottom of the column. For example, the code might say "page 63, left column, word 6 down." Tom then found the word indicated on page sixty-three and wrote it down along with its definition. The computer generated three codes in response to each inquiry.

Friends began imploring Tom to given them a reading with his marvelous divination instrument. He soon learned that the oracle did not respond to every inquiry with clear answers. There seemed to be a connection between the sincerity of the inquirer and the quality of material that appeared on the screen. Those who asked flippant questions often got incoherent results. Interestingly these individuals never seemed to mind receiving senseless messages. Perhaps they never expected to get anything from the session except merriment. It was as though everyone, including the oracle, was content to enjoy a bit of entertainment.

But divination results were very different for those who took the activity seriously or had a genuine need for guidance. The words they received almost always provided something helpful. One day a woman named Jill was brought to Tom's house by friends. She said very little and did not join in the laughter of those who were having fun with the program. When her turn came, she only said that she had a problem and that professionals could not help her solve it. The question she typed was, "Please give advice on how to solve my problem." When they looked up the codes, three words emerged: "transport," "spouse," "consultation."

Jill's hand flew to her mouth, for she immediately perceived their meaning. "I'm supposed to transport my spouse for a consultation with the doctor," she said. Then Jill explained that she had a serious vaginal yeast infection that she couldn't seem to cure. Medications made it ease up for a little while, but then it would come back soon thereafter. A friend had suggested that she was getting reinfected by her husband, but she dismissed this theory because he showed no symptoms. When Jill followed the oracle's advice, she learned that her husband did indeed carry a yeast culture. After he was treated, her ailment never returned.

The computer oracle also proved to be a fine detective agent. Months earlier, Tom had run into an old acquaintance named Robert whom he had not seen for years. Their talk was hurried because both of them were rushing to appointments. Tom learned that his friend had just moved into town, but addresses were never exchanged. Now he felt a strong impulse to contact Robert again, but the phone company recorded no listing under his name.

Not knowing what to do, Tom turned to his oracular guide for help. "How can I find Robert?" he asked. The words he received were "night," "train," "pathway." An association leaped into Tom's mind. "Night Train" was a brand of cheap whiskey that transients often drank in an abandoned hotel near the beach. Tom had seen empty bottles of the alcohol littering a pathway near the hotel. "Why, that's the 'pathway'!" he suddenly realized. But then a worry came into his mind. "Do you mean that Robert has sunk into alcoholism?" he typed into the computer. His answer was "vista," "parking lot," "wait." Indeed, there was a parking lot near the hotel that opened to a beautiful vista of the sea. Tom often sat there on misty days and looked out over the peaceful water. But how all of this related to Robert was unclear. He had no choice but to do as the oracle said and "wait."

Two weeks later, Tom found himself with an extra hour to spare before he had to return to work. He drove to his favorite vista point overlooking the ocean, unpacked his lunch, and listened to music on the radio. At 2 p.m., Tom knew that it was time to go, but he could not bring himself to turn the ignition key. He simply sat there gazing into the blue, as though in a trance state. Suddenly, he saw a figure pass by. Robert was walk-ing up the trail from the hotel! Tom was so overcome with excitement that he leaped out of the car and practically tackled his friend. During their long conversation, he learned that Robert was working on a crew renovating the hotel. "Yes," the friend confirmed, "I've had to shovel out many bottles of Night Train in that place!"

How Can Divination Work?

Tom's encounters with the computer evoke many questions about underlying principles of divination. Trying to explain the accuracy of these messages is interesting because the issues are uncluttered by considerations of telepathy or interpersonal influence. For example, no one can say that a computer shrewd-ly reads Tom's nonverbal cues and tells him what he wants to know (a charge often made against palmists, card readers, and other practitioners). Let's look at three possible explanations for Tom's experiences and see how they each contribute to a deep-er understanding of oracles. I will present each argument in the most convincing light possible.

The Skeptic:
"Divination Is the Art of
Making Something Out of Nothing"

Would any reasonable person believe that Tom's computer intentionally selected certain words for certain people at certain times? By what conceivable means could it do this? In designing the program, Tom made sure that words would be generated at random in response to questions. He could have instructed the system to select words that related in some way to the question's content—perhaps by matching synonyms or using grammatical cues. But he used a randomizer. And that's what he got: random

words. As to why some of his friends found great personal meaning in the results, this is explained easily. Those individuals
who had specific problems or questions on their minds were
eagerly awaiting helpful responses. They read personal meaning
into the words they received. Tom himself provided evidence
for this theory. He noted that frivolous questioners who treated
the activity as mere entertainment received nonsense responses, whereas sincere or needful inquirers got helpful responses.
Clearly, one group of participants was highly motivated to
read meaning into a set of random words, whereas the other
group was not.

However, there are two other possible explanations for how
the program, even though it was designed to be random, might
have called up words in a nonrandom fashion, though they are
both implausible. Some might say that god or otherworldly force
took control of the program, but this theory is not very useful,
since one cannot explain a mystery by pointing to an equally
unexplainable mystery. Since such an occurrence can't be
proved or disproved, the "god in the machine" theory negates
the whole issue. Or, it could be argued that human brain waves
somehow influenced the action of the microchips. While certain people have claimed to possess this type of power, there is
as yet no scientific evidence that can support such a claim. At
present we must accept the theory that divination results carry
no significance in themselves. Any meaning or utility we derive
from them are creations of our own imagination.

The Spiritualist:
"Divination Is the Instrument
of Supernal Forces"

Those who must find a physical, observable cause for everything are hopelessly out of touch with reality—ancient *and*
modern! Decades ago, theoretical physicists demonstrated that

matter and energy are interchangeable, that seemingly solid objects are but impulse patterns, and that forces invisible to the human eye shape the universe as we know it. These insights would have come as no surprise to citizens of the ancient world. For them every observable event had its origin in the unobservable world of spirit. Didn't the Vedas teach that everything we see around us is a projection from the great minds of the *asuras* (deities and demigods)? Therefore, the reasonable person seeks solutions to problems at the level of *cause* (the invisible realm) rather than at the level of *effect* (the things and events we see around us).

From the beginning of time, divination has provided an excellent means of focusing attention on the spiritual underpinnings of reality. Divination is like a demonstration laboratory: it shows us how the elements of daily life are moved and shaped by the greater force of Primary Reality. The Roman philosopher Plutarch expressed this position well when discussing augury. "Birds are the veritable instruments of divine power," he said. "It is the gods who determine the variety of their movements and elicit their cries and twitterings. Sometimes they hold them suspended in the air; sometimes they hurriedly dispatch them to hinder (or assist) the purposes of men."[4]

Tom's divination program operates upon the same principles that Plutarch assigned to augury. Supernal Forces control the selection of words in response to questions. It is they who determine the variety of their electronic movements, who hold them suspended or hurriedly dispatch them to the screen for our purposes. Why should this task be regarded as difficult"? If Cosmic Consciousness can generate universes, it certainly can pop up a few word-finders on a screen. The Great Ones are everywhere present. We cannot always understand their ways and means, but we can be sure that "in them we live and have our being."

The Matrix Makers:
"Divination Is an Acausal Synchronicity"

Skeptics and spiritualists have more in common that they think! Both seek the causes behind oracles. Both agree that *something* prompted the words "consultation" and "spouse" to appear on Tom's computer screen. The skeptic says, "A randomizer caused it"; the person of faith says, "Supernal Forces caused it." Both are viewing events from a linear viewpoint and concluding that one event led to another.

But what if we view divination from a nonlinear, acausal viewpoint? Carl Jung explored this perspective extensively in this work with *I Ching*, and it became a foundational concept in his theories on synchronicity.[5] The ancient Chinese, Jung said, were masters at thinking in terms of fields. They were keenly interested in looking at the pattern of events formed during a particular moment of observation. According to their view, no single event exists in isolation, but it rises from the larger matrix to which it belongs. What appears to be an isolated event is really part of a larger whole. And each event speaks for the larger whole.

The field perspective was an ideal explanatory framework for Chinese divination. When bones were rolled or yarrow stalks tossed, the diviner assumed that these objects would fall in a pattern characteristic of that moment in time. If meaning could be found in their configuration, then much larger patterns of meaning would be revealed. Marie-Louise von Franz, a colleague of Jung's stated the view succinctly. One does not ask, "Why has this come about, or what factor has caused this effect?" she said. The key question is, "What likes to happen together in a meaningful way in the same moment?"[6] Jung called this view "acausal" because one event does not cause the next event to happen.

Divination makes sense when viewed from a field perspective. Signs that present themselves in answer to our inquiries are always the perfect signs, for they arise from the larger configuration of All-That-Is. When Tom received the words "parking lot", "vista", "wait," on the computer screen, they gave expression to many interior and exterior realities that belonged to the "shape of things." The oracle showed a perfect moment in time when Tom's waiting and gazing at the vista would fall naturally together.

Viewed from the acausal perspective, divination needs no scientific proofs or godly forces to lend it validity. The past, present, and future are available in each unique moment, reflecting each other like faceted mirrors. Or, put another way, the results of divination are always "valid" because they are holographic. Just as the smallest bit of a holographic image contained the whole image within it, the simplest divinatory message contains all the answers we need. Our task is to let the larger field (of which we are a part) play upon us and speak through us. Then divination becomes an act of communion as well as communication.

Synthesizing Opinions:
Divination Is a Complex Phenomenon

Which of these explanations is the most valid? We do not have to choose among them for each one contributes something valuable to our understanding of divination. The skeptic reminds us that we ourselves bring meaning to oracles. Cards, sticks, and dictionary words tell us nothing at all unless we "read" them. Our own intuitive and interpretative powers play a large role in all divination work. However, skeptics are wrong when they say we make meaning out of nothing. The results of divination often speak in a manner that's strikingly clear, precise, and helpful. Then we *know* we are not making up the whole thing.

The spiritualist also contributes a valid point. Oracles are given to us by a power beyond the personal self, and their assistance is often so elegant that we can only breathe a prayer of gratitude. But we also must exercise good judgment in the way we act upon the advice we receive. Those who give up their free will and follow the lead of any message open themselves to danger. There are many tragic stories about people who allow spirits and unknown forces to take over their lives. Common sense is an essential ingredient in any divination practice.

Matrix makers tell us that things fall together in patterns of "just so," possibly without reason. This viewpoint keeps the world fresh and full of wonder. It relieves us from always trying to find causes, predict outcomes, and make things happen in a certain way. We can throw the dice with a shout of freedom, knowing that the way they fall is the only way they *could* fall in that cosmic moment. But we should never forget that our own intentions and desires are also part of the cosmic moment. We, too, are part of the universal matrix, and so we also bear some responsibility for the shape it takes. By paying close attention to our deepest motivations, we cocreate the universe in more conscious ways.

Divination remains a powerful tool whether or not we understand its nature. But our practice is strengthened by giving thought to the conceptual underpinnings of what we do. When critics give simplistic reasons why divination cannot work, we can answer them with intelligent responses. And we may remind them that some of the most illustrious people in history, such as Moses, Socrates, Confucius, Plutarch, and C. G. Jung, have taken the art seriously.

Oracular Space and Divination: A Personal Account

In the beginning of this chapter, I related the experience of having my cards read for the first time. From that moment on, the cards and I established a deep bond that remains strong

When Destiny Was Written upon the Liver

ONE OF THE MOST ANCIENT AND WELL-DOCUMENTED divination systems is haruspicy, the art of inspecting entrails from sacrificed animals. The earliest evidence for this practice is a liver-model almost four thousand year old, dating from the Old Babylonian period.[7] Petitioners seeking divine guidance brought an animal, usually a sheep, to the Baru ("one who sees"). The animal was then sacrificed at the altar as prayers were offered to the deities. It was believed that Divine Presence joined with the animal at the moment of death, leaving its imprint on the body. The liver was an especially sensitive recording instrument, for it was considered to form a juncture between body and soul. It was thought that the petitioner's soul also joined with the sacrifice in a mystical way, for when the Baru read signs written in the entrails, he would say (as though speaking for the sheep), "My master will complete his journey safely," or "My lord will meet with strong opposition." Haruspicy was an exceedingly complex art. Hundreds of documents have been found that provide explicit directions for interpreting nuances of shape, color, texture, size, and appearance in an animal's organs. This form of divination survived well into Roman times and guided the decisions of many nations.

today. They speak to me in ways unparalleled by any other divination instrument. When I close my hands around a deck, I know exactly where I am and who I am. Entering into "oracular space" is easy when I lay the cards out before me, especially if another attuned person is near. Why this particular means of divination should affect me so powerfully is a mystery. Perhaps timing played a role in the course of events. I was fortunate to be initiated into the art during adolescence, a period of intense spiritual awakening for many young people. Oracular abilities may develop very rapidly between the ages of about ten and eighteen if a person is given the proper stimulation and support.

I felt strangely off-center for several weeks after my first card reading. Daily chitchat at school fell hollow on my ears, and class studies seemed more pointless than usual. Parties, loud music, and noisy crowds (which I never liked anyway) now tortured me with their harsh clamor. At night, a wheel turned in my chest like a great round thing with life of its own. I found myself thinking again and again about red hearts and black spades, kings and jacks in royal array, queens gazing out at me, mother to daughter. Then one morning I woke up knowing what I must do. I would ask Mrs. Cavallero to teach me the cards.

"Learning the cards and learning to read the cards are two different things," my teacher said. "I'll be glad to teach you everything about the system. As for the rest, you'll discover it yourself." I had no idea what these statements meant, but it didn't matter, for I was thrilled to be sinking into that familiar gold armchair again, reaching for the little enameled box.

Card by card, Mrs. Cavallero and I went through the deck, talking about the meaning of each. Nine of hearts denotes a wish coming true, but look at the middle heart, for if it is reversed, there will be a wait. Seven of spades whispers a secret or hidden thing kept "under the table"; if five of those spades are pointing up, the matter will be revealed, even if people try to keep it cloaked. Many cards shifted in meaning when they fell near other cards. Some symbols carried more than one interpretation, and the reader had to use her or his intuition to know which one was correct. I diligently wrote down everything she said and could not wait to try my hand at the art.

Mrs. Cavallero told me she had learned to read cards around the year 1915 when a group of Gypsies took up residence in her little town for several months. They earned a bit of money by "telling fortunes" to all who were interested. How attracted the young Midwesterner felt to those Gypsy wagons lined inside with rich carpets and tapestries! She spent every free moment in the band's company, longing to know more about the mysterious craft they practiced. One kindly woman agreed to teach her a method of reading cards that had been passed down through many generations. Strangely, Mrs. Cavallero was exactly my age at the time.

Armed with my twenty pages of notes, I set off to become a cardomancer. I memorized the meaning of each card in its upright and reverse forms fairly quickly, mostly by giving myself readings day and night. So many friends clamored to sample the art that I never fell short of practice opportunities. My style of reading was straightforward. After laying out a row of cards (various methods could be used), I related the meaning of each symbol as I had learned it, sometimes combining a few interpretations in a creative way. I was pleased when the person I read for drew in a breath of surprise because the cards matched her or his life situation so precisely. I saw that this method of divination really seemed to work for me.

But after a year of constant reading, I felt that something was missing. Many of the cards did not connect with one another in a meaningful way, and as I recited their interpretations, my words sounded mechanical. What was I doing wrong? The answer came with a shock one day as I was reading for a seventeen-year-old student whom I had never met before. Peering at the three cards she drew, I recited their meanings. "Two of clubs, that's a place of school or work," I began. "And, uh, there's a new opportunity coming by fate; that's the seven of clubs. Then a nine of spades, well, we usually have a disappointment or painful situation of some kind there. Now that doesn't quite make sense, does it. . . . "My voice trailed off, for I couldn't see how the cards connected.

I was further blocked by a welter of feelings and images playing somewhere on the edge of my awareness. I sensed forces tugging in two directions: some were trying to go and some were being pulled back. Someone, an older woman, felt horribly empty and scared. I saw her pulling on a younger person, her daughter, trying to keep her home. Then I realized that the daughter was this high school student sitting before me. Yes, it had to do with going off to college; the mother didn't want her to go.

I decided to take a risk and say what was in my mind rather than follow the cards precisely. "Let me suggest something here," I began. "I wonder whether a new opportunity is in the air for you to go to college, maybe a very special college. But something is pulling you in two directions. Someone is in grief about your leaving. Could it be your mother?" The girl's mouth dropped open. Her eyes gaped at me as though I were an apparition. Then she told me about the partial scholarship she had been offered from the state university three hundred miles away. Her mother had expected her to attend the local community college.

"I'm the only one who hasn't moved out of the house," the girl said. "Nobody else can handle Mom's drinking," I listened to her story. Then I said that only she could decide what to do, but the cards strongly indicated that this college opportunity had come by fate and could change her life for the better. I later learned that she did leave home and go to the university. It made me feel good to think that perhaps the work we did gave her a little extra strength to make a positive decision.

For the first time, I understood the difference between reading the cards and reading between the cards. The true message of any divination cannot be found only in the signs and symbols appearing before us. If we merely recite their assigned meaning, we lose the heart of the communication. Symbols should be used as springboards into oracular space, where the real story will be found. When I had read cards in the past, many feelings, pictures, and situations always played through my mind. But I ignored them. In fact, I blocked them out because I thought they would get in the way of my interpretations. Now I discovered that my job as a diviner (and later as a psychotherapist) was to trust the field of shared imaginations that sprang up between me and the other. Perhaps this is what archetypal psychologist Stephen Aizenstat means when he advises us not to "interpret" dreams or reduce them to symbols but to "tend" them. By opening a wide space for the realities that pay us a visit in dreams, oracles, and other mysterious domains, we will be met by many guides to the soul.

Divination's Timeless Bones

My experience as a card reader has helped me understand divination practices from ancient and modern times. On the surface these methods look very different from one another, but they all have the same aim: to help consciousness enter oracular space. When a Viking wise-woman strikes her divination ax into the ocean (see sidebar, page 201), a haruspex peers at an ox liver (see sidebar, page 211), or a preacher opens the Bible at random for guidance, they are doing something quite similar. Each diviner shifts into a special state of mind where signs speak to them with intent and meaning. Regardless of what divination tools are used, one must cultivate a relationship with this special state of mind in order to obtain results. Here are four suggestions for strengthening our own relationship with oracular knowing as we practice divinatory arts.

1. *Remember the Divi in divination; always approach your practice with reverence.* To divine is to seek revelation from supernal ("belonging to the beyond or higher") sources. These sources need not be imagined as heavenly, for some cultures make use of underworld or otherworld agencies to provide guidance. But participation of something beyond the personal self must be assumed.

Holding an attitude of reverence does not mean carrying a long face. We need not be somber or mirthless during divination proceedings. In fact, it is said that the deities love to laugh, and that you can recognize enlightened beings by the twinkle in their eyes. Alan Watts, a modern teacher of Zen Buddhism, once remarked that angels can fly because they take themselves lightly.[8] We, too, can enter a light spirit during divination while still remaining fully within sacred intention. What truly impairs this work is an attitude of flippancy or disdain. I refuse to undertake even the simplest divination if someone in the room is making disparaging remarks. Before touching any instrument of divination, I survey the environment and ask, "Would I invite a deity into this setting?"

The best way of inviting sacred Presence into our work is through a simple request or prayer. Uttering an invocation changes the atmosphere in the room completely. I personally like the many-name approach used by countless ancient practitioners. Rather than call upon Divinity as a single entity, its many identities and aspects are named out loud. I often say something like, "We respectfully invite all beings into our presence who would assist us with this work. Devas, guides, teachers, animal spirits, and plant-life souls, we ask your protection and assistance. Entities from this world and the Otherworld who would help us, we thank you. Only those who serve the highest good may enter here."

Each practitioner should fashion an invocation that kindles devotional feeling. In general, it should contain three elements: a request to be joined by sacred Presence(s), a request to be aided and protected, and a request that our work serve the highest good. These are the three prayers that practitioners from earliest times have made before undertaking any divination. We can only benefit by following their example.

2. *Give divination a chance to claim you.* Freely acquaint yourself with as many divination methods as possible, trying your hand at approaches borrowed from many centuries and cultures. Fortunately, information and supplies are more available today than at any period in modern history. Experience freely until a certain method strongly attracts you. How and why this bonding happens is an enigma. The divination system may or may not fit with your ancestral heritage, cultural background, or conscious preference.

I doubt I would have chosen playing cards as my first choice among oracular instruments. (Something a bit more esoteric and romantic would have been nice!) But they chose me.

How might you know when a divination approach calls you personally? It often begins when you use an instrument (or another person uses it in your presence) and an uncanny fascination takes hold. You want to learn everything you can, and the learning never feels like drudgery. Each symbol you study opens a portal into ever-expanding meanings. You intuitively understand things about the art that no one ever taught you. This is a sign that the "daimon of the system" is joining with your own interior patterns and instructing you even in your sleep. You cannot wait for free time so that you can play with the method some more. I say "play" because you feel a sense of joyful engagement and pleasure in this work. You are never tired at the end of a session, for it seems to give you energy rather than deplete your resources. If these experiences seem familiar, you have been claimed by a divinatory art. In all likelihood you will practice it for the rest of your life in one form or another.

Many people do not connect to divination in such an engrossing way. If you have experimented with numerous approaches and found that none of them have come to life for you, you might go to a skilled practitioner and ask the Sources whether divination is indeed your calling. Not everyone is drawn to learning a musical instrument or an athletic sport or a foreign language. We must trust our soul's noncallings as well as its callings. Destiny seems to have very specific ideas about what each of us should be doing on the planet, and our greatest personal fulfillment always lies in those directions and none other.

3. *Honor the materials and symbols of divination, but never get tethered to them.* It is important to create a personal link with the instruments of divination, for they serve as the physical "body" of oracular guidance. Before using stones, cards, coins, books, or any other divinatory materials, I lay my hand upon them and say, "I acknowledge you as an oracle. Thank you for your help." This simple act seems to change the psychic field around my materials, and I look upon them with greater sense of awe after affirming their power.

Few individuals need to hear the cautionary statement I will make next, for modern diviners (unlike ancient diviners) rarely become obsessed with their materials. But for those who may need reminding: Your materials play an important but not an all-important role in the art of divination. Just as the beauty of a fine painting does not live in its pigments alone, the light of divination does not reside wholly in its materials. You do not have to locate a fifteenth-century tarot deck or wrap engraved symbols in three layers of black silk in order for divination to work. What your materials lack, spirit will supply. I have used old beat-up decks with cards missing, and the reading worked just as well. It is fitting to treat divination instruments with ritual honor, but our real homage belongs to the ineffable joining of the seen and the unseen.

All divination methods utilize a preestablished scheme of meanings. The scheme may be quite simple, as when we toss a coin and say, "Heads mean yes, tails mean no." Or it may have immense subtlety and complexity, like the sixty-four *I Ching* hexagrams and their many permutations. Any method of divination works best if you memorize its symbols and integrate them deep into psychic awareness. Then their meanings become part of your mind's own pattern of operation. Intuitive connections spark easily from image to image, from the divination sign to its fuller implications. This is why a skilled astrologer can look at one conjunction and see an entire situation or story unfold. Signs are meant to be springboards into fuller oracular knowing.

One of the best exercises I know for developing this "springboard" ability utilizes a common dictionary: Lay the dictionary on your lap, open it at random, and let your finger impulsively land on a word. Say the word and read its definition out loud. Then keep on speaking, saying anything that comes to mind that's been triggered by the word.

For instance, I tried this technique while writing this passage, and when I opened the dictionary (after fumbling for a moment when one of the pages stuck), my finger landed on the word "portionless." I read the definition, "having no portion, especially having no dowry or inheritance," and let my thoughts branch out as I continued to speak, saying "No inheritance, cut off, left out, family doesn't care, abandoned, sad, angry, I'll show them, will make it on my own." At this point I stopped, but clearly my associations were heading into a story of some kind. With a bit of practice, nearly any word you nudge will start rolling in an interesting direction. Sometimes you may get stuck on a word (especially if it is something like "gamma-aminobutyric acid")! In that case, skip the word and open the book again.

With this exercise, you are not asking a question or trying to gain divinatory information. You are merely strengthening your ability to make associations and think in metaphors. Try to leave your mind blank while choosing a word. And allow yourself to explore connections and images that range outside of your personal life. Practicing this exercise gives life to the mythopoetic dimension of words and images.

You may later add an oracular dimension to the exercise. First quiet your mind and take the dictionary in your hands. Place one hand upon its cover and say, "I acknowledge you as an oracle." This will foster a bond with the source of information. Say a brief invocation asking for presence, protection, and helpful results. Now formulate a question that has genuine meaning for you. Open the book, light upon a word, and read it aloud. Use the same technique of letting thoughts branch in all directions. If possible, tape-record the words you say or have a friend write them down. During the process you may suddenly get a strong hit about what the word means for you. If this happens, shift your attention to the insight and explore its significance. You may ask for clarification and open the book to another word. But an old rule of divination says that you shouldn't ask the same question twice in a row. Keep good notes on your results, for often the meaning of a word becomes even clearer with the passage of time. End the session by thanking the oracle for its assistance.

4. *Always maintain a structured ritual setting for divination.* Ritual has been defined as "a system of actions and beliefs that has a beginning, a middle, and an end and is directly related to sacred intention."[9] The practitioner begins by marking out a special place and time to contain the work. As we have seen, ancient diviners were skilled at creating "sacred space." They traced a ritual circle on the ground, entered a temple, offered a sacrifice, uttered a mantra or prayer, or merely sat quietly for a few moments. Rituals such as these serve to separate the

practitioner from the rhythms of ordinary life and to help create a field of consciousness suitable for the work ahead. Many diviners in native cultures put on masks or costumes to aid their transition from the ordinary to the nonordinary world.

Selecting a quiet setting with minimal disturbances is the first step in creating a ritual space for divination. Objects of beauty and meaning should be placed nearby, for they contribute their own power and influence to the psychic field. During divination proceedings, clear demarcations should be made between one question and another. For example, after each question, materials are gathered up, a breath is taken, and the next question is asked with full focus. The Sources are thanked after guidance is received on an issue. Take care that divination sessions don't run on too long, or else spiritual energy may fragment, opening the door for undesirable influences to enter. I have found that ninety minutes seems to be the upper limit for any session, no matter how inspired everyone feels.

Closing a divination ritual properly is very important. When time is drawing to a close, you should say, "This will be the final question for now." Stating the intention aloud enables everyone present (perhaps even the Invisibles) to begin pulling back their consciousness from the oracular field they share. Once the final question has been asked, don't yield to the temptation of asking another. To do so extends the session beyond your intention and loosens the ritual framework. Remember that the Mighty Counselors are always willing to return when asked. We need not grasp desperately at their presence in any given session.

The divination ritual is completed with a prayer or invocation of thanks. I have modeled my own closing utterance after that of Nepalese shamans whose work I have observed. They thank each deity, spirit, and entity by name. These acknowledgments preserve the bond between practitioners and their sources of spiritual help. Because shamans interact with so many different entities, their closing prayer of thanks sometimes lasts for thirty minutes! I have opted for a shorter version, speaking only those names that carry special meaning for me. If a special Presence has joined the work during a divination and indicated its name, I acknowledge its participation.

My closing prayer might sound like this:

> We thank You who have joined us today and assisted this work. I thank my own guides and guardians, as well as those of [name each person present in the room]. We are grateful to you, [name any entity who identified itself during the session], for communicating with us today. We deeply honor those angels, earth devas, ancestors, and sacred denizens of the Otherworlds who share our lives. In the days and weeks to come, we ask that the guidance we received today continue to unfold its wisdom and to the highest good for all. Blessed be.

A feeling of such warmth permeates the room at the close of a properly crafted ritual that participants often feel the flow for days afterward. The experiences they share will help generate a special field of consciousness in which oracular guidance will flourish. Then they will appreciate, as we shall see in the next chapter, what a valuable place oracles may have in everyday life.

Ancient Germans Consult a Tree Oracle

AMONG THE EARLY GERMANIC TRIBES, NO IMPORTANT
decision was made without submitting the matter to
divination. One method utilized wood from an oak,
hazel, or beech. These nut-bearing trees were revered
as highly magical and sacred. After offering prayers
and propitiations, the diviners cut a branch from the
chosen tree. The wood was sliced into thin strips, and
each strip was marked with a different sign. When
completed, the tokens were gathered up and tossed at
random upon a white cloth spread across the ground.
Someone in a leadership position served as the lot
selector. With eyes cast upward toward the heavens,
the agent reached down and selected three slips of
wood, one at a time. Their symbols were read aloud,
and from their meanings, an answer to the inquiry was
obtained. If the divination forbade the carrying out of
an enterprise, the plan was dropped without further
discussion. But if the inquirers were told to proceed,
they sought confirmation of the reading through further divination.

This divination method is described by Tacitus
in the early second century c.e., and scholars say it is
consistent with descriptions from other sources.[10]
Nut-bearing trees were widely worshiped for thousands
of years all over northern Europe. The signs drawn on
wooden slips were probably similar to the runic symbols used by Germanic and Scandinavian peoples
long into Christian times. Not only were these runes
symbols *of* something, but they were regarded as living
forces *in themselves* that participated in human affairs
and shaped our destinies.

Chapter 8

Making a Place for Oracles in Everyday Life

A s I pour over ancient accounts and native legends, a
change sometimes steals over my awareness. Objects
take on more three-dimensional clarity than usual. Pictures on
the wall gaze out at me as though they know I am there. Life
shines forth from each leaf with such verve and beauty that I
could kneel before them the whole day long. The air is heavy
with promise, and I would not be surprised if a spirit took shape
before my eyes. Because I am not used to experiencing the
world so keenly, this state of mind is a little hard to bear. Then
a veil falls and I see things in their old accustomed way again.

The consciousness I touch at these moments was very well
known to premodern peoples. They *lived* in it most of the time.
Why else would the Ashanti of West Africa sing a funeral song
for each tree after cutting it down? For what other reason would
the Irish of former days bow three times to the new crescent
moon and say, "Lady moon, I hail thee"?[1] People worship only
that which seems holy to them. In a sacred world, every tree is
alive and each new moon winks with divine intention.

Oracles come to us abundantly when we notice how much soul everything has. But since modern culture constantly steers us away from an ensouled way of experiencing, we must correct our direction and turn back to our origins. The task is easier than it may seem. At the edge of awareness we already know how it feels to be addressed by the visible and invisibles who share existence with us. Knowledge pooled from the vast collective experience of humanity is lodged in our deep memory, just waiting to be called into service.

Childhood recollections may lead us back to oracular knowing. As youngsters, we saw, heard, and felt through senses enchanted by *anima mundi*. The sense of relationship we felt with existence has been expressed with tenderness by the archetypal psychologist Mary Watkins:

> What happened to those imaginary playmates of ours who ate more from the family dinner table than we did? And those secret places that we found down the alleys and in the woods where we were not supposed to go? Remember the long hours spent talking to the trees and to our dolls? Of gazing in the mirror at ourselves, wondering what we would grow up to be, trying on the costumes of our fancies?[2]

Watkins goes on to say that when we get older, we are pushed into separating the imaginary from the real, the mythical from the scientific, and metaphor from matter. Eventually we lose touch with the wild, creative universe we used to know. But imaginal realities never die. They continue to find expression through our dreams, fantasies, irrational passions, creative urges, and even our psychological symptoms. And where the imaginal lives, oracles flourish.

This chapter contains numerous exercises for strengthening oracular ways of knowing. Each procedure is easy to carry out

From earliest times, the moon has been revered as a living force that interacts with us in a direct, personal way. People such as these women dancing in ecstacy under the moon's spell were called "loonies" by those who sought to suppress ancient folkways. (17th-century drawing)

and can be completed in less than fifteen minutes. I recommend selecting one or two a day and practicing them when you are in a relaxed mood. Like homeopathic remedies, small amounts will often have a better effect than large doses. Oracles need only the slightest encouragement to come back into our lives.

Exercise:
Greeting the Living World

Upon awakening, greet everything you see or hear for a period of one full minute. Say aloud or to yourself, "I greet you, picture on the wall. I greet you, dresser. Hello, sun coming through my window. Hello, bird I hear in the distance. I greet you, cars in the street." Allow objects and sounds to come into your awareness in their own way, in any order. Each morning you will greet some things and ignore others. Do this exercise for seven days. If you forget a day, pick up the practice again the next morning. After seven days, switch to saying goodnight for one minute to things you see or hear before going to bed. Then do the morning practice again for a week. Before long, you will find yourself mentally greeting things you encounter in the course of a day. This is a sign that you are entering an *anima mundi* state of mind.

Purpose of the Greeting Exercise

Native peoples have always forged a personal bond with everything around them. Objects and creatures are not merely things but conscious beings in their own right. We see this attitude reflected in nearly every Native American legend. For example, in a Sioux tale, Bear goes traveling with a group of his companions. They camp for the night under a tree. But before going to sleep, Bear calls out the following words:

"Good night, Mountains. You must protect us tonight. We are strangers but we are good people. We don't mean harm to anybody. Good night, Pine Tree. We are camping under you. You must protect us tonight. Good night, Owl. I guess this is your home were we are camped. . . . Good night, Grass People. We have spread our bed right on top of you. Good night, Ground. We are lying right on your face. You must take care of us. We want to live a long time."[3]

How different the world would seem if we experienced the mountain as being alive and the ground as having a face. Like the traditional Sioux, we would be careful how we treated them. It would become obvious that we needed Nature's protection in order to survive. Then the environment around us would become a place of dialogue and connection. Though many of the old ways have slipped from memory, we can strengthen our natural bond with creation simply by remembering to say, "Hello."

Exercise:
Letting Clouds Uncloud Your Vision

This exercise builds upon a pastime we all enjoyed in childhood: gazing up into the clouds and seeing pictures. Select a day when clouds are abundant overhead. Lie on the ground or recline in a chair so that you can gaze comfortably at the sky without straining your neck. Address the clouds as you would address a living being. Speak naturally in your own style of expression. I say something like, "Beautiful cloud-beings, I love the way you move above me, gathering and dissolving in the most mysterious ways. I ask you to become an oracle for me now." Adopt an attitude of quiet watching. Don't strain to see something. Dissolve your focus and soften your eyes, just drifting with the clouds.

Soon a particular area of the sky may attract your attention. Often this area lies at the edges of your vision, not directly in the place where you were looking. Allow your eyes to rest upon the area of interest. Staying somewhat unfocused, watch and see what the clouds will do. Faces, animals, objects, or scenes may take shape. Let these images do what they wish to do. Don't try to control them. Your consciousness will begin to become as soft and swirling as the clouds themselves as it reveals new images. Relax into this state of being for a while. If concrete thoughts about daily life interfere with your thinking, gently let them go and return your attention to the clouds. Each session you devote to this practice should last a little longer, heading for twenty minutes. At the end of the exercise, you might say something like "Thank you for being with me today, cloud-beings. Let my eyes continue to see your magical forms in all of life."

Purpose of the Cloud Exercise

Our eyes are over stimulated by the modern world. Too many objects of too many different colors speed by too quickly. Television shoots images at our brain faster than a machine gun. Oracular vision is always going on inside us, but it gets crowded out of consciousness by aggressive competitors from the external field. Gazing at clouds slows down our visual processing. It provides gentle stimulation to the eyes while giving the inner senses ample space to move.

Opening up space for the quieter senses helps us enter a state of being that has been called the "contemplative moment" by Jungian analyst Charles Asher. Contemplation is "the attentive pause at the heart of human life, a gazing upon what is immediately given," Asher says. "It is the breath taken away by beauty, the moment after love making, the little death."[4] In contemplation we witness the self's unfolding with little attention to what has been or might be. This focus constellates a place where we, from moment to moment, find our rest and watch the world create itself anew.

Gazing at clouds also affirms the imaginal dimension of psychic life. I always feel awed when I see faces and figures forming in the billows overhead. I wonder how they can take on such unique character. Rarely will two people see exactly the same formation, even when comparing the same area carefully. But our companions witness their own vivid pictures. Are the images only in our minds, we wonder? No, for clearly they are fashioned of cloud matter; we would not see them against a clear blue sky. But are the images really "in" the clouds? No, for the organizing power of our own perceptions transforms vapor into meaningful patterns. It becomes evident to us the cloud pictures occupy a position somewhere between "out there" and "in here." They arise when imaginal presence intersects with physical matter.

Understanding that matter and spirit constantly meld into each other is a key to receiving oracles. Like the clouds, oracular messages come from that realm between the material and the nonmaterial, between the known and the unknown. Philosopher Henry Corbin has called this order of reality *mundus imaginalis*, world of the imaginal.[5] This word is perceived not with the ordinary senses alone but with a faculty he calls imaginal consciousness. Corbin reminds us that this realm is not *imaginary* in the sense of being unreal. Archetypal images, emblems, and dramas come into our lives as primary and irreducible facts. We can gain practice in hosting these visitors by letting clouds reveal the contours of our greater soul.

Exercise:
Touching the Soul of an Animal Being

For this practice you will need to be in a setting where you can gaze at an animal for ten minutes without being interrupted. For example, you can arrange to be alone with a companion animal at home, or you can go to a zoo, horse stable, or pet store. This exercise works better if you select a mammal to focus upon because of the human body's kinship with other mammals. However, selecting a fish, bird, or reptile as your partner also can be rewarding.

Your goal for this practice is to experience the animal as a fully conscious, aware, ensouled being. You will invite your own body to feel its kinship with the animal's body, thereby creating a direct link between the two of you.

If possible, determine the animal's gender so that you can address it as he or she. (In this example, we will suppose that the animal is female.) Now look into her eyes and notice how alive and liquid they are. Become aware of her nose and the moist breath moving in and out. Imagine how warm her body would feel if you touched her. Imagine your hand stroking her head, running down her neck and back, rubbing the underside of her belly. See whether you can savor her scent.

Tell the animal (mentally or out loud) how beautiful you find her to be. Describe her to herself, using whatever words come to you. The idea is to witness the animal with all of your senses and communicate your experience to its soul.

When you think you have conveyed your appreciation fully, shift your perspective and try to imagine how it would feel to be inside this creature. What if you moved your head and shoulders as she moves hers? How would you feel walking on four legs rather than your own? If you looked out through the creature's eyes, how might you see the world? Imagine what it would be like to watch a human being staring at you! This part of the exercise is the most difficult, for we cannot truly depart from our own viewpoint and enter another. But if you experience flashes of "otherness," you have succeeded.

Now shift your perspective one more time. Become yourself again and look at the creature before you. Imagine that a human soul is living behind those eyes. Perhaps (as in the myths of old) a beautiful prince or princess had decided to inhabit that body for a period of time in order to accomplish a certain goal. Now you are gazing not into the eyes of an animal but into the eyes of someone similar to yourself. Try to experience the being you see as completely conscious and present. When this idea takes hold, you may feel a slight shiver go through you. The space between you and the animal may seem unusually charged or "thick." It may be hard to keep looking at your companion. Then you will know that you have made contact with something important. Even if you don't feel a strong reaction, your experience of the animal will have deepened.

It's time to close the meditation. Say to the animal who has been your host, "I honor you and I thank you." Take in three long, steady breaths and let the last one out rapidly with a bit of extra force. This procedure will help pull you out of the psychic field you have generated. If you still feel entranced or drawn strongly to the animal, take another three breaths, then pause until you feel clearheaded.

Purpose of the Animal Meditation

Animals help us reawaken to an ensouled world. Their bodies bear so much biological resemblance to our own that a natural arc of connection leaps between us when we draw near. This arc penetrates into deep instinctual recesses of the psyche. Ways of experiencing that belonged to our archaic ancestors may suddenly come into memory. Because these sensations seem foreign to our customary feelings, we tend to break our connection with them. By staying focused on an animal's essential being for a sustained period of time, we will give new experiences a chance to emerge.

Our kinship with nonhuman entities may also be strengthened through service in the world. As a result of your growing rapport with animals, you may feel strongly moved to do something on their behalf. This action might take the form of volunteering in animal shelters or sending contributions to wildlife defense groups, humane societies, and environmental protection causes. You may consider writing letters to elected officials supporting proanimal legislation. These actions will not feel like a burden; in fact, they will rest upon you lightly because you are being carried by something bigger than yourself. Each one of us discovers our own way of demonstrating love for the natural world. Even the smallest of these expressions nourishes oracular awareness and helps to restore ancient bonds with the matrix of life.

Exercise:
Seeing, Hearing, and Feeling the Source of Oracles

The following practices stimulate creative powers and help us see the world as a place where different realities merge in and out of one another. Select one of these procedures each day and practice it in a short session lasting from three to fifteen minutes. Since the exercises may be somewhat disorienting, I do not recommend sustaining them for long periods unless you are accustomed to meditating regularly.

Seeing: Sit or stand in a quiet place and gaze out upon the scene before you. Imagine that everything you see sprang into being only moments ago. Imagine that the air around you is not merely air but a luminous fluid that can coalesce itself into all kinds of shapes and objects. See the walls, buildings, shrubs, and people around you as having been made from this fluid. They are not solid; at any moment they could melt back into the original medium and disappear. Picture how it would look if part of the scene before you suddenly melted away.

Look at an empty place in the air. Imagine that it begins to thicken, take on color, and shape itself into an object that was not there before. Your eyes probably will not see these things actually happen. But you can work with them in your mind's eye and attempt to overlay your inner images on the outer ones. If at any point you feel a mild sense of wooziness or confusion, as though everything suddenly seems unreal, this is a signal that you have achieved an important perceptual shift. Stay relaxed and speak to the medium that looks like air. Say something like, "I want to see more of who you really are. In the days and weeks ahead, show me what my eyes should see." You may feel a warm pulse of affirmation within you, as though something has assured you of a good outcome. End the exercise by closing your eyes and breathing steadily three times.

Hearing: Sit or lie down in a place where you will be alone and no phones will ring. An outdoor setting is preferred, but stationing yourself indoors next to an open window is a good alternative. If possible, choose a place where the sounds of nature will not be drowned out by traffic or harsh noises. It is best to place an eye mask or bandana over your eyes to block out your visual field. Listen to the sounds around you. Allow anything and everything to make itself known to you. Don't pull away from any sound you hear, even if it seems grating or unpleasant. When your attention wanders to the concerns of the day, simply bring it back to the sounds around you. If you hear something beautiful, like a bird singing, gently let that go and become diffuse again so that everything has an equal place in awareness.

Soon you will notice how interesting and complex your auditory field has become. Float along in it as you would drift in warm seawater. Sounds may begin to transmute into feelings and sensations. The stirring of treetops may reach you as a throaty whisper, or the gunning of a motorcycle engine may hit you like a body blow. This transformation signals that a shift in perspective has occurred. Observe the experiences that arise for a few more minutes. Rather than dwelling on any one experience, continually return your attention to the overall pattern of sound. Now address the auditory field directly. Say something like, "I want to listen to you more fully. In the days and weeks ahead, tell my ears what I should hear." Breathe deeply a few times, focusing on the sound of your breath. End the meditation by opening your eyes.

Feeling: Since most of us lack practice in attending to the body as a channel, this exercise requires a little longer than the others, about fifteen minutes. The procedure will gain power if you do it while receiving a massage. Body-knowing is brought to life at the touch of a human hand. But since massage is usually a luxury to be enjoyed only at certain times, it's fine to do the procedure alone.

Find a place where your body will feel perfectly safe even when you cannot see or hear your surroundings. Use a pair of ear plugs to block sound and use an eye mask or bandana to block all light. Now relax your body. Surrender it comfortably to the place you have chosen. Turn your attention to the soft pressure of support against your buttocks, back, legs, and other areas. Notice the gentle weight of your clothes against your skin. If any breezes or temperature changes from the outside brush against you, attend to them also. Certain areas of your body will suddenly become present to you and then may fade again. For example, your abdomen may call attention to its deep, interior mystery. Or you may feel a slight ache behind your eyes. Whatever arises, allow it to be there but do not fix your interest in any one place. Stay loose and free-ranging. Emotions and memories may rise up along with physical sensations. Promise to explore them later, but do not get sidetracked at this point.

As you continue in this state of consciousness, your body may seem to take on a life of its own. Its field of experience may awaken into a rich pulsing of feelings and sensations. Then you will know that your consciousness has shifted into closer align-ment with the body-self. Address your body directly and say, "I want to receive your communications more keenly. In the days and weeks ahead, let me feel what I should know. Stretch your body from head to toe and take in three deep breaths. Remove your ear plugs and mask. Make sure that you are fully oriented to the outside world before returning to your activities.

Purpose of the Seeing, Hearing, and Feeling Practices

In the first meditation we gain practice in seeing the world as a medium that can generate and dissolve forms. Rigid boundaries begin to melt. If we can begin to experience all of creation as a fluid, living intelligence, oracles will spring into awareness everywhere. You will know that your visual field has loosened up when you suddenly see ordinary objects as new and fresh. Glancing at the keys of your old piano, you may suddenly feel struck by their lean black and whiteness, by the smooth perfection of their surface, by the way they pose cunningly in threes and twos as though ready to dance. If you find yourself seeing this way, oracles will soon follow.

The hearing meditation endeavors to open a larger space for sounds to live. In daily life, most of our energy is directed toward screening out sounds, not taking them in. Have you ever tape-recorded or videotaped a conversation with someone in a restaurant? At the time, you only hear yourselves speaking. But when you listen to the tape later, you will be shocked by the terrible clatter of dishes and the roar of voices nearly drowning you out. Goal-directed tasks (such as focusing on a conversation) require a narrowing of the auditory field. But oracular work requires an opening of the field.

The "sensing" meditation brings awareness to an area often ignored: the body and its ways of knowing. Oracular messages frequently enter through senses other than sight and hearing. They register in and through the cells themselves. Physically felt oracles may be one of the oldest forms of guidance known to humankind. Jungian analyst Robert Bosnak was told by Australian aborigines (the Pitjantjatjara) that they often received clairvoyant messages through various parts of their bodies.[6] One woman said that when she felt strange sensations in her hip, she knew that something important was going on with her husband. A twitching feeling in the nose signaled that a stranger would soon arrive at her house. The area of her upper arm communicated information about her sister or aunt. These sensations provided very accurate information. As we become more intimately acquainted with the subtle presses and workings of our own bodies, a new field of oracular perception will open wide.

Exercise:
Looking for Enchantment in All the Right Places

The wanderer in you is always ready to take off for parts unknown, pulled forward by a promise of enchantment at the next turn. In this exercise, you will let your oracular knowing serve as trail master and lead you to an enchanted place. Select a day when you do not feel rushed. Go to an area where you will be safe, and let your body steer you in any direction that feels right. You may wish to stroll down a city street or wander in a park. Even your own backyard may hold enchantment at times. Stroll around (or ride in a conveyance, if walking is a problem) in a relaxed way, taking in the terrain around you but not focusing on anything in particular. Stay aware of what is going on in your body. Do tensions press anywhere? Do you feel light? Weighted down? Attend to the signals you receive, especially if your body wants to stop, turn, or backtrack. Follow its lead.

At one point you may see or hear something that draws your attention. Go to the area and dwell there for a few moments. Does the place hold enchantment for you? If so, you will be drawn in by its special qualities. Wonder or awe may steal over you, and the rest of the world will face away temporarily. Your intuition will register a sense of rightness, of "this is it." You probably will lose your desire to wander further that day. A message or illumination about something important may come to you, but do not expect to receive a specific oracle. The experience may be one of wordless rapport between you and the *genius loci*, the soul of the place. Stay in its presence for a while without trying to interpret or understand.

Your place of enchantment might look quite ordinary to the outer eye. It may not be a thatched earthen hut nestled near the brook beneath emerald trees. (Where did that hut go, anyway? We keep searching for it!) Your destination may prove to be a white cement wall dancing with shadows or a slobbering gargoyle peering from the old bank building. But the place will carry a certain charge for you that will be easy to identify once you have experienced it a few times. When you feel the time has come to leave, acknowledge your enchanted spot by leaving a small offering or by respectfully saying good-bye. If possible, keep notes about your impressions because they may later shed light on other intuitive experiences you have.

Purpose of the Enchanted Place Exercise

This exercise provides practice in recognizing places of power for you. By noticing the way your body, mind, and emotions feel in different physical locations, you will learn to utilize a deep instinctual way of knowing. Our relationship with "place" is older than our relationship with tools or words, from an evolutionary standpoint. Many traditional cultures still preserve knowledge of how to commune with the *genius loci.* Shamans in many parts of the world often scout out an area with their interior vision to determine what invisible forces dwell there. Sometimes they peer through an empowered human bone to clarify their perception. They advise people not to build houses or perform ceremonies in negative spots. But place-spirits often can be negotiated with to make an environment favorable for human endeavors.

Being able to "feel places" will open a wide arena for oracular messages to enter. It may even save your life someday. A remarkable demonstration of this fact was experienced by Peter Skafte during a canoe trip on the Delaware River. Peter and several companions had been paddling all morning and were ready to stop for lunch. As luck would have it, in the middle of the river they spotted a small beautiful island perfect for camping.

An enormous tree rose from the sandy beach, providing cover over a nice flat beach. The group pulled their canoes up on the shore and walked around to get a better look.

The tree was a stately old thing, almost completely hollow in the center. Its heavy branches spread in all directions. Right under the tree were plenty of places for sitting comfortably. But nobody in the party sat down. They paced back and forth, around and around. Peter felt that something wasn't right. An uneasiness seemed to creep up from the ground itself. It registered strongly in his stomach and made him feel very peculiar. Even though the afternoon was hot, a chill penetrated his body—or perhaps his soul. It almost seemed as if the place didn't want them there. He couldn't imagine building a fire or spending the afternoon under that tree. Without saying a word, Peter walked back to the canoe and sat down. The others followed in silence and pushed off into the water.

The party had not paddled more than twenty-five yards when they heard a thundering boom. It sounded as though dynamite had blasted off directly behind them. They whirled around and saw the old tree crashing in on itself, branches exploding everywhere. Tons of weight smashed down upon the sandy campsite. The fallen tree littered the ground with mounds of debris higher than a building. If Peter and his friends had lingered there for two minutes longer, most of them might have been crushed to death. How did they know that the place was not right"? Eye and mind could detect no danger, but the body called upon its ancient ability to feel the psyche of a place and act with wordless wisdom.

Exercise:
Letting Your Head Be Turned by Beauty

Go to the produce section of a grocery store and look at the fruits and vegetables. Try to forget about how they taste or are used in cooking. See them as beautiful works of art on display. Appreciate the inventiveness of their shapes and the subtlety of their hues. Few artists could ever have thought up so many shades of flecked gold and pale green and blood purple. Unfocus your eyes a little and let them drift across the display. You may find that one particular section attracts your attention. Go to that section and let your hand be drawn to a particular fruit or vegetable. It may not be the most "attractive" item at first glance, but trust the prompting that brought you there. Pick up the work of art and buy it.

Once at home, spend ten minutes or so pouring your attention into the item you selected. Study it up close and from a distance. Hold it up to the light, pass it across your cheek, feel it with your lips. With reverence, cut open the fruit or vegetable and gaze at the mysteries of its interior chamber. If it is edible in present form, take a piece of it into your mouth as you would a ritual offering. When you think you have fully appreciated the beauty of this creation, thank it for being with you. Words might come to you, such as, "Extraordinary plant-being, I never knew your full beauty until this moment. Thank you for existing, and for giving yourself to me this day."

Purpose of the Beauty Exercise

From the earliest times, oracles have been associated with beauty and the arts. Aesthetic pleasure is intimately linked with oracular perception. Guidance often comes through aesthetic channels. You may have had the experience of wandering in a bookstore and suddenly becoming attracted to a particular volume. The cover (or even just the spine) looks so beautiful to your eyes that you must reach out to it. Impulsively, you buy the book. Soon you find that there is something very important for you in that work. Perhaps you learn crucial information to help you make a decision. Or the writing offers a clarifying perspective on a problem of yours. Later, you look at the book's cover and it may not seem beautiful at all. In fact, its teal and pink colors might seem downright ugly. Did your taste change in the space of a few short weeks? No, the "signal light" went out of the object as soon as you received its intended message.

Oracular forces cast a halo around things and people we are supposed to notice. I have learned from many trials to pay attention when I see this special brightness surround an object. One day I dashed out my back door and saw an old flashlight sitting on an outdoor shelf. Though I had passed by that shelf a hundred times, I never noticed the flashlight before. But now it stood out in my visual field with unusual clarity. Knowing that I was seeing an oracular halo, I grabbed the light and tossed it into my car. My mind thought the whole thing was a little foolish, for I already had a flashlight with me. That evening I worked past dark at the school. As I drove up the winding canyon road leading to my house, my engine sputtered and stopped running. I knew I would have to walk a half mile along a totally dark road before I could get home and call a tow truck. I clicked on the flashlight I usually carry in the car and found that it was dead. But the old rusty one I had snatched from the shelf guided me all the way back.

Not every oracular showing leads to a dramatic outcome. Often our attention is called to small details, and sometimes we never learn the reason why we were led in a particular direction. But I have found that the most serious errors result from ignoring the oracular shining, not from following its prompting

We may ask why aesthetic qualities should tell us so much about the deeper nature of reality. Archetypal psychologist James Hillman suggests that beauty is not an abstract quality above and beyond the things of the world. Instead, it "refers to the luster of each particular event—its clarity, its particular brightness."[7] Beauty is the very sensibility of the cosmos, the manifest *anima mundi*, with all its textures, tones, tastes, and attractiveness. Hillman points out that beauty has been called a *Deus Revelatus*, a God-Revelation. Divine Presence reveals itself through embodiment of the beautiful. From this perspective, it is not hard to see why the oracular light should suddenly come to our service and light the way. When we see, hear, or feel the aesthetic qualities of the world, we draw closer to the faces of God.

Working with Divination: Quick and Cosmic Practices

As we recall from chapter 7, divination was once a sacred art designed to open a line of communication with Supernal Forces.

Thousands of methods have been used to obtain answers to questions, make decisions, see into the future, and understand the deeper meaning of issues. Extensive lists have been drawn up of the various "mancies" (divination procedures) known to us. Aeromancy (reading atmospheric conditions), alectoromancy (watching the movement of roosters), aleuromancy (placing slips of paper into cakes such as fortune cookies), arithmancy (using numbers), austromancy (divining by the study of winds), and axinomancy (cracking agate stones on a hot surface) are only a few of the practices classified under the letter A!

We find encouragement for our own work by realizing how many forms of divination have been practiced worldwide. Everything under the sun (and moon) has been used as an oracular channel. Each of us can select our instruments with freedom, trusting that the world will speak through our chosen methods. No material is too inglorious to be used in service of the divine arts.

We honor the sacred underpinnings of divination by bringing sincerity and mindfulness to our practice. But the spirit of play also has a place in all sacred endeavors. Ramakrishna, the god-intoxicated mystic who lived in nineteenth-century India,

Singing Funeral Songs for a Tree

THE TRADITIONAL ASHANTI PEOPLE OF WEST AFRICA regard trees as ensouled beings worthy of respect and consideration.[9] In their view, taking the life of these beings is a very grave affair. When the Ashanti need to cut down a tree to obtain material for their work, they often break an egg upon the trunk as an offering and ask for its forgiveness. "I am coming to lay my axe upon you and carve you up," the executioner says. "Receive this egg. Eat this egg and forgive me." He beseeches the departing soul not to harm him in the same way he is harming it. After the tree is cut down, a funeral rite is held for the fallen body. *"Damirifa! Damirifa! Damirifa!"*—Alas, alas, alas! the people cry in plaintive voices. This heart-wrenching lament is also sung at the funeral of human beings.

But fallen trees have a chance to live again in the creations made from their bodies. After wood carvers finish making their drums, stools, masks, and other objects, they perform a rite of consecration to invite the departed tree-soul to come back into the wood. "Don't wander forever," they call to it. "Come into your new home. We will honor you here." Thus, each drum or carved artifact becomes a living shrine for the tree-spirit who inhabited it. Clearly, the Ashanti and other native peoples do not experience the objects they create as mere things but as the embodiments of spiritual presence.

used to say that the universe was a "mansion of mirth" and that human beings were meant to join the playful sporting of the gods.[9] We should feel at liberty to experiment with different kinds of divination and to create our own procedures during inspired moments.

None of the following divining exercises depends on boards, cards, or other manufactured instruments. I enjoy working with commercial oracle systems found in stores, but I also take pleasure in using simple methods based on ancient folkways. You might try these procedures and use them as models for your own creative exploration.

Divination:
Trusting a Stone to Speak

Using stones to read the will of destiny is among the oldest divination practices known. We may continue the tradition by submitting our questions and concerns to the lot method of revelation. Lots are objects drawn at random from a group of similar objects. In the simplest procedures, inquirers reach into a container and draw a stone (or slip of wood) that carries a designated meaning.

Creating your own lot divination can be immensely satisfying. Browse around your immediate area and locate natural materials such as rocks, pods, shells, or pieces of wood. Then decide upon the type of answers you wish to build into the system. For example, you may choose three different color stones, signaling "yes," "no," and "cannot answer now." Make sure that the coding cannot be detected by touch. That is, avoid using qualities like rough and smooth, or small and large, as a carrier of meaning because otherwise your hand will be tempted to select a favored answer.

Though the structure of this divination seems simple, it can yield profound results. Lots were trusted by adepts in all ancient cultures, and they are still used by native peoples worldwide. You will discover that nearly any issue can be explored by asking a series of yes or no questions. Binary (either-or) answers are restricting, but they force us to probe our thoughts about a matter carefully so that we can make the right queries. This process usually leads to important insights about our underlying motivations and desires.

If you wish to develop a more elaborate divination system, you may inscribe symbols, words, or images on your lots. A psychotherapist I know, Holly Adams-Matthews, created an oracular tool to use in her work with women's groups. Holly first went to the beach day after day looking for smooth, hand-sized stones. She had to draw upon her own oracular knowing to choose these materials, for they had to feel just "right." Sometimes she picked up a stone that looked good, but its attractiveness soon faded, or its weight seemed out of balance in her hand. Holly said that her intuitive abilities became increasingly keen as she practiced using them each day.

After Holly felt sure that a stone had called her, she sat with it for a long time and asked, "What qualities will you hold for us? What wants to be inscribed on you?" As images began to form in her mind's eye, she drew them on the surface with colored markers. For example, the figure of a woman emerged with a spiral turning at her throat and also in the palm of each hand. Holly knew at once that the woman was a healer. Other archetypal images, such as the queen self, the warrior, the nymph, the mother, and various goddess figures, came forth. Many of the designs bore resemblance to those uncovered by archaeologists in Neolithic sites from many thousands of years ago. Women who desire guidance on various life issues approach the stones and ask, "What do I need to assist me in this situation?" Each stone evokes a different archetypal resource that Holly helps the woman explore.

Finding your materials and putting inscriptions upon them can be a spiritual practice in itself. Remember that symbols and images have a life of their own independently of you, and yet they also absorb some of your psyche into their dynamic structure. Your oracular tool becomes a unique creation that is partly you and partly "other." After you work with the tool for a while, it begins to shift and change in unexpected ways. Certain symbols may fade in importance; they may even vanish mysteriously. Others grow in power, and their meaning expands each time you connect with them. The personal relationship you form with your divination system becomes a central part of the work. You will not be able to tell where you begin and it ends. This process is similar to alchemical transformation where, in the words of Jung, "the psychic and the physical become blended in an indissoluble unity."[10]

Divination:
Oracles Written on the Leaves

According to the legend, the sibyl of Cumae sometimes wrote each word of her oracle on a leaf and placed the precious inscriptions at the mouth of her cave. But sometimes the mischievous wind picked up the leaves and scattered them in all directions. Then people would have to use their own powers of understanding to piece them together and discover the message's intent.

You can borrow from this ancient image and create a wind-sibyl oracle of your own. I value the procedure because of its sweeping energy and spaciousness. Nothing is more exhilarating than throwing your inscriptions into the wind and letting the air swirl them into a wise answer. I have noticed that this divination method works especially well for important, complex questions involving many factors. For instance, if you must decide whether or not to move to another city, and the lives of other people will be affected by your choice, the wind-sibyl can offer insight on how the pieces can "fall" together in the best way.

Gather between twenty and thirty medium- or large-sized leaves from the ground. They should be rather dry but not crumbly. If no leaves are available, cut twenty to thirty leaf shapes from paper. Brown paper bags are ideal for this purpose. As you assemble your materials, ask them to help you in your oracular quest. You might address the tree as follows: "Great tree-soul, I thank you for giving me these parts of your body. Each leaf carries your power and presence. Please speak to me as an oracle today." If you cut shapes from paper, you could invoke a blessing, saying something like, "I cut these paper leaves in honor of great tree-souls everywhere. I ask you to infuse these images with your spirit. Please speak to me as an oracle today." Now take an indelible marking pen (thin tipped) and write a separate word on each leaf, one side only. The words should relate to the question on your mind. Concerns, fears, wishes, choices, and possible outcomes can be noted. Include some action words in your selection, like "give," "take," "accept," "tell," "stop," and so forth. Your expectation is that some of these words will fall together and form a message.

After the leaves are inscribed, hold them in your hands and say, "I acknowledge you as an oracle. I thank you for your help today." Go outside and find a place where you can throw the leaves into the air and have them land in a clear area. A patio, lawn, beach, or clearing in the woods is suitable. There should be a breeze stirring in the air, but not a strong wind blowing. Now address the wind. You might say, "Eternal wind, I don't know where you come from or where you go. But I ask you to help me now and speak through these leaves. I release the following matter into your care . . ." Now state your question, problem, or concern and toss the leaves into the air.

Once your oracle leaves have settled back to the ground, look at each one without disturbing it. Notice that some have landed with the inscription facing upward. Read all of these words and survey their positions to see whether they communicate added meaning in connection to one another. You do not have to study every single leaf; just try to get an overall idea of their meaning. Very often the first thing that comes into your mind as you survey the pattern is the correct oracular message. Sketch a diagram of the position of the words, for you may glean a more detailed understanding later. You may gather up the leaves and use them again if you wish. But the same question should not be asked twice. At the end of the procedure, don't forget to thank the wind and the leaves for the attention they have given you.

Divination:
For Your Ears Only—Seeking a Cledon

Some oracles come to us through chance words heard in a crowd. They may also be delivered through the lips of speakers who have no idea they are uttering words of counsel. The Greeks called these messages *cledons* (see chapter 1). After submitting a query to the deities, they would step outside into a public place and accept the first words they heard as the divine answer.

Many cledons come to us spontaneously, answering questions or providing guidance at just the right moment. But you may also seek this type of oracle intentionally. It is best to wait until a specific issue presses on your mind forcefully. You will feel the pressure build up within you. "I *must* have an answer to this question now!" you suddenly say to yourself. Or perhaps you find your attention narrowing in on the problem like a high-intensity beam. It concentrates your awareness, and you feel that the time is right, perfectly right, to gain illumination. Signals such as these tell you than an oracle is near. Address your source(s) of guidance: "I am ready to receive clear and helpful guidance on the issue of. . .[describe the issue in a few words]. Tell me what I should know in the next words I hear."

Now go directly into a place where you will hear people talking. A sidewalk, restaurant, office, or store will work well. If you are in a private home when the cledon mood comes over you, wait for the next voice you hear. In Greece and Rome, the utterances of children were highly prized as oracles. Should a delivery person or solicitor appear at your door, listen carefully to the first words that person speaks.

Some of the best cledons I have received have come from the television or radio. One night I was sitting in bed trying to read, but I kept losing my concentration. I realized then how worried I was about a friend who had just had a biopsy done on a lump in her breast. Would she be diagnosed with cancer? Or would the report give her a clean bill of health? It seemed unbearable to wait until the lab results were announced. I felt an urgent need to know the answer. And suddenly I felt that I *could* know, at that very moment. I quietly said, "Please give me an oracle about my friend's biopsy. I pray that she will be all right." Then I reached for the remote control of my television. Flipping it on, I tuned my ears to the first words I would hear. Newly washed shirts and pants marched across the screen as a voice shouted gaily, "Clean, clean, clean! That's the good news—all clean!" With happiness and relief, I closed my eyes and said out loud, "I accept the oracle! Thank you." The next evening, my friend called me with the "good news" that her lump was a harmless cyst. "So you're clean!" I exclaimed. Soon after, I told her about my splendid television oracle.

Cledons remind us that ordinary events contain different layers of reality within their structure. Even a detergent advertisement can deliver words of wisdom under the right conditions. An oracular perspective helps us probe below (or beyond) the surface of things and touch another kind of order rich in meaning. As we learn to feel our way into this other order, everyday events become less important and more important at the same time. They lose some of their power to control us because we see them as only one small portion of reality. Yet we honor them as tips of the iceberg whose invisible undersides are awesome in dimension. Paying attention to cledons and other spontaneous oracles will help us form a closer relationship with the matrix of life. But as always, we rely on common sense to keep our oracular work in balance. Not every voice in the crowd bears a message for us. Dozens of birds flutter in the trees above, but we can't assume that each movement is a personal sign. Just as a wise counselor remains silent for a while and then offers direction at the right moment, oracles speak when the psyche is ready to hear. They follow an enigmatic timetable of their own. To over-invest meaning in everyday events will drive us a little crazy, for the mind will get pulled in too many different directions. Oracular presence doesn't want us to jump at its command like a slave. It wants to join with us in a dance.

Listening to the Oracle

Our exploration of oracles has led us deep into the territory of dreams, divination, messages from nature, and other mysterious domains. We have surveyed oracular practices from many periods in history, trying to identify the secret kinship they share. While admitting that the source of oracles is forever unknowable to us, we have witnessed the way they provide beneficial guidance and restoration to the soul.

Oracles appear in a thousand forms and use any instruments available to communicate their messages. But oracular consciousness itself—the state of knowing through which we receive oracles—seems to operate in universal patterns across many cultures and centuries. The first pattern may be called "divine distraction." Oracles are most likely to appear when we enter into a drifting, musing, entranced mood. The mind needs to be slightly displaced from itself so that a different kind of awareness has room to operate. Divine distraction may be triggered through prayer, meditation, ritual, or body-centered practices. Repetitive action (such as driving) may lull us into a state of displacement. Emergencies or strong emotions also serve to whack us outside of ourselves temporarily and open a portal for the oracle's appearance.

Another universal feature of oracular knowing might be referred to as "poetic heat." Oracles communicate with us through images, symbols, comparisons, metaphors, and direct emotional impact. We must approach them in the same way we approach poetry or art. When the poet says, "Black, black, black is the color of my true love's hair," we know that something more than the color black is being celebrated. Our imagination takes flight from the words and leads us into experiences of our own. In the same way, when we throw the *I Ching* and receive the image of "biting through," we cannot understand the image unless we allow it to play upon our poetic sensibilities. It branches in all directions, generating both familiar and strange associations. Then suddenly, we hit upon the right meaning and know without question what the hexagram is saying to us.

Finally, oracular knowing always leads us into mystical connection. It unites the personal soul with mysterious realities beyond the self. When Maili the shaman (chapter 7) saw her patient's illness patterned in the grains of rice, she knew that a force greater than her own knowledge was lending its wisdom. When the architectural consultant Rosmarie Bogner (chapter 1) was driven off the land scheduled to be developed, she had no doubt that something beyond the ordinary was issuing warning. Oracular knowing erases our sense of isolation. Oracles speak to the heart, engage the senses, and dream up endless ways of making their presence known.

Many thoughts and feelings arise as I endeavor to summarize what I have learned from our wanderings. I remember how it all began, when a camellia blossom fell and startled my consciousness into a new world. Perhaps the finest gift I have received from that world is a sense of abiding companionship. They know us, these uncanny "others" who show themselves in dreams, signs, and wonders. They are the strangers who are not strange. We will never understand who they are or to what realm they belong. But each time they make an appearance, I discover once again that something more intimate than a lover shares this life field with me.

Oracles offer counsel for issues great and small. But their most important message is one of comfort. Be assured, they tell us, for you are not alone. Look how we greet you at every turn. Listen to how we call your name through a hundred voices, and call you by names that still lie sleeping in your future. The world is greater than you know. So be comforted, and let us talk awhile.

Notes

CHAPTER 1: RECEIVING AN ORACLE

1. Thomas Moore, *Care of the Soul: A Guide for Cultivating Sacredness in Everyday Life* (New York: HarperCollins, 1992).

2. The term "numinous" was coined by the German theologian Rudlof Otto in *The Idea of the Holy* (London: Oxford University Press, 1958).

3. My account of Appian's experience is developed from research by W. R. Hallidax, *Greek Divination: A Study of Its Methods and Principles* (Chicago: Argonaut, 1967).

4. George Rawlinson, trans., *The History of Herodotus* (New York: Tudor Publishing Company, 1928), 100.

5. These superstitions about a white-footed horse are from Iona Opie and Moira Tatem, *Dictionary of Superstitions* (Oxford: Oxford University Press, 1992).

6. H. W. Parke, *The Oracles of Zeus* (Berkeley: University of California Press, 1981).

7. Rosmarie Bogner, "House with Soul: A Reminder to Incorporate Psyche in Dwelling and Building" (master's thesis, Pacifica Graduate Institute, 1992).

8. I thank Rosmarie Bogner for a follow-up letter recounting these events.

9. Richard Tarnas, *The Passion of the Western Mind* (New York: Ballantine, 1991), 444.

10. Carl G. Jung, *Dreams*, trans. R. F. C. Hull (Princeton, N.J.: Princeton University Press, 1974), 96.

CHAPTER 2: LISTENING TO THE ORACLES OF EARTH

1. Martin Buber, *I and Thou* (New York: Scribners, 1958).

2. I thank Mrs. G. A. Read from Dorset, England, for relating the account of Annie Burt and the bees.

3. These stories about bee worship are from Hilda Ransome, *The Sacred Bee in Ancient Times and Folklore* (Boston and New York: Houghton Mifflin, 1937).

4. William L. Cassidy, "Crow Augery" http://users.deltanet.com/-ncassidy/astro/crow.html, 1984/1996).

5. The story of the Coeur d'Alene Indians is from Catherine Feher-Elston, *Ravensong: A Natural and Fabulous History of Ravens and Crows* (Flagstaff, Ariz.: Northland Publishers, 1991).

6. James Redfield, *The Celestine Prophecy: An Adventure* (New York: Warner Books, 1993).

7. J. Allen Boone, *Kinship with All Life* (San Francisco: HarperSanFrancisco, 1976).

8. Boone, *Kinship with All Life*, 79–80.

9. Marija Gimbutas, lecture at the Pacifica Graduate Institute, Santa Barbara, May 1993.

10. Maria Leach, ed., *Standard Dictionary of Folklore, Mythology, and Legend* (San Francisco: HarperSanFrancisco, 1949/1972), 351.

11. C. Nadia Serematakis, *The Last Word: Women, Death, and Divination in Inner Mani* (Chicago: University of Chicago Press, 1991).

12. Sogyal Rinpoche, *The Tibetan Book of Living and Dying*

(SanFrancisco: HarperSanFrancisco, 1994).

13. Thomas Berry, *The Dream of the Earth* (San Francisco: Sierra Club Books, 1988), 195.

CHAPTER 3: DELPHI'S ENDURING MESSAGE

1. The story of the founding of the oracle at Delphi is adapted from Diodorus Siculus, *World History* V, bk. 16, para. 26, in *Diodorus of Sicily*, trans. C. H. Oldfather (Cambridge, Mass.: Harvard University Press, 1956), 309.

2. Aeschylus, *The Eumenides*, trans. Philip Bellacott (Baltimore: Penguin Books, 1962), 47.

3. For valuable reflections on the importance of Apollo, Dionysus, and the center at Delphi, see David Fideler, "The Voice from the Center: The Oracle of Apollo and the Oracle of the Heart," *Gnosis* 5 (Fall 1987): 23–27.

4. Joseph Fontenrose, *The Delphic Oracle* (Berkeley: University of California Press, 1978). Fontenrose provides an analysis of all the known oracular statements from Delphi.

5. The attitudes of church fathers toward the oracle are discussed in Giulia Sissa, *Greek Virginity*, trans. A. Goldhammer (Cambridge, Mass.: Harvard University Press, 1990).

6. This translation of the last Delphic oracle is found in Peter Hoyle, *Delphi* (London: Cassell and Company, 1967), 142.

7. H. P. Blavatsky, *Isis Unveiled*, ed. Boris de Zirkoff, 2 vols. (Wheaton, Ill.: Theosophical Publishing House, 1972); *The Secret Doctrine*, ed. Boris de Zirkoff, 3 vols. (Wheaton, Ill.: Theosophical Publishing House, 1993); *The Voice of the Silence* (Wheaton, Ill.: Theosophical Publishing House, 1992). Observations about Blavatsky's ability to quote from unseen texts is found in *Collected Writings* (Wheaton, Ill.: Theosophical Publishing House, 1982), 13:285.

8. William Dalrymple, "Living Like a Thakur," *Conde Nast Traveller* (December 995): 80–91.

9. Geoffrey Arnott, "Nechung: A Modern Parallel to the Delphic Oracle?" *Greece and Rome* 36, no. 2:153–57.

10. Lionel Corbett, lecture at the Pacifica Graduate Institute, Santa Barbara, tape recording, summer 1995.

11. Viktor Frankl, *Man's Search for Meaning: An Introduction to Logotherapy* (Boston: Beacon Press, 1963).

CHAPTER 4: DREAMS AS ORACLES

1. Synesius of Cyrene, *On Dreams*, trans. Isaac Myer, in *The New World of Dreams*, eds. Ralph L. Woods and Herbert B. Greenhouse (New York: Macmillan Publishing Co., 1974), 160.

2. The Yansi approach to dreaming is discussed in E. M. Jedrej and Rosalind Shaw, *Dreaming, Religion, and Society in Africa* (New York: E. J. Brill, 1992).

3. Amy Tan's method of imagining is discussed in Naomi Epel, *Writers Dreaming* (New York: Carol Southern Books, 1993).

4. An account of Elias Howe's dream is found in Montague Ullman and Stanley Krippner, *Dream Telepathy* (New York: Macmillan, 1973), 219.

5. Tartini's dream is discussed in many sources, including L. S. Ginzburg, *Tartini: His Life and Times* (New Jersey: Paganiniana Publications, 1981).

6. Samuel Coleridge, preface to *Kubla Khan*, in *The Portable Coleridge*, ed. I. A. Richards (New York: Viking Press, 1950), 156–58.

7. Brian Inglis, *The Power of Dreams* (London: Grafton Books, 1987), 112.

8. Inglis, *Power of Dreams*, 141.

9. Patricia Miller, *Dreams in Late Antiquity* (Syracuse, N.Y.: University Press of Syracuse, 1995).

10. The invocation to Apollo is recounted in C. A. Meier,

Healing Dream and Ritual: Ancient Incubation and Modern Psychotherapy (Einsiedeln, Switzerland: Daimon Verlage, 1989), 51.

11. Ancient Near Eastern dream incubation is discussed extensively by Robert Karl Gnuse, *The Dream Theophany of Samuel: Its Structure in Relation to Ancient Near Eastern Dreams* (Lanham, Md.: University Press of America, 1984).

12. Meier, *Healing Dream and Ritual*, 55.

13. Henri Cocteau quoted in Inglis, *Power of Dreams*, 17.

CHAPTER 5: THE SHADOW SIDE OF ORACLES

1. C. G. Jung quoted in Connie Zweig and Jeremiah Abrams, *Meeting the Shadow* (Los Angeles: Jeremy P. Tarcher, 1991), 4.

2. Research on self-disclosure from S. M. Jourard and P. Lasakow, "Some Factors in Self-Disclosure," *Journal of Abnormal and Social Psychology* 56 (1958): 91-98.

3. The idea of banks as temples is from Lewis Lapham, *Money and Class in America: Notes and Observations on Our Civil Religion* (New York: Weidenfeld and Nicolson, 1988).

4. Alex Owen, *The Darkened Room: Women, Power, and Spiritualism in Late Victorian England* (Philadelphia: University of Pennsylvania Press, 1990).

5. Florence Cook's story is told in Owen, *The Darkened Room*.

6. Bruce T. Grindal, "Into the Heart of Sisala Experience: Witnessing Death Divination," *Journal of Anthropological Research* 39 (1983): 60-80.

7. James Hillman, *Re-Visioning Psychology* (New York: Harper Colophon, 1975).

8. Lionel Corbett, *The Religious Function of the Psyche* (London and New York: Routledge, 1996), 181.

9. Dion Fortune, *Psychic Self-Defense* (York Beach, Maine: Samuel Weiser, 1996).

10. Patrick Harpur, *Daimonic Reality: A Fieldguide to the Otherworld* (London and New York: Penguin, 1994).

11. The Neanderthal burials were discovered by Ralph S. Solecki, Shanidar, *The First Flower People* (New York: Alfred A. Knopf, 1971).

12. Malidoma Somé, *Ritual: Power, Healing, and Community* (Portland, Oreg.: Swan/Raven and Company, 1993), 43.

13. The exercise of tracing the pentagram is from Fortune, *Psychic Self-Defense*, 189.

CHAPTER 6: SIBYLS

1. Stephen Aizenstat, "Jungian Psychology and the World Unconscious," in *Ecopsychology: Restoring the Earth, Healing the Mind*, eds. T. Roszak, M. Gomes, and A. Kanner (San Francisco: Sierra Club Books, 1995), 92-100.

2. H. W. Parke, *Sibyls and Sibylline Prophecy in Classical Antiquity* (London and New York: Routledge, 1988). Parke offers the most extensive and scholarly study of sibyls available.

3. The story of the old sibyl is from Dionysius of Halicarnassus, *The Roman Antiquities* 4.62.1–5, trans. Earnest Cary (Cambridge, Mass.: Harvard University Press, 1939).

4. Virgil, *The Aeneid*, verses 60–215, trans. Allen Mandelbaum (Berkeley: University of California Press, 1981).

5. Par Lagerkvist, *The Sibyl*, trans. Naomi Walford (New York: Random House, 1958), 49.

6. Mariana Monteiro, *As David and the Sibyl Say* (Edinburgh: Sands and Co., 1905), 119.

7. Toni Wolff, *Structual Forms of the Feminine Psyche*, trans. Paul Watzlawik (Zurich: C. G. Jung Institute, 1956).

8. Rachel Carson, *Silent Spring* (New York: Houghton Mifflin, 1962).

9. Wolff, *Structural Forms of the Feminine Psyche*, 9.

10. Mary Watkins, "In Dreams Begin Responsibilities: Moral Imagination and Peace Action," in *Facing Apocalyse*, eds. V. Andrews, R. Bosnak, and K. Goodwin (Dallas, Tex.: Spring Publications, 1987).

11. Mary Watkins adapted this exercise from the work of Robert Jay Lifton, who has called attention to the "double life" we lead in relation to urgent social issues. See R. J. Lifton, "Psychological Effects of Nuclear Weapons and Nuclear War," in *Proceedings of the Harvard Medical School Conference: The Medical Consequences of Nuclear Weapons and Nuclear War* (Cambridge, Mass.: Harvard Medical School, 1981).

12. Martin Luther King's "I Have a Dream" speech was delivered before the Lincoln Memorial in 1963. See James M. Washington, ed., *The Essential Writings and Speeches of Martin Luther King, Jr.* (San Francisco: HarperSanFrancisco, 1990).

CHAPTER 7: RESTORING DIVINATION TO THE DIVINE

1. G. M. Foster, "Divination," in *Standard Dictionary of Foklore, Mythology, and Legend*, ed. Maria Leach (San Francisco: HarperSanFrancisco, 1949/1972), 316.

2. My discussion of the Urim and Thummim is drawn primarily from Cornelis Van Dam, "The Urim and Thummim: A Study of Old Testament Means of Revelation" (Ph.D. diss., Uitgeverij VanDenBerg-Kampen, Holland, 1986); and C. Houtman, "The Urim and Thummim: A New Suggestion," *Vetus Testamentum* 40, no. 2 (1990): 229–31.

3. The wise-woman warrior story is from *Ljosvetninga Saga*, a medieval Scandinavian narrative. This version is from Hilda Ellis Davidson, "The Germanic World," in *Oracles and Divination*, eds. Michael Loewe and Carmen Blacker (Boulder, Colo.: Shambhala, 1981).

4. Plutarch quoted in Robert Flaceliere, *Greek Oracles*, trans. Douglas Garmans (London: Elek Books, 1965).

5. Carl Jung, foreword in *The I Ching or Book of Changes*, ed. Richard Wilhelm, trans. Cary F. Baynes (Princeton, N.J.: Princeton University Press, 1950).

6. Marie-Louise von Franz, *On Divination and Synchronicity: The Psychology of Meaningful Chance* (Toronto: Inner City Books, 1980), 8.

7. H. Dillon, *Assyro-Babylonian Liver Divination* (Rome: Pontificio Instituto Biblico, 1932).

8. Alan Watts, lecture at the University of Colorado, Boulder, April 2, 1971.

9. This definition of "ritual" comes from Jonathan Z. Smith, ed., *The HarperCollins Dictionary of Religion* (San Francisco: HarperCollins, 1995), 930.

10. Tacitus, *Germania*, in *Tacitus*, trans. M. Hutton (Cambridge, Mass.: Harvard University Press, 1930).

CHAPTER 8: MAKING A PLACE FOR ORACLES IN
EVERYDAY LIFE

1. There is a long history of this custom in Ireland. See Iona Opie and Moira Tatem, *Dictionary of Superstitions* (Oxford: Oxford University Press, 1992), 280. In 1979, an old man was quoted as saying that he still bows to the waxing crescent moon when it makes its appearance each month.

2. Mary Watkins, *Imaginal Guests* (Dallas, Tex.: Spring Publications, 1972), 1.

3. The Sioux tale is recounted in Gilbert Voyat, *Cognitive Development Among Sioux Children*, Cognitive Language Series, ed. R. W. Rjieber (New York: Plenum Press, 1983).

4. Charles Asher, *The Contemplative Self* (Big Sur, Calif.: New Camaldoli Publications, 1995), 4.

5. Henry Corbin, "*Mundus Imaginalis*, Or the Imaginary and the Imaginal," *Spring: An Annual of Archetypal Psychology and*

Jungian Thought (1972):1–19.

6. Robert Bosnak, *Tracks in the Wilderness of Dreaming* (New York: Delacorte Press, 1996). 22.

7. James Hillman, *The Thought of the Heart and the Soul of the World* (Woodstock, Conn.: Spring Publications, 1981/1992), 43.

8. R. S. Rattray, *Religion and Art in Ashanti* (London: Oxford University Press, 1959), 5–7, 183–86.

9. Swami Nikhilananda, ed., *The Gospel of Sri Ramakrishna* (New York: Ramakrishna-Vivekananda Center, 1942).

10. Carl G. Jung, *Psychology and Alchemy.* In *Collected Works of C. G. Jung,* R. F. C. Hull, trans. (London: Routledge and Kegan Paul, 1968), paragraph 394. (Jung's original monograph was published in 1944.)

Further Reading

ANIMALS AS ORACLES AND GUIDES

Boone, Allen J., and Paul H. Leonard. *Adventures in Kinship With All Life.* Joshua Tree, Calif.: Tree of Life Publications, 1994.

Bruchai, Joseph. *Native American Animal Stories.* Golden, Colo.: Fulcrum Publishing, 1992.

Green, Miranda. *Animals in Celtic Life and Myth.* New York: Routledge, 1998.

Laland, Stephane. *Animal Angels: Amazing Acts of Love and Compassion.* Berkley: Conari Press, 1998.

Malotki, Ekkehart, ed. *Hopi Animal Tales.* Lincoln: University of Nebraska Press, 1998.

McElroy, Susan C. *Animals as Guides for the Soul: Stories of Life-Changing Encounters.* New York: Ballantine Publishing Group, 1998.

———. *Animals as Teachers and Healers.* New York: Ballantine Publishing Group, 1997.

McGinnis, Mark W. *Lakota and Dakota Animal Wisdom Stories.* Chamberlain, S. Dak.: Tipi Press, 1994.

O'Sullivan, Patrick V. *Irish Superstition and Legends of Animals and Birds*. Chester Springs, Pa.: Dufour Editions, 1991.

Smith, Penelope. *Animal Talk: Interspecies Telepathic Communication*. Hillsboro, Oreg.: Beyond Words Publishing, 1999.

Titsch, Twylah. *Creature Teachers: A Guide to the Spirit Animals of the Native American Tradition*. New York: Continuum Publishing Company, 1997.

DIVINATION (GENERAL THEORY AND SPECIFIC TRADITIONS)

Abiola, Kola. *Dilogun: The Sixteen Cowries Divination System*. African Traditional Religion Series. New York: Zungo Publications, 1996.

Aburrow, Yvonne. *Auguries and Omens: The Magical Lore of Birds*. Edmonds, Wash.: Holmes Publishing Group, 1994.

Berchman, Robert M. *Mediators of the Divine: Horizons of Prophecy, Divination, and Theurgy in Mediterranean Antiquity*. Atlanta: Scholar's Press, 1998.

Blum, Ralph. *Oracle, The Book of Runes: A Handbook for the Use of an Ancient and Contemporary Oracle*. Venice, Calif.: Oracle Books, 1982.

Cicerco, Marcus Tullius. *The Nature of The Gods and Divination*. Translated by C. D. Yonge. Amherst, N.Y.: Prometheus Books, 1997. Original text written in the first century, B.C.E.

Connor, W. R., ed. *Roman Augury and Etruscan Divination*. Ancient Religion and Mythology Series. Manchester, N.H.: Ayer Company Publications, 1979.

Greer, John M. *Earth Divination, Earth Magic: A Beginners Guide to Geomancy*. St. Paul: Llewellyn Publications, 1999.

Karcher, Stephen. *The Illustrated Encyclopedia of Divination.* New York: Barnes and Noble Books, 1997.

Karcher, Stephen, and Rudolf Ritsema. *I Ching: The Classic Chinese Oracle of Change.* Shaftesbury, England: Element Books, 1994.

Lake, Medicine Grizzlybear. *Native Healer: Initiation into an Ancient Art.* Wheaton, Ill.: Quest Books, 1991.

Peek, Phillip. ed. *African Divination Systems: Ways of Knowing.* Bloomington: Indiana University Press, 1991.

von Franz, Marie-Louise. *Divination and Synchronicity: The Psychology of Meaningful Chance.* Toronto: Inner City Books, 1980.

Webster, Richard. *Omens, Oghams, and Oracles: Divination in the Druidic Tradition.* St. Paul: Llewellyn Publications, 1999.

DREAMS

Artemidorus. *Oneirocritica: The Interpretation of Dreams by Artemidorus.* Translated by Robert J. White. Torrance, Ga.: Original Books, 1990. Original text written in the second century, C.E.

Bond, Alma, and others. *Dream Portrait: A Study of Nineteen Sequential Dreams as Indicators of Pretermination.* Madison, Conn.: International Universities Press, 1992.

Bulkeley, Kelly. *Spiritual Dreaming: A Cross-Cultural and Historical Journey.* Mawwah, N.J.: Paulist Press, 1995.

Cowan, James C. *Mysteries of the Dreamtime: The Spiritual Life of Australian Aborigines.* Nashville, Tenn.: Associated Publications Group, 1989.

Gouda, Yehia. *Dreams and Their Meanings in the Old Arab Tradition.* Chicago: Kazi Publications, 1996.

Harris, Monford. *Studies in Jewish Dream Interpretation.* Northvale, N.J.: Aronson, 1994.

Hillman, James, and Margot McLean. *Dream Animals.* San Francisco: Chronicle Books, 1997.

Rogers, L. W. *Dreams and Premonitions.* Santa Fe: Sun Publishing Company, 1993.

Rossi, Ernest Lawrence. *Dreams, Consciousness, Spirit: The Quantum Experience of Self-Reflection and Co-Creation.* Malibu, Calif.: Palisades Gateway Publishing, 2000.

Tenzin, Wangyal Rinpoche. *Tibetan Yogas of Dream and Sleep.* Edited by Mark Dahlby. Ithaca, N.Y.: Snow Lion Publications, 1998.

Ullman, Montague, and Claire Limmer, eds. *The Variety of Dream Experience: Expanding Our Ways of Working with Dreams.* SUNY Series in Dream Studies. Albany, N.Y.: State University of New York Press, 1999.

Wolfe, Fred. *The Dreaming Universe: Mind-Expanding Journey Where Psyche and Physics Meet.* New York: Touchstone Books, 1995.

ORACLES

Dempsey, T. *Delphic Oracle: Its Early History, Influence, and Fall.* Manchester, N.H.: Ayer, 1972.

Hogue, John. *Nostradamus: The New Revelations.* Shaftesbury, England: Element Books, 1995.

Lowe, Michael, and Carmen Blacker, eds. *Divination and Oracles.* Boulder: Shambhala, 1981.

Staewen, Christoph. *Ifa: African Gods Speak: The Oracle of the Yoraba in Nigera.* Somerset, N.J.: Transaction Publications, 1996.

Westcott, William, ed. *The Chaldean Oracles Attributed to Zoraster.* Edmonds, Wash.: Holmes Publications, 1984.

Word, Charles. *Oracles of Nostradamus*. Santa Fe: Sun Publications, 1981.

SHAMANIC TRADITIONS

Balzer, Marjorie, ed. *Shamanic Worlds: Rituals and Lore of Siberia and Central Asia*. Armonk, N.Y.: M. E. Sharpe, 1996.

Bean, Lowell J., and Sylvia B. Vane, eds. *California Indian Shamanism*. Anthropological Papers no. 39. Novato, Calif.: Ballena Press, 1992.

Bernstein, Jay H. *Spirits Captured in Stone: Shamanism and Traditional Medicine Among the Taman of Borneo*. Boulder: Lynee Reinner Publishing, 1996.

Castaneda, Carlos. *Magical Passes: Practical Wisdom of the Shamans of Ancient Mexico*. New York: Harper Collins, 1998.

Conway, D. J. *By Oak, Ash, and Thorn: Modern Celtic Shamanism*. St. Paul: Llewelyn Publications, 1995.

Covell, Alan C. *Ecstasy: Shamanism in Korea*. New York: Hollym Corporation Publishing, 1983.

Elk, Wallace B., and William S. Lyon. *Black Elk: The Sacred Ways of a Lakota*. San Francisco: HarperSanFrancisco, 1991.

Halifax, Joan. *Shamanic Voices: A Survey of Visionary Narratives*. Bergenfield, N.J.: Viking Penguin, 1991.

Kharitidi, Olga. *Entering the Circle: Ancient Secrets of Siberian Wisdom Discovered by a Russian Psychiatrist*. San Francisco: HarperSanFrancisco, 1997.

Labee, Armand J. *Guardians of the Life Stream: Shamans, Art, and Power in Prehispanic Central Panama*. Santa Ana, Calif.: Bowers Museum of Cultural Arts, 1995.

Index

Note: Page numbers in italics refer to illustrations.

Illustration and Photo Credits

Cover image: Springtime fresco, Akrotiri, Santorini, c. 1500 B.C., Minoan, courtesy Nimatallah/Art Resource, NY.

QUEST BOOKS

are published by

The Theosophical Society in America,

Wheaton, Illinois 60189–0270,

a branch of a world fellowship,

a membership organization

dedicated to the promotion of the unity

of humanity and the encouragement of the study

of religion, philosophy, and science, to the end that

we may better understand ourselves and our place

in the universe. The Society stands for complete

freedom of individual search and belief.

For further information about its activities,

write, call 1–800–669–1571,

e-mail olcott@theosophia.org,

or consult its Web page:

http://www.theosophical.org

The Theosophical Publishing House

is aided by the generous support of

THE KERN FOUNDATION,

a trust established by Herbert A. Kern

and dedicated to Theosophical education.